Being and Becoming a Management Education Scholar

A volume in
Research in Management Education and Development
Charles Wankel, *Series Editor*

Being and Becoming a Management Education Scholar

Charles Wankel
St. John's University

Robert DeFillippi
Suffolk University

INFORMATION AGE PUBLISHING, INC.
Charlotte, NC • www.infoagepub.com

Library of Congress Cataloging-in-Publication Data

Wankel, Charles.
  Being and becoming a management education scholar / Charles Wankel, Robert
DeFillippi.
      p. cm. – (Research in management education and development)
  Includes bibliographical references.
  ISBN 978-1-60752-346-8 (pbk.) – ISBN 978-1-60752-347-5 (hbk.) – ISBN
978-1-60752-348-2 (e-book)
1. Management–Study and teaching (Higher) 2. Business education. 3.
Business teachers. I. DeFillippi, Bob. II. Title.
  HD30.4.W36 2009
  658.0071'1–dc22

                                                          2009043798

CONTENTS

CHAPTER 1

BEING AND BECOMING A MANAGEMENT EDUCATION SCHOLAR

An Overview

Charles Wankel and Robert DeFillippi

Being and Becoming a Management Education Scholar is a volume that examines what it takes to succeed in academic management education and development scholarship, presenting perspectives on the opportunities, constraints and requirements of contemporary research in management education. Issues that are discussed in this volume include the changing career implications of coming to be a researcher on management education rather than on management topics and leveraging leadership roles in management education scholarship and its venues including journals, book series, handbooks, textbooks and scholarly societies. The chapter authors address these issues through research grounded in personal biography, institutional history, and critical reflection.

As the study and practice of management is advancing and in some ways converging, the advance of research on professional education (that is, in

Being and Becoming a Management Education Scholar, pages 1–9
Copyright © 2010 by Information Age Publishing

business, law, medicine, engineering, etc.) is a global endeavor (Elimimian, 1987, Anonymous, 2005). Indeed, current topics in professional education research include clarifying what transnational professional education is (Lebel-Grenier, 2006) and how professional education can be transnationalized (Jukier, 2006). In recent years, it has become increasingly clear that the scope and rigor of management education research, in particular, needed to expand in the face of the increasingly globalized environment. Qualitative in additional to quantitative methods were found to be required to best address the research questions that arose (Beukenka 1972). Management education research had to confront the issue of whether it is hard or soft research. This issue of the stature of research on education versus that of the study of professional practice and theory is also being dealt with by education research in other professions (Gruppen, 2008a; Albert, Hodges, & Regehr, 2007). The importance for the various professions of focusing on the betterment of their educational endeavors through solid research has been widely discussed (Vickers, 2000; Fortenberry, 2006; Streveler & Smith, 2006; Cook, Bordage, & Schmidt, 2008; Christiaanse et al., 2008; Borrengo, Streveler, Miller, & Smith, 2008; Gillespie et al, 2008; Gruppen, 2008; Koro-Ljungberg & Douglas, 2008; Skelton & Buckley, 2008; Borrengo, Douglas, & Amelink, 2009; Dornan, Peile, & Spencer, 2009; Eva, 2009a; Jesiek, Newswander and Borengo 2009; Schifferdecker & Reed, 2009; Walsh & Sandars, 2009; Watson, 2009). The chapters of this volume are reports on the issues and meaning associated with the commitment to turn, at least to an extent or for a time, one's scholarly research on cutting-edge issues in management education, grappling with the changing nature of contemporary professional education and how it is offered, and looking toward the interdisciplinary concerns of 21st century professional education and research thereof.

In professional education research, differences have been found in the perceptions of the endeavor by novices and experts (Pugsley, 2008). One issue that arises in researching management education is what is missing from management education that should be added to it (cf. Tienari & Laurila, 2007; Murray, 2009). One of the useful results of the efforts of leaders in management education research dissemination has been to alert scholars of alternative research approaches for research in management education. This has occurred in the wider context of similar events in other education research in other professions (Boyer, 1974; Siegfried & Sweeney, 1980; Schifferdecker & Reed, 2009). The authors of this volume approach the issues in management education research from a variety of perspectives, offering up analyses of the state of current scholarship, what is lacking in it, and how best to engage in management education research in a way that is sensitive to the interests and perspectives of teachers and learners, as well as novice and expert researchers.

The research in this volume can be divided into three distinct approaches. Chapters 2, 4, and 5 of this volume provide insights into management education scholarship through biographical accounts of the authors. Chapters 3, 7, and 8 assess the institutional influence and prevailing opportunities for publication on management education scholarship and the institutional and evolutionary history of leading journals for management education scholarship and an academic handbook. Chapters 6 and 9 offer perspectives from communities of management education scholars who offer alternative perspectives on how management education and management scholarship might be joined and implemented.

In Chapter 2, "Shifting Paradigms Through 'Letting Go': On Allowing Oneself to Become a Management Education Scholar," Robert Chia argues for an appreciation of the unexpected efficacy of an indirect and circuitous professional route to becoming a management education scholar in cultivating a nuanced and tempered attitude towards life and the often counterintuitive nature of the human predicament. Chia suggests that becoming a management education scholar requires balancing the path of the normal academic scholarly career (one that is likely to support academic scholarship that is appropriate for publication in the "right" journals but runs the risk of a preoccupation with publishing in prestigious academic journals rather than the practical value and relevance of what they teach in their classes; see Bennis & O'Toole, 2005) with a more exploratory path based on five principles he identifies by drawing upon his rich biography of becoming an internationally renowned management education scholar. Chia suggests that his five principles (shifting paradigms through 'letting go'; detouring to gain access; cultivating 'negative capability'; valuing naivety and 'learned ignorance'; and developing 'upstream' thinking) lead to the appreciation of the value of the indirect route to management education scholarship.

In Chapter 3, "Scholarly Outlets and Scholarly Identity: A Narrative of the Founding of the Academy of Management Learning & Education," James Bailey, William Ferris, Roy Lewicki, and David Whetten discuss the history and key decisions about the founding, launch, and early years of the journal *Academy of Management Learning & Education*, based on their experiences as the founding editors and editorial board members. One of the things incumbent upon the editors of journals focused on management education research is challenging the boundaries that circumscribe research in management education issues. Certainly the *Academy of Management Learning in Education* journal had to negotiate its territory with other Academy of Management journals (cf. Nielsen, 2008). Their account parses important debates concerning the journal's domain, quality standards, and innovations; notable articles of AMLE's early years that attracted a wide management audience and built the reputation of the journal; and their analysis of the overall impact of *AMLE* on the field of management education scholarship and their own personal aspirations for the future of *AMLE*.

In Chapter 4, "I Get By with a Lot of Help from my Friends": Reflections of an Accidental Management Education Scholar," Ben Arbaugh chronicles his decade-long career development from an entrepreneurship scholar to a management education scholar, characterizing it as idiosyncratic and conditioned by chance opportunities that were recognized and exploited through a regularly expanding network of colleagues and collaborators representing the top researchers in the field of management education scholarship. Arbaugh concludes with the suggestion that management education scholars should actively pursue innovative cross-disciplinary academic scholarship grounded in his unique and successful professional development.

An area that professional education research might be more developed might be in curricula (Rover, 2006; Bourguignon, Pleskovic, & Elkana, 2007). In Chapter 5, "When Legitimizing Teaching Methods Becomes an Opportunity to Develop Management Education Scholarship in Negotiation and Collective Decision Processes Pedagogy: 'Bringing it into Action'— The Narrative of a French Business School Professor's Experience," Laurence De Carlo discusses her experience as an educator and management education scholar and the challenges she faced in integrating the processes and principles underlying her scholarship with her pedagogic practices in the environment of the ESSEC Business School. She presents how the French *grandes écoles* higher education establishment presents challenges to practice-oriented education through a cultural bias in favor of abstract theoretical knowledge. She recounts how she overcame the environmental and cultural constraints in order to develop a non-classical way of teaching negotiation in complex decision processes and creating several innovative pedagogical projects. She concludes that the current professional pressure for French business professors to publish in Anglophone academic journals has discouraged innovative pedagogical research. She argues that it will take time for faculties, administrators and students in French higher education to cultivate the belief in the value of management education scholarship.

Many scholar teachers like the notion of integrating research and teaching (McClelland, 1974; Ray, 1976). In Chapter 6, "Interpreting the Scholarship of Teaching in Management Education and Learning: A Critique of the Domain," Gordon Dehler, Joy Beatty, and Jennifer Leigh engage the problem of integrating effective teaching with world-class management educations scholarship. They begin by distinguishing three kinds of teaching: good teaching, scholarly teaching, and teaching as scholarship, in order to advance two related positions concerning the needs of current management education and scholarship. First, they argue that the standard of good teaching is insufficient for the needs of contemporary management students. In order to educate world-class 21st century managers, educators should adopt a standard of scholarly teaching that is focused on developing independent student learning. In the authors' assessment, meeting the challenge of shifting pedagogical standards to the level of scholarly teaching has the additional academic benefit of legitimizing management education scholarship in the academic community. They argue that legitimizing management education scholarship is possible through the transition from a teaching-as-technique pedagogical paradigm to the paradigm of teaching as scholarly practice. Their central claim is that practice is commodified when teaching is viewed narrowly as technique and, as a result, cannot achieve the credibility required to be a legitimate scholarly domain within organization and management studies.

In Chapter 7, "The Emergence of the Scholarship of Management Teaching and Learning as a Field in Its Own Right: The Development of Scholarship in Learning, Education, and Development," Cynthia Fukami and Steven Armstrong present an account of the creation and development of the SAGE *Handbook of Management Learning, Education and Development* from both the biographical perspective of the editors' distinct background and experiences and the institutional perspective of the planning, development, and execution stages of the Handbook's development. They introduce the research process they undertook to determine key historical, current, emerging, and future issues surrounding the field of management education scholarship. This process included a comprehensive review and content analysis of leading scholarly journals in management education as well as a review of ten years of programs of the Management Education and Development division of the Academy of Management and soliciting a large number of chapter proposals from scholars identified within each of these domains. They also describe the editing process, which involved fourteen leading scholars as anonymous reviewers and the individual chapter authors providing suggestions for revision and the identification of more suitable scholarly contributions. They provide an integrated summary of the contents of the entire Handbook. In conclusion, they investigate opportunities for achieving academic success in management education and development scholarship, which ensures quality and relevance in the overall student experience and consider some of the constraints, challenges that impacted this type of scholarship, and suggestions for overcoming them.

The selection of reviewers in management education research presents different issues to editors than those confronted by research in management topics (cf Eva, 2009b). In Chapter 8, "Pioneering and Fostering the Scholarship of Teaching and Learning in the Organizational Sciences: The Journal of Management Education," Jane Schmidt-Wilk and Cynthia Fukami present the origin and development of the *Journal of Management Edu-*

cation (JME) from its genesis in 1975 as the newsletter *Organization Behavior Teaching Society* up through its rechristening in 1991, sharing their insights as editors of the journal. They compare the relative positions of the *Journal of Management Education* with the *Academy of Management Learning and Education* in the academic field and discuss the relevance and increasing rigor of the contents of the *JME*. They provide a window into the thinking of the editorial staff of the *JME* and give an insider's perspective into how decisions are made in the editorial review process and how research advances their academic goals for research of increasing rigor and relevance. The authors conclude with predictions about the future trends in scholarship of teaching and learning and the editorial policies and practices of the *JME* based on observations on the current dialectic between relevance and rigor in management education scholarship.

One of the endeavors of the leaders in management education research in this volume has been to build a community of management education scholars. This issue has been addressed by other professional disciplines; for example, in engineering, see Lohmann (2005) and Borrengo, Douglas, and Amelink (2009). Communities of practice need to be fostered to better enable researchers to collaborate and widely disseminate good practice (Pugsley, 2008). In Chapter 9, "Sharing Expertise About Educational Innovation in Economics and Business: A Case History of the EDiNEB Network," Wim Gijselaers and Richard Milter describe the challenges and innovative solutions associated with the creation of the EDiNEB Network (**ED**ucational **IN**novation in **E**conomics and **B**usiness), an international community of educators and advocates of problem-based learning. This community grew out of a need for rethinking how scholarly teaching and learning practice can be implemented in academic intuitions. EDiNEB was organized at a 1993 conference on problem-based learning; it is funded by Maastricht University and administered by an advisory board including members from European and American universities. The roots of EDiNEB are traced back to 1983, when Maastricht University in the Netherlands created a Faculty of Economics and Business Administration that featured problem-based learning as an integral component of the four-year curriculum. This chapter addresses the issues of how to support innovation in business schools through encouraging research with goals focusing on the application of results in a teaching context beyond the traditional goal of publication. The EDiNEB Network is presented as providing a platform to further teachers' understanding of the innovation and development of ownership.

The perspectives presented in this volume represent only a few of the numerous issues that exist in management education research. Research in other disciplines of professional education offers insight into topics for management education research. An issue in research on management education is the need for consistency. Other professional disciplines are dealing with this in studying their own pedagogical and research methods. For example, in medical education research, there is a movement to use a standardization of patients' reports to facilitate replication and comparison of results (Wilson, Ward, & Ward, 1994; Howley, Szauter, Perkowski, Clifton, & McNaughton, 2008). Indeed, some professional disciplines are more advanced than management education researchers in consistently integrating practitioners' reports with those of academicians. For example, reports by clinical professors of their training of medical students are more common than practitioners reporting on interns in business (Albert, Hodges, & Regehr, 2007). An endeavor that the gatekeepers of management education research might undertake is to explore the common issues in professional education research and to strive for a symbiosis between management education research and those of other disciples (McClelland, 1974, Ray, 1976). This has been one of the strategies in medical education research (Eva, 2008) that business education research might follow.

REFERENCES

Albert, M., Hodges, B., & Regehr, G. (2007). Research in medical education: Balancing service and science. *Advances in Health Sciences Education, 12*(1), 103–115.

Anonymous (2005). Advancing engineering education research worldwide. *Journal of Engineering Education Research, 94*(3), 283–284.

Bennis, W. G., & O'Toole, J. (2005). How business schools lost their way. *Harvard Business Review, 83*(5), 96–104, 154.

Beukenka, P.A. (1972). Case-method and case-research in European marketing education. *Management International Review, 12*(6), 115–128.

Borrego, M., Douglas, E.P., & Amelink C.T. (2009). Quantitative, qualitative, and mixed research methods in engineering education, *Journal of Engineering Education Research, 98*(1), 53–66.

Borrego, M., Streveler, R.A., Miller, R.L., & Smith, K.A. (2008). A new paradigm for a new field: Communicating representations of engineering education. *Journal of Engineering Education, 97*(2), 147–162.

Bourguignon, F., Pleskovic, B., & Elkana Y. (Eds.). (2007). *Capacity building in economic education and research: Lessons learned and future directions.* Washington, DC: World Bank Publications.

Boyer, B.B. (1974). American legal education: Agenda for research and reform. *Cornell Law Review, 59*(2), 221–297.

Christiaanse, M.E., Russell, E.L., Crandall, S,J., Lambros, A., Manuel, J.C., & Kirk, J.K. (2008). Development of an asset map of medical education research activity. *Journal of Continuing Education in the Health Professions, 28*(3), 186–193.

Cook, D.A., Bordage, G., & Schmidt, H.G. (2008). Description, justification and clarification: A framework for classifying the purposes of research in medical education. *Medical Education, 42*(2), 128–133.

Dornan, T., Peile, E., & Spencer, J. (2009). In defence of the existing strengths of medical education research. *Medical Education, 43*(4), 391.

Elimimian, J.U. (1987). A factor analytic-based methodology for evaluation of research in education in less developed countries. *Research in Education, 38,* 87–106.

Eva, K.W. (2008). The cross-cutting edge: Striving for symbiosis between medical education research and related disciplines. *Medical Education, 42*(10), 950–951.

Eva, K.W. (2009a). Broadening the debate about quality in medical education research. *Medical Education, 43*(4), 294–296.

Eva, K.W. (2009b). The reviewer is always right: peer review of research in Medical Education. *Medical Education, 43*(1), 2–4.

Fortenberry, N.L. (2006). An extensive agenda for engineering education research. *Journal of Engineering Education Research, 95*(1), 3–5.

Gillespie, C., Zabar, S., Truncali, A., Paik, S., Lee, J., Jay, M., Ark, T.K., Bruno, J.H., & Kalet, A.L. (2008). Building the evidence for medical education: Database for research on medical education in academic medicine (dream). *Journal of General Internal Medicine, 23*(2), 196.

Gruppen, L. (2008). Is medical education research 'hard' or 'soft' research? *Advances in Health Sciences Education, 13*(1), 1–2.

Howley, L. Szauter, K., Perkowski, L., Clifton, M., & McNaughton, N. (2008). Quality of standardised patient research reports in the medical education literature: Review and recommendations. *Medical Education, 42*(4), 350–358.

Jesiek, B.K. Newswander, L.K., & Borrego, M. (2009). Engineering education research: Discipline, community, or field? *Journal of Engineering Education, 98*(1) 39–52.

Jukier, R. (2006). Transnationalizing the legal curriculum: How to teach what we live. *Journal of Legal Education, 56*(2), 172–189.

Koro-Ljungberg, M., & Douglas, E.P. (2008). State of qualitative research in engineering education: Meta-analysis of JEE articles, 2005-2006. *Journal of Engineering Education, 97*(2), 163–175.

Lebel-Grenier, S. (2006). What is transnational legal education? *Journal of Legal Education, 56*(2), 190–195.

Lohmann, J.R. (2005). Building a community of scholars: The role of the Journal of Engineering Education as a research journal. *Journal of Engineering Education Research. 94*(1), 1–6.

McClelland,W.G. (1974). Integration of research and teaching in management education. *Management International Review, 14*(2), 47–60.

Murray, P. (2009). Infusing alcohol research into medical education: A perspective from NIAAA. *Alcoholism-Clinical and Experimental Research, 33*(6), 218A.

Nielsen, C.H. (2008). Challenging the boundaries of medical education research. *Medical Education, 42*(11), 1137–1138.

Pugsley, L. (2008). Expectation and experience: Dissonances between novice and expert perceptions in medical education research. *Medical Education. 42*(9), 866–871.

Ray, G.H. (1976). Use of case studies in integration of research and teaching in management education. *Management Decision. 14*(1), 63–68.

Rover, D.T. (2006). Engineering education: Research and development in curriculum and instruction. *Journal of Engineering Education, 95*(3), 255–256.

Schifferdecker, K.E., & Reed, V.A. (2009). Using mixed methods research in medical education: Basic guidelines for researchers. *Medical Education, 43*(7), 637–644.

Siegfried, J.J., & Sweeney, G.H. (1980). Bias in economics education research from random and voluntary selection into experimental and control-groups. *American Economic Review, 70*(2), 29–34.

Skelton, J., & Buckley, S. (2008). What is the value of good medical education research? A reply to Bligh and Brice. *Medical Education, 42*(10), 1045.

Streveler, R.A., & Smith, K.A. (2006). Conducting rigorous research in engineering education. *Journal of Engineering Education, 95*(2), 103–105.

Tienari, J., & Laurila, J. (2007). Special topic forum on "Management education: Research and practice." *Scandinavian Journal of Management, 23*(1), 1–3.

Vickers, M.H. (2000). Australian police management education and research: A comment from "outside the cave." *Policing—An International Journal of Police Strategies & Management, 23*(4), 506–524.

Walsh, K., & Sandars, J. (2009). Competing interests and research in medical education. *Postgraduate Medicine Journal. 84*(989), 113–114.

Watson, K. (2009). Change in engineering education: Where does research fit? *Journal of Engineering Education, 98*(1), 3–4.

Wilson, T.E., Ward, D.R., & Ward, S.P., (1994). Use of self-reported college aptitude-test scores in accounting education research. *Psychological Reports, 74*(1), 327–328.

CHAPTER 2

SHIFTING PARADIGMS THROUGH "LETTING GO"

On Allowing Oneself to Become a Management Education Scholar

Robert Chia

ABSTRACT

This chapter explores an oblique, circuitous, and non-linear approach to attaining wisdom and scholarship in management education. I maintain that becoming an accomplished management education scholar involves a much more colourful, rich, and digressive intellectual journey than is generally acknowledged: Detours, dead-ends, fortuitous encounters, and accidental discoveries are an inevitable feature of the process of intellectual maturation. Appreciation of the surprising efficacy of such an indirect and circuitous route helps cultivate a more nuanced attitude and tempered predisposition towards life and the paradoxical and counterintuitive nature of the human predicament. In this chapter I emphasise the importance of *letting go* to gain insight and wisdom; the approach of *detouring* in order to gain *access*; the importance of *negative capability* in dealing with uncertainty; the role and significance of *ignorance* and intellectual *naivety* in facilitating paradigm-shifts; and the impor-

Being and Becoming a Management Education Scholar, pages 11–41
Copyright © 2010 by Information Age Publishing
11

tance of moving *upstream* and away from the spectacular *downstream* happenings to changing the course of things with a minimum of effort and attention. Drawing on my own personal life experiences I shall show how each of these paradoxical stances has led me to appreciate the value of this less direct and circuitous approach to achieving management education scholarship.

> *You cannot force a plant to grow. . . . You must allow it to grow . . .*
> *allowing things to happen constitute active involvement...this discretion*
> *makes the "doing" very hard to apprehend.*
> —Francois Jullien (2004)

Much of the current emphasis on attaining competence, proficiency, or even mastery in a particular field of endeavour presupposes a linear, cumulative view of knowledge and skill acquisition, assimilation, and deployment. Progress in learning is presumed to be generally a smooth, uninterrupted, and causally efficacious one, moving us almost inexorably from the novice stage to eventual mastery of a practice. Such an incrementalist attitude towards knowledge, skill, and wisdom pervades management research and education and underpins the more established attempts to produce capable and effective management education scholars. In this chapter I shall explore an alternative more oblique, circuitous, and less linear approach towards attaining wisdom and scholarship in management education. Becoming a management education scholar involves a much more colourful, rich and elliptical intellectual journey than is generally acknowledged. Such an indirect route helps precipitate a more nuanced attitude and tempered predisposition towards life experiences and it incorporates a number of paradoxical or counterintuitive stances: the importance of *letting go* to gaining insight and wisdom; the approach of *detouring* in order to gain *access*; the importance of *negative capability* in dealing with uncertainty; the role and significance of *ignorance* and intellectual *naivety* in facilitating paradigm shifts; and the importance of moving *upstream* and away from the 'spectacular' *downstream* happenings to changing the course of things with a minimum of effort and attention. Drawing on my own personal life experiences I shall show how each of these paradoxical stances have led me to appreciate the value of a less direct and circuitous approach towards achieving management education scholarship.

TWO ROADS TO PERSONAL GROWTH AND DEVELOPMENT

> *Two roads diverge in a wood, and I—*
> *I took the one less travelled by,*
> *And that has made all the difference.*
> —Robert Frost (1916/1993)

There are two roads one can take in any field of inquiry or endeavour; one leads us on the 'royal' road, moving almost inexorably towards convergence, competence, and technically efficient exploitation. The other is a road less taken, one that unintentionally and often serendipitously leads us towards a more richly textured appreciation of difference, diversity, and the role of luck and chance in shaping human destinies. This more *circuitous* route, although often seemingly less efficient, is nevertheless associated with profound insights, wisdom, and an enriched appreciation of the human condition. Allowing oneself to become a Management Education Scholar entails balancing the latter with the former. Management education scholarship is not so much a 'job' or 'career' as it is a 'vocation'—a commitment one makes in upholding the search for truth, authenticity, personal growth, and integrity. It involves boldly engaging with the world of ideas and bringing to bear the insights they offer on the world of practical affairs. It is to follow Immanuel Kant's invective '*sapere aude*': to 'dare to know' even and especially if such knowing generates doubts, troubles and disturbs us, and makes us restless and anxious. For it is this very intellectual restlessness and doubting that propels us forward in the interminable search for an adequate comprehension of the human condition. The outcome is the attainment of a level of maturity in which we ourselves create the very condition of doubt and do so with a sense of irony and humour. Without doubt there is no willingness to *unlearn* and, hence, no real capacity for learning. Without doubt we descend almost invariably into dogma. To seek out the critical differences that make a genuine difference to the quality of our lives and the lives of others we must be acutely tuned to the possibility of otherness—that things can always be other than they are.

Allowing oneself to come into awareness of the "difference that makes a difference" (Bateson, 1972) to our comprehension of life situations requires an openness and almost innocent naivety that paradoxically comes from being on the 'margins' or periphery of established cultures, paradigms, norms and social systems. It is to accept the need for constantly oscillating between being an 'insider' and an 'outsider' to any dominant societal norm, worldview, perspective, or frame of comprehension and to endure the constant threat to individual identity that such oscillation entails. For it is such interminable oscillation that serves to heighten sensitivity and consciousness and to educate our attention to the differences and discriminations in social practice that account for the richness and diversity of the knowing we encounter across cultural, institutional, and ideological divides. Thus, paradoxically, we cannot know who we are or how well or badly our institutional system operates or how oppressive/liberating our political systems are; nor are we generally aware of the peculiar idiosyncrasies of our inherited cultures and predispositions, unless we have some basis of first-hand comparison with a foreign other, an experience of 'otherness.' We learn and gain insight through contemplating difference *and* sameness. It is the oscillatory movement *between* differences and sameness that heightens our understanding and comprehension of the complexities of our modern life-worlds.

The idea that difference and oscillation structure consciousness and hence our capacity to discriminate and discern is not new. Sigmund Freud posited it as the necessary basis for a newborn child becoming aware of its own individuality, and he came to this understanding while observing his young nephew playing with a spool; throwing it under the bed uttering "gone" and then retrieving it with a delighted "there!!" This is a game all parents know about: the absence/presence couplet that is constantly played that babies and young children find endless pleasure in re-enacting. Jacques Lacan (1986) maintains that such oscillation between absence/presence provides the unconscious meta-structuring needed for our entry into language and socialization. In other words, the more we are exposed to a highly differentiated and varied field of lived experiences that are "pre-conceptual" and even pre-linguistic, the more subtle and well-honed are our powers of observation and discrimination within a social domain. This is not something sufficiently encouraged in social life in general and in management academia in particular.

The unspoken truth about many management educators in business schools is that a great majority have had a very limited range of exposure to life's predicaments in general and management predicaments in particular. In Britain and North America in particular, the traditional route to becoming a management academic is an unbroken linear progression from undergraduate studies to an MBA and then to a doctoral degree in a relevant sub-field of business before assuming an academic position. It is true that in the course of a PhD research there is usually a requirement for empirical investigation and even for prolonged contact with business and industry, in the form of research collaborations and even consultancy work. Yet in all these, the researcher/consultant remains effectively outside the realm of the actual practice of management: His or her role is more that of an observer/analyst than of an absorbed and active participant who is necessarily emotionally engaged, having to take risks and often making unpopular decisions that they have to subsequently live with because the consequences of such actions and decisions do not go away but remain ever-present in future considerations. As such the mode of preparation that currently exists for management educators is not by any means ideal. As Bennis and O'Toole (2005) have noted, business school academics are more preoccupied with writing and publishing in prestigious academic journals than with the practical value and relevance of what they teach in their MBA classes.

This situation can be partially rectified if the path towards becoming an effective management education scholar is clarified and the aspiring academic is encouraged to explore the conditions of possibility of knowledge as much as exploiting previously established forms of understanding (March, 1996). It is often the road less expeditious, much more circuitous and ser-endipitous—often leading to *cul-de-sacs* and paths that are much more reli-ant on chance than on purposeful venture to attaining crucial insights. It is ultimately a "road less travelled." I identify five elements that mark out the contours of this circuitous passage towards a fulfilling lifelong vocation in management education scholarship: shifting paradigms through "letting go"; *detouring* to gain *access*; cultivating "negative capability"; valuing *naivety* and "learned ignorance"; and developing "upstream" thinking.

SHIFTING PARADIGMS THROUGH "LETTING GO"

> *In order to grasp, it is necessary first to release.*
> —Lao Tzu in Chan, 1963, p. 157

Refugees, immigrants, entrepreneurs, and new settlers in a community share a common predicament: They have to move away from clearly de-fined zones of comfort and familiarity with the material and social environ-ment they have come from, however stark or unsavoury that might have been, letting go of an embedded lifestyle they have been born into and embracing new routines, new social configurations and patterns of inter-actions in order to forge and discover their new social identities. There is often a deep sense of loss, of bewilderment and of heightened anxiety, and of a deep doubting of one's own capability to cope with the challenges to one's sense of individuality and self-worth the new circumstances may throw up. This is particularly more acutely felt in adults, often weighted down with their burden of responsibility, than for young children who, by and large, find it much easier to adapt to new and foreign circumstances. It involves a painful process of *letting go*. But like all life-changing experiences it is a profound source of learning; about oneself, about the ingenuity and inexhaustible capacity for adaptation and survival, about one's values and one's attachments to cultural, social and symbolic idiosyncrasies, and about one's ingrained habit of thought. It involves a genuine paradigm shift: not something one chooses, but something one is forcibly thrown into—a "throwness" that elicits our deepest existential anxieties and thus an almost primordial instinct for survival.

Thrown into an alien environment in unfamiliar circumstances—not in a privileged position as an expatriate transferred to a developing country or as a casual visitor spending time in a different country, but as one de-privileged, seeking refuge or even as an aspiring individual seeking to forge a career or to enrich one's life—one experiences a certain vulnerability; a fragility and an acute sense of "constructedness" in one's previous sense of identity, culture, and belonging. An existential crisis is almost inevitable. Here, chance and happenstance play a much more crucial role in shaping mentalities than otherwise is the case. Take the case of Nassim Nicholas Taleb, author of the much acclaimed book *Fooled by Randomness* (2004) and a new book called *The Black Swan* (2007) that is set to revolutionize our thinking about significant events in the world. Taleb's wonderful and penetrating insights into the weaknesses of our dominant "conformist" mode of linear causal thinking with its unquestioning reliance on Gaussian distributions and Bell curves, and the conceptual blindness thereby brought about by it, has won him many thoughtful admirers worldwide. Taleb grew up in war-torn Lebanon, obtained a baccalaureate from the French *lycée*, did an MBA at Wharton, spent time as a foreign exchange trader before becoming a Dean's Professor of the Sciences of Uncertainty at University of Massachusetts at Amherst. While it would be tempting but unwise to assert direct causality of his unusual and refreshing thinking to his rich and diverse set of life experiences, it would not be too far-fetched to recognize the effect of such a diverse formative background on his sensitivity to crucial differences in attitudes and habits of thought generally unexamined by those totally immersed in a specific socio-cultural and institutional context. Taleb's vital contribution derives from the very fact that he is an "outlier" having to constantly oscillate between different cultures, mentalities, and systems of thought.

That our individuality and personhood is socially constructed and precariously sustained through habits, norms, and cultural practices is well appreciated in much of social theory, not least by what has come to be called Actor-Network theory (ANT), whose function it is to "explore and describe local processes of patterning, social orchestration, ordering and resistance" (Law, 1992, p. 8). For ANT, "what counts as a person is an effect generated by a network of heterogeneous, interacting materials….People are who they are because they are patterned networks of heterogeneous materials" (Law, 1992, p. 5). Instead of assuming that individuals are self-identical, autonomous, and purposeful agents in their own rights, ANT maintains that we are who we are because of the often invisible background social practices that operate continuously to support and sustain our social identity and sense of personhood. This security of identity provided by our cultural origins is shattered by the forcible dislocation from one social domain to another as in the case of refugees, immigrants, new settlers, and even entrepreneurs.

Loosing our previously secure social self and having to let go forms a vital step in the path towards maturity of self, personhood, and an existential sense of knowing who we really are, and hence the confidence and conviction to moderate the need for being wanted, or to be popular and liked.

Authenticity in action comes from a hard-won overcoming of an existential crisis—a crisis of security and self-identity. Jean-Paul Sartre's (1966) *Being and Nothingness* and Herbert Marcuse's (1964) *One Dimensional Man* are ideologically worlds apart, but they share one common insight: that most people most of the time live inauthentic and unfulfilling/unfulfilled lives because they are existentially insecure, prisoners of social norms, expectations and aspirations. Instead of owning and taking responsibility for their personal circumstances and relishing the challenge, they spend all their energies lamenting their plight and in maintaining status quo. Either they remain blissfully unaware of the one-dimensionality of their own thinking or they continue to operate in bad faith, refusing to acknowledge their own complicity in the circumstances they find themselves and/or justifying why they are not where they would prefer to be by citing conditions and circumstances beyond their control. There is "social inertia" (Bourdieu, 1990) involved in maintaining this disingenuous and intrinsically unsatisfying form of existence. Yet the familiarity and pseudo-security it offers is seductive, much like how management academics have a tendency to cling to simplified representations (often in a quantifiable form) of management reality rather than to confront the inherent flux and uncertainty that is the actual experience of managing.

Letting go allows us to shift paradigms from one of inauthentic existence where the truth lies outside us and must therefore be told to us, to one where the pain and existential endurance associated with living authentically constantly reminds us that to be true to life we must suffer the consequence of knowing that there is no ready outside explanation for justifying our actions—that we have no choice but to choose and to live with the consequences of our choice. It is to appreciate the Kierkegaardian axiom that life must be "lived forward" even as we make sense of it backwards, and that to truly live is to be necessarily "emotionally disturbed." This is the existential price that must be paid in a genuine paradigm shift.

PERSONAL REFLECTIONS

I am originally from Singapore, now settled in academia in the United Kingdom having arrived here to study and live in the later half of the 1980s as a mature student after a successful career in business. Before that, until the age of 30 I had *never* been outside Singapore/Malaysia—never flown or taken a boat trip beyond those shores. On my first trip to Britain in 1979, sponsored by my then employer, a British multinational, I arrived at Heathrow Airport after a 24-hour flight involving stops at Dubai and Athens. On arrival at the airport lounge waiting for connection to a domestic flight to Manchester, I discovered to my amazement at a news-stand no less than six different newspapers reporting on an event the day before, all with spectacularly different takes. That such plurality of interpretations existed at all was a source of bewilderment for me having come from a small nation where a single national newspaper reported authoritatively on all events that were deemed important and relevant. It was for me, the stark difference of this experience from my own previously closeted world that made a difference in me having to revise my comprehension of the world around me. My subsequent six-month stay at the parent company in Britain after that was a constant eye-opening experience and a rich source of novel insights into cultures, lifestyles, and aspirations of a people vastly different from my own.

Six years after my first experience of Britain I returned as a mature student to do a one-year Masters in Organization Studies at Lancaster University. Here my intellectual appetite was whetted. With the encouragement and support of my lecturers I explored the wider world of the humanities and social sciences even though the course was ostensibly about Organization Studies. Herbert Marcuse's (1964) *One Dimensional Man,* Jean-Paul Sartre's (1966) *Being and Nothingness,* and John Berger's (1972) *Ways of Seeing,* in particular, were a revelation to my consciousness. Life could never be the same thereafter. I returned to work in my company for another two years.

Two years later, in 1988, nine years after my first visit to Britain, I made the momentous decision to give up a successful business career to live in Britain and to experience a different lifestyle from that of the work-driven one which up till then had defined my entire life. The opportunity came from an acceptance by the University of Lancaster for me to do a PhD in Organization Studies. It was, initially, an excuse to get away from the weariness of a lifestyle entirely defined by work priorities. Selling my house to pay for my PhD was a gamble with no possibility of a fall-back position. Becoming a student again, after enjoying the privileges of being a senior manager in a multinational was a humbling experience. Whereas I had previously had eager staff always available at my beck and call, now I had to stand for hours at the photocopier with a stack of five-penny coins copying book chapters and journal articles to bring home to read. More humbling was the loss of status and the threat to my own self-worth. I was jobless with a wife and a very uncertain future ahead. She too had sacrificed her career to be with me. Without her confidence and unflinching support it would have been impossible for me to have successfully completed my studies. These things weigh heavy on your shoulders when things do not go as well as you hope. Many a time, I harboured deep self-doubt and wondered if it had been a reckless move, and if I should give up altogether the idea of a PhD and return home shameful and empty-handed.

"Letting go" may be easily thinkable in conceptual terms, but it is emotionally draining in practice. It means deliberately moving from the known to the unknown and openly embracing the vagaries associated with an as-yet-undefined future. The future might be well be orange, but there is no guarantee that it will be bright.

DETOURING TO GAIN ACCESS

Does not detour—which is anything but gratuitous—exert a certain power, which is all the more forceful for its discretion?
—Jullien, 2000, p. 7

Capitalism is the dominant political economic system widely credited as the primary cause of the overwhelming success in wealth-creation among developed countries and the subsequent the rise of the global economy. Communism and socialism, in their unadulterated forms, are no longer considered seriously viable options. The capitalist instinct teaches us that it is a direct, focused, and purposeful self-interested approach, characterized by clarity of intentions and the means and resources to effect the desired outcome, which invariably produces the most successful results. Probably the most vital principle of capitalism that Adam Smith identified in *An Inquiry into the Wealth of Nations* (1776/1976) is the idea of the division of labor and the emphasis on specialization it encourages. Specialization means focusing attention on a specific aspect of phenomena to the exclusion of other aspects and then repeatedly concentrating effort on it to exploit its possibilities in order to achieve a desired outcome. This approach breeds a focused, instrumental, means–ends logic of action.

Such means–ends thinking implies, on the one hand, a wide range of available assets and resources, in the form of tools, equipment, information, expertise, competencies, capabilities, and so on, and on the other some distant end away in the far horizon towards which we unswervingly march and by which we measure and judge the effectiveness of our actions, as would a helmsman judge his course by a landing pier on the far shoreline. The expenditure of effort is hence directly linked to the perceived efficacy of purposeful action. Action in this sense carries with it an aura of "heroism," of the transcendental capability of human agency, the ability to accomplish things against, or in spite of the run of nature.

This kind of means–ends, or what James March (2003) calls "consequentialist" thinking, promotes a directness of approach in dealing with affairs of the world: It pervades modern capitalist societies and it is deeply imbibed in the collective psyche of university business schools and systematically promoted therein. It presupposes that success in any endeavour requires selecting and choosing a particular course of action; clarity of goals and objectives, carefulness in charting out the most direct and expeditious plans for action, and thoroughness in implementing the latter with the full force of our intelligence and capability, are key aspects of this approach. Effective action is generally associated with the direct, visible, and decisive intervening into the natural course of things. It suggests the imposition of individual *agency* and *will* onto a recalcitrant and obdurate reality, of overcoming resistances and obstacles in order to obtain a pre-determined, more desirable state of affairs. It elevates the visible, the spectacular, and the sensational over the mundane everydayness of day-to-day practical coping in accounting for events and social transformations.

The encouragement of such a direct interventionist view of managerial action is intimately linked to a deeply embedded habitual line of causal reasoning, initiated by Plato in the *Republic*, in which an ideal form or "model" (paradise, absolute beauty, eternal love, unrivalled riches, indisputable conquest, highest status, global supremacy, maximum profits, market-dominance, etc.) is used as the basis for dealing with the imperfections of reality. This ideal is taken to be the *goal*, the all-consuming end to be relentlessly pursued and attained. Human *will* is then purposefully deployed in the realization of this ideal. Ideal, goal, will, and presumed efficacy of intervention thus channels, drives, and gives meaning and purpose to human judgement and action, and generates the pattern of choices and decisions that ensue. An instrumental form of thinking is set up to enable the bridging of the perceived gap between the ideal and the actual, the theory and practice.

This preference for directness in dealing with human affairs and events through such heroic action is the life and soul of the Greek-inspired modern Western mind (Jullien, 2004). Both democracy and capitalism emphasize free and open debate, competition and confrontation, and the seeking of a desired end though decisive action, whether in war, public debate, or business dealings. This has been the *sine qua non* of the liberal democracies. Such a preference for direct face-to-face confrontation, in war and in public debate, has its equivalent in the world of business strategizing exemplified by phrases such as "new market captures," "hostile takeovers," "price wars," "acquisitions," and the very idea of a "competitive strategy." Yet, whether success or failure can be directly attributed to these decisive, spectacular doings remains contentious. The question of the overall efficacy of direct visible intervening actions into the course of things remains a point of in-tense debate. Could it be that there are other more mundane and effica-cious strategies in operation in actual practice but that because they do not function according to the means–ends logic of heroic strategizing and are thus more quiet and elusive they remain unnoticed and hence unappreci-ated as the actual driving force producing seemingly favorable outcomes? Could it be that a more oblique and circuitous approach in dealing with affairs of the world, as in human inquiry, be actually more efficacious in the long run than a direct spectacular means–ends approach?

The effectiveness and unparalleled success of the means–ends instru-mental rationality in a variety of human circumstances is without question. Modern civilisation and the various technologies we have developed owe much to this cultivated capacity for deliberate, focused and systematic ex-ploitation of our natural and mental resources. As a species, we would not be as advanced as we are without the development of these innate capaci-ties. Yet, for all its accomplishments, there is a troubling aspect; a dark un-derside which remains understated. The very directness of a means–ends interventionist approach can often unwittingly generate undesired side-ef-fects; it is invariably disruptive. Direct action is always external to the course of things and so constitutes an 'intrusion'; there is wastage involved because such spectacular intervention is, of necessity, to a degree incompatible and hence turbulence-generating in its very act. It often results in destruction and displacement of assets, capabilities and resources. By imposing itself on the otherwise smooth, unspectacular laminar flow of reality, such inter-ventions tears at the tissue of things and upsets their internal coherence. It breeds a resistance that often work counterproductively to blunt its intend-ed effect. Direct, heroic action helps crystallize interest and may provide a convenient narrative 'hook' for hanging a story-line justifying the very means-ends thinking that inspires its elevation (Jullien, 2000, pp. 35–53). Yet, there is a sense in which this spectacular aspect of action only accentu-ates its artificiality and superficiality.

In the realms of management scholarship and inquiry, the instrumen-tal means-ends form of thinking and the direct 'heroic' interventionist ap-proach associated with it still predominates in business schools. It eschews a more oblique and circuitous approach in dealing with affairs of the world and in engaging with the world of ideas as well as in the educational pro-cess. March (2003: 205) laments the loss of a sense of vocation and an up-holding of the values of scholarship and inquiry, not for direct instrumen-tal reasons, but *for their own sake*. He reminds us of an alternative 'grand tradition' of scholarship and inquiry which 'sees action as based not on anticipations of consequences but on attempts to fulfil the obligations of personal and social identities and senses of self'. It is one that cannot be justified by a means-ends logic of action. It is 'a tradition that speaks of self-conceptions and proper behaviour, rather than expectations, incentives, and desires'. March uses Manuel Cervantes's Don Quixote as an example of this kind of behaviour which carries its own logic of justification: a justification which shows that in vocations such as management scholarship and education, exploration and intellectual forays and 'detours' from the mainstream literature and the kind of thinking associated with it can help us gain a much more rounded appreciation of what it means to be a within a university tradition and what genuine scholarship might entail. March himself resorts to literature, poetry, philosophy and the arts, rather than the traditional business and management disciplines to illuminate the human predicament (see, for example, March and Weil, 2005). For him, the arts and the humanities, despite their apparent remoteness, have much insight to offer about the nature and causes of human behaviour, which, after all, is what management studies attempt to comprehend. Criticising the direct, exploitative and instrumentalist approach pervasive in business schools, March writes:

> Great enthusiasms, commitments, and actions are tied not to hopes for great outcomes but to a willingness to embrace the arbitrary and unconditional claims of a proper life.... When we recognize ourselves as sharing a human identity that is intertwined with traditions of scholarship, we are led to view business schools in ways that are somewhat less consequentialist than are the ways that have become familiar to contemporary discussions. . . .

> A university is only incidentally a market. It is more essentially a temple—a temple dedicated to knowledge and a human spirit of inquiry. It is a place where learning and scholarship are revered, not primarily for what they contribute to personal or social well-being but for the vision of humanity that they symbolize, sustain, and pass on.... Higher education is a vision, not a calculation. It is a commitment, not a choice. Students are not customers; they are acolytes. Teaching is not a job; it is a sacrament. Research is not an investment; it is a testament. . . .

> But in order to sustain the temple of education, we probably need to rescue it from those deans, donors, faculty, and students who respond to incentives and calculate consequences and restore it to those who respond to senses of themselves and their callings, who support and pursue knowledge and learning because they represent a proper life, *who read books not because they are relevant to their jobs but because they are not, who do research not in order to secure their reputations or improve the world but in order to honor scholarship*, and who are committed to sustaining an institution of learning as an object of beauty and an affirmation of humanity. (March, 2003: 206, emphasis added)

It is not always the case that a direct mean–ends instrumentalist approach to things is most efficacious or leads to the most satisfying outcomes. Particularly in human situations, an oblique, less direct and more digressive approach may ultimately prove to be more fruitful and enriching. Such "*obliquity* of the trajectory leads to a *depth* of meaning" (Jullien, 2000, p. 53) that is usually inaccessible, unattainable, or glossed over by a more direct frontal form of engagement. Many deeply insightful and pleasurable experiences derive from an aesthetic principle in art, poetry, music and writings, for instance, in which meaning is not exhausted at the first glance but is allowed to develop endlessly and speculatively in the process of contemplation. This is the real secret of great artistic masterpieces, great writings, and great teaching and education. Each time one engages with these great works, a new meaning is revealed. Similarly, in the educational process, students may long have graduated before they begin to fully appreciate the full import of what was learned in their university life that they did not fully understand at that time. Moreover, such retrospective insights are not limited to the formal learning that was necessarily featured in the main curriculum. Insight may have come from a cursory throw-away remark by a particular teacher or an infectious enthusiasm and commitment displayed in certain lectures that left a lasting impression. The allure of a genuine university education process lies in the immanent potentiality of the as-yet-unrevealed. University education is as much the communication of possibilities as it is of actualities. In this way, a fact communicated under such circumstances is no longer a bare fact. Instead, it is suggestively pregnant with possibilities. It is no longer a "burden on the memory; it is energising as the poet of our dreams and as the architect of our purposes" (Whitehead, 1932, p. 139).

This awareness of the subliminal qualities both in effective educational processes and in great works of art is something that the art critic John Ruskin deals with in *Modern Painters*. Here Ruskin reminisces on his experience of standing at the foot of an old Church tower in Calais and reflects on why he felt more drawn to the gnarled and rugged contours of an old wasted building rather than to the surface orderliness and neatness of which the eye naturally seeks.

Ruskin was writing in reaction to the advent of modernism and representation when the immediate sense of neatness, orderliness and trimness had taken hold of Victorian England and threatened to "artificialize" the human sensibilities by an over-emphasis on the visible, the direct and the manifest. He coined the term *noble picturesque* to allude to this deep awareness and appreciation of the intricate richness and multiplicity of contours and detours which lie beneath the immediate and the apparent.

> I cannot find words to express the intense pleasure I have always in first finding myself, after some prolonged stay in England, at the foot of the old tower of Calais church. The large neglect, the noble unsightliness of it; the record of its years written so visibly, yet without sign of weakness or decay; its stern wasteness and gloom, eaten away by the Channel winds; and overgrown with the bitter sea grass. . . . I cannot tell the half of the strange pleasures and thought that come

about me at the sight of that old tower...it is the epitome of all that makes the Continent of Europe interesting, as opposed to new countries....We, in England, have our new streets, our new inn, our green shaven lawn, and our piece of ruin emergent from it,—a mere *specimen*....put on a velvet carpet to be shown...that spirit of trimness. The smooth paving stones; the scraped, hard even rutless roads; the neat gates and plates, and the essence of border and order, and spikiness and spruceness....now I have insisted long on this English character, because I want the reader to understand thoroughly the opposite element...the *noble picturesque*, its expression, namely of suffering, of poverty, or decay, nobly endured by unpretending strength of heart. Nor only unpretending, but unconscious...the picturesqueness is in the unconscious suffering. (Ruskin, 1903-1912/1996, Vol. VI: 11, emphasis added)

It is this noble picturesque that invites a "detour" in our thinking to attending to what is not immediately apparent. It is what defines the works of great artists, writers, and thinkers and suggests the richness and variety of their sustained efforts to display, through their interminable struggles with representation and expression, their deepest insights, which are largely invisible to the less initiated who are more distracted by the superficial content of representation itself. Pausing to reflect, preparedness to let oneself "soak in" the circumstance one finds oneself detouring for a moment, to gain genuine access; that is the open exploratory and infinitely satisfying approach towards management education scholarship. The tortuous route is also the more satisfying, enriching and fulfilling one.

NEGATIVE CAPABILITY: RESISTING THE HASTE-OF-WANTING-TO-KNOW

Negative Capability, that is, when a man is capable of being in uncertainties, mysteries, doubts, without any irritable reaching after fact and reason.
—John Keats in G. F. Scott (Ed.), 2002: 46

We live in a world of instant information, instant communication, instant "MacDonaldized" services and instant "canned" expertise. If we are in any doubt we recourse to the internet for information, to the mobile phone for immediate contact and clarifications wherever we are in the world, and to the experts and consultants for advice on our problems and ailments, and increasingly we have cultivated an expectation for instant customer satisfaction even in university business schools. Convenient textbooks, e-library access, handy lecture guides, concise power-point handouts, and even direct video-conferencing are now the order of the day. Gone are the days when physically browsing laboriously through dusty old manuscripts in the library, formally read lectures, untidy handwritten notes and scribbles, and struggling mightily to comprehend the seemingly obscure thoughts of dead, great thinkers, defined universities and the life of the mind. We are socially conditioned into expecting clarity, certainty, and predictability as an intrinsic feature of everyday life. As a result, we have developed an impatience for clarity and transparency and have great difficulty dealing with the ambiguous, the uncertain, and the not-yet-realised. We have internalized a "haste-of-wanting-to-know" and lack the necessary patience and resilience to wait for situations to unfold and clarify themselves before we act. This cultivated impatience is a weakness.

In our modern world of instant gratification, quick results, and the immediate satisfying of needs, within the context of management education, there is no longer any requirement for sustained engagement with ideas, or for prolonged pondering, savouring, doubting, and intellectual struggle. Being kept in ambiguity and suspense is no longer an acceptable state of affairs; paradoxically, these days, only a good movie or novel can draw out this sense of suspense and intrigue in us. Books, especially text-books, and journal articles are expected to clearly state their objectives, lay out their plan, delimit the management "problematic" and plainly and clearly set out the issues for consideration, contemplation and appropriate action. There is no longer any urgency or concern for the nuanced, the implied, the inarticulate, the unspoken—that underbelly of tacit understanding that grounds all forms of human communication which like the lining of a kimono keeps it in shape but yet is invisible to the eye (Nishida, 1921/1990). In other words, we have not learned how to endure uncertainty and doubt because we have surreptitiously privileged the overt, the visible, and the manifest over the invisible, the covert, and the latent. All the former aspects lend themselves to quick clarification and empirical confirmation. We are seduced by quantity, numbers, and neat figures. We fail to appreciate the importance of the need for close careful reading, of "mulling over," and of feeling the mood and sentiment of the author; of seeking out the invisible and the inarticulate underlying our sense of things. We fail to value what the English poet John Keats calls "negative capability."

Keats arrived at this insight when after a night out with his companions he recalled having "not a dispute but a disquisition with Dilke [one of his companions] on various subjects; several things dovetailed in my mind and at once struck me, what qualities went to form a Man of Achievement especially in literature and which Shakespeare possessed so enormously" (John Keats, in G. F. Scott (Ed.), 2002: 46). For Keats, what makes an individual a "man of achievement" is a cultivated ability to endure not knowing without getting overly anxious about what to think or do to resolve a situation. To him, the possession of a 'negative capability' is a sign of intellectual and practical maturity; the ability to resist the urge for premature closure and finality and hence the openness to new possibilities and new insights. Keats' negative capability involves the ability to bask in the totality of experience without questioning or seeking some specific answer to it: in other words to take the world around us and appreciate it simply as it is. This notion of 'negative capability' is well illustrated in Keats' own encounter with a Grecian urn on a visit to the British Museum and his pondering over the mysteries associated with it.

In *Ode on a Grecian Urn*, Keats contemplates on the mysterious origins and meanings of the surface depictions on the side of an ancient Grecian urn. The pictures contained are frozen in time and beg for an explanation. He describes the urn as a "historian" that can tell a story and wonders about the figures on the side of the urn and asks what legend they depict and from where they come: "What mad pursuit? What struggle to escape?/ What pipes and timbrels? What wild ecstasy?" The Grecian urn, passed down through countless centuries to the time of the Keats' viewing, exists outside of time in the human sense—it does not age, it does not die, and indeed it is alien to all such concepts. In Keats' meditation, this creates an intriguing paradox for the human figures carved into the side of the urn. They are free from time, but they are simultaneously frozen in time. This paradox and ambiguity is what pervades all of human experiences and the cultivation of "negative capability" allows us to live that experience for what it is without necessarily willing it to speak conveniently to us on our own terms. Negative capability is that state of intentional open-mindedness to accept that not all things in life can be straightforwardly resolved and is a quality possessed by great poets and thinkers.

In late 1970s I was a production superintendent with a large can manufacturing plant in Singapore. This was a time of industrial strife in Britain where we were getting our regular supply of tinplate (at that time tinplate and not aluminium was largely used in can manufacturing outside the U.S.) from British Steel in Britain. On one occasion, the port workers in Britain went on strike so much so that all shipment of tinplate bound for Singapore was held up. This caused us much anxiety and concern as our local customers—the breweries and soft drinks manufacturers—were expecting their regular monthly supply of cans for their own processing and export. But because of the port strike we were unable to carry on production and to meet delivery deadlines and hence incurred the wrath of our customers who threatened to take their business elsewhere. Frantically, three of us—the factory manager, the marketing manager and I—went in to the office of the managing director to seek his advice on what to do under these dire circumstances. We had already tried various alternative suppliers to no avail. To our surprise and astonishment, we found

---

him calmly playing with his train set on the mahogany table where he usually held his monthly management meetings. When we confronted him with the problem he basically told us that since there was nothing much else we could do to meet the demands of our customers, it was best to use this period to carry out maintenance work that we had had to push back because of constantly having to meet delivery targets. For him this was an opportunity, not to frantically scurry around like headless chickens but to use it as an opportunity to prepare ourselves for what came after once the strike had been resolved.

The impulse to act quickly or do something to resolve a pressing problematic situation is so ingrained that sometimes we forget that biding time, allowing things to mature, ripen, or unfold and develop without intervening, counterintuitive though it may seem, may be actually the best course of action to adopt. Here is my own experience of the value of negative capability.

Not doing, and the capacity to not act, to restrain from premature action and final conclusion (i.e., a *negative* capability) is sometimes much more efficacious than plunging in and intervening directly to change the course of things. Yet the problem with not acting, or non-doing, is that it is hardly ever recognized in positive terms especially in a culture where spectacular action is highly regarded. Negative capability is linked to an economy of effort and an appreciation of the importance of *timing* and *timeliness* in producing a desirable outcome.

NAIVETY AND "LEARNED IGNORANCE"

The more he knows that he is unknowing, the more learned he will be.
—Nicholas of Cusa, 1996, p. 12

We live in a world awash with information, images and representations—an impressive accumulation of documented knowledge. It is frequently asserted that in a knowledge economy such explicit forms of information and knowledge have become the fundamental building blocks of modern society. Knowledge and information are critical to all modes of economic progress and development because it is believed that attainment of higher levels of knowledge is what leads to higher levels of performance, output, and productivity and hence higher standards of living. The more we know and understand the better off we will be. By "knowledge," as opposed to mere opinion, we generally mean a set of organized propositional statements of facts or concepts and ideas that is a result of rigorous, reasoned judgement and/or systematic and thorough observation and verification.

This idea that proper knowledge is only considered so when it can be explicated in propositional form is attributable to Aristotle (1998) who insisted that the ability to explain and articulate the *cause* of things is what clearly distinguishes the knowledgeable person from the merely experienced one. To know, therefore, is to possess the answer to the question "Why?" and not just the "What?" of a phenomenon. This privileging of *causal* explanation over experience has meant that the art of "doing" has been overshadowed by the "science" of reasoning and justification. Yet many of our life experiences teach us that living itself offers deep insights and tacit understandings which are not always amenable to representation or rational forms of explanation. Pure experiencing itself provides us with a primordial form of knowing that has not been sufficiently acknowledged in contemporary epistemology. Oftentimes, there can be a deeper awareness about what we do not know, or what cannot be expressed in linguistic terms, that nevertheless constitute genuine and profound insights into the human condition. This was something Socrates was acutely aware of.

Unlike Aristotle or Plato, Socrates was wise because he was acutely aware of his own ignorance and of how much it took to confront this ignorance. Socrates understood that all knowledge lies on a bed of ignorance; to know is also to "owe," to incur a debt to what one does not know. To know that one does not know, as Socrates concluded, is to begin to acknowledge the inherent *owing* in kn*owing*—the ignorance of knowledge. The literary critic Barbara Johnson echoed this insight when she wrote:

> Ignorance, far more than knowledge, is what can never be taken for granted. If I perceive my ignorance as a gap in knowledge instead of an imperative that changes the very nature of what I think I know, then I do not truly experience my ignorance. The surprise of otherness is that moment when a new form of ignorance is suddenly activated as an imperative. (Johnson, 1989, p. 16)

Only when we become painfully aware that it is *ignorance of our ignorance,* and not merely a simple gap in knowledge, that prevents profound insights—only then do we develop and mature as individuals and begin to glimpse that illusive realm called wisdom. It is this Socratic idea of a state of heightened awareness of ignorance that is implied by the term *learned ignorance.*

Learned ignorance is a cultivated humility, meekness of demeanour, and openness of mind that is distinct and different from the aggressive and relentless pursuit, acquisition, and exploitation of knowledge. In contrast to the current emphasis on knowledge-creation, acquisition and accumulation as the basis for enlightened decision-making and performance, learned ignorance inclines us toward the performative value of intellectual naivety.

It is a reminder that formal learning and knowledge is not the be-all and end-all of human understanding and action. In a book written in the early fifteenth century, entitled *Idiota de sapienta* (*The layman on wisdom and knowledge*), Cardinal Nicholas of Cusa, a German cleric, describes a conversation between a scholar and a layman as follows:

> **Layman:** I am amazed at your pride because although in perusing countless books you tire yourself with continual reading, you have not yet been brought to a state of humility.... True knowledge makes one humble....
>
> **Orator:** [Oh] poor, utterly unschooled Layman, what is this presumption of yours [that leads] you thus to make light of the study of written learning, without which study no one makes progress?
>
> **Layman:** [Oh] Great Orator, it is not presumption, but love, that does not allow me to keep silent.... The opinion of authority has held you back, so that you are as a horse that by nature is free but that by contrivance is tied with a halter to a stall, where it eats nothing but what is served to it. For your intellect, restricted to the authority of writings, is fed by strange and unnatural food.
>
> **Orator:** If the nourishment that comes from wisdom is not present in the books of the wise, then where is it present?
>
> **Layman:** ...I maintain that no *natural* nourishment is to be found there. For those who first devoted themselves to writing about wisdom did not derive their growth from the nourishment of books, which did not yet exist; rather by means of natural foods they were brought unto the state of being grown men. And by far they excel in wisdom those others who suppose that they have learned from books.
>
> [The dialogue eventually ends with the scholar suitably persuaded of the superior wisdom of the layman.]
>
> **Orator:** You relate such beautiful things. Explain now, I ask, how can I be elevated into some kind of tasting of Eternal Wisdom? (Nicholas of Cusa, 1996, pp. 497–503)

The basic point that seems to be made repeatedly here is that knowledge, information, and symbolic representations, rather than help us to grasp pristine reality, often distract and distort our understanding of the latter. Because we ordinarily think of our lack of knowledge in terms of a "gap" in representation that must be filled, our instinctive tendency is to seek more such forms of abstract knowledge. Paradoxically, in that very process, we lose touch of that which is most near and dear to us—the very richness of life experience itself. Rather than lead us on the path toward greater understanding, wisdom, and fulfillment, more knowledge and possessions actually distances us from our life experiences. As the philosopher Alfred North Whitehead perceptively points out in *Science and the Modern World*: "When you understand all about the sun and all about the atmosphere and all about the rotation of the earth, you may still miss the radiance of the sunset. There is no substitute for the direct perception of the concrete achievement of a thing in its actuality" (Whitehead, 1926/1985, p. 248). Paradoxically, the more we "know," in its formal intellectual sense, the more we are likely to mistake representations for reality and hence lose the intimacy and richness of lived experiences.

This loss of innocence through intellectualizing experience is something that was deeply understood in ancient China and is well encapsulated in the enigmatic sayings of the ancient mystical Chinese figure Chuang Tzu:

> The knowledge of the ancients was perfect. In what way was it perfect? There were those who believed that nothing existed. Such knowledge is indeed perfect and ultimate and cannot be improved. The next were those who believed there were things but there was no distinction between them. Still the next were those who believed there was distinction but there was neither right nor wrong. When the distinction between right and wrong became prominent, Tao was thereby reduced. Because Tao was reduced, individual bias was formed.... In reality Tao has no limitations, and speech has no finality.... Therefore there are things which analysis cannot analyze, and there are things which argument cannot argue.... Therefore it is said that argument arises from failure to see. (Chuang Tzu, in Chan, 1963, p. 186)

In a more accessible and recognizable form, the pragmatist philosopher William James has written extensively about this kind of "naïve" knowing that precedes symbolic representation and formal knowledge in his exploration of "pure experience": "'Pure experience' is the name I give to the immediate flux of life which furnishes the material to our later reflection with its conceptual categories. Only new-born babes, or men in semi-coma from sleep, drugs, illness, or blows, may be assumed to have an experience pure in the literal sense of a *that* which is not any definite *what*" (James, 1912/1996, p. 93).

However, while James is doubtful about the our normal capacity for achieving this "pure experience," others like the art critic John Ruskin, the Japanese philosopher Nishida Kitaro, and the Japanese industrialist Konusuke Matsushita insist that this is a prerequisite for outstanding performances of any kind. For Ruskin, the power of great works of art lies in the painter's capacity for achieving what he calls the "innocence of the eye" (Ruskin, 1927, *Works,* Vol. XV: 27). Likewise, for Matsushita, arguably the most successful and influential Japanese industrialist of the 20th century, the attainment of this pure innocent seeing is what makes for a good business decision-making: an ability to attain a clear and uncluttered vision of things as they are.

The untrapped, open mind—*sunao*—of which I often speak is a temperament that allows one to see things as they really are. Without this open, receptive mind, we lack true strength. We have made it a regular management policy at Matsushita Electric to cultivate this *sunao* mind, in the conviction that it enables us to perceive the real state of things in society. If one views the world with a narrow and grasping mind, one becomes fixed on and distracted by extraneous aspects of things, often losing sight of their true character.... you just always try to see white as white, blue as blue, black as black—without prejudice or distortion. That way you will not err in judgement. Approaching things with such a straightforward spirit makes a person strong, upright, and wise, and thus able to grasp the true state of things. (Matsushita, 2002, p. 45)

There may be some who will be sceptical about the ability to attain this "innocent" or naïve seeing and to act accordingly. Yet, as Matsushita points out, this pure awareness is consistent and resembles the achievements of Zen training. "Zen training with its austere life-style and stress on meditation, seeks to free the mind from material concerns and prejudices, and in this sense the Zen mind bears a certain resemblance to the *sunao* mind" (Matsushita, 1978, pp. 63–65). This Zen-like awareness involving the purging of thought and conceptual categories is something extensively cultivated in the East as the German philosopher Eugene Herrigel discovered during his stay in Japan learning the art of archery.

In the relentless perfecting of action exemplified by sustained practice in the art of archery, the object is to arrive at that moment of 'artless art' which transcends technique when the archer, his/her equipment and the target are no longer experienced as discrete entities but form one reality in a unified, singular and effortless movement. "... Bow, arrow, goal and the ego, all melt into one another, so that I can no longer separate them. And, even the need to separate has gone. For, as soon as I take the bow and shoot, everything becomes so clear and straightforward and so ridiculously simple" (Herrigel, 1953/1985, p. 86). As the Zen master advised Herrigel, it is not the "I" that shoots; rather it is the trans-individual "it" that shoots: Performance is no longer something *willed* by a deliberate and conscious agent, but results from a spontaneous outpouring of action. Contrary to the common belief that better decisions and excellent performance in whatever field of endeavour are better achieved by more knowledge and information, oftentimes it is intellectual naivety and learned ignorance which accounts for such superior performance. This is because a heightened sensitivity to actual goings-on more than compensates for a lack of proper verifiable knowledge. Too much knowledge and information can desensitize us from the realities of what is actually going on—cluttering our minds, confusing and paralysing us from the ability to spontaneously respond to the immediacy of a given situation.

As a very mature student setting foot into high academia for the first time at the age of thirty-six (I did a technician's diploma in Mechanical Engineering at a local polytechnic in Singapore), I enjoyed an exhilarating and unforgettable experience when I got to Lancaster University in the UK to do my Master's despite not having done a first degree. Indeed, in retrospect, I am of the view that not having done a first degree, particularly in a discipline like management, actually encouraged me to explore the wider intellectual concerns of academic scholarship. Being intellectually naïve can be an asset in that it does not stop us from "straying" away from the specified course of study. Although my masters was in Organizational Analysis and Behaviour and although my initial expectation was to learn something that I could then apply back at work, it soon became clear quite early in the course that the questions that I was seeking answers for barely scratched the surface of the human condition. This new-found awareness came from reading well beyond the confines of the degree I was studying for. With encouragement from my mentors, I spent more time in the philosophy section of the library than I did in the management section. Until then, I had never heard of Popper, Kuhn, or Bateson, let alone Marx, Freud, Levi-Strauss, Lacan, and Derrida. As I mentioned previously, Jean-Paul Sartre's *Being and Nothingness*, Herbert Marcuse's *One Dimensional Man* and John Berger's *Ways of Seeing*, which dealt with art and perception, had a deep influence on me and awakened my awareness of the universality of the problem of perception. I ended up writing a 140-page dissertation on "Concepts of Self and their Implications for the Human Sciences" which, to this day I am quite pleased by the quality of the piece considering the fact that it was my very first serious academic piece of work. Although I found the work of writers like Whitehead, Bergson, Lacan, Lyotard and Derrida almost impenetrable and struggled mightily to even begin to glimpse what they were getting at, I began to gradually appreciate the kinds of issues and questions these writers, especially the more recent "poststructuralist" were addressing and the fundamental nature of their critique. Only then did I realize that they were critiquing the insidious pervasiveness of our reliance on representations at the expense of reality. Only then, did I realize how close, paradoxically, they were to the thinking of the ordinary practitioners who were instinctively suspicious of neat and glib explanations and prescriptions proffered by academics and consultants. I am not the only practitioner-turned-academic who has found profound resonances in the intellectual counter-movement initiated by poststructuralists.

Such profound insights are summarily dismissed by many mainstream management academics, most of whom have never actually read or followed closely the intellectual reasoning of the Derridas, Foucaults, Lyotards, Deleuzes, and Levinas of this world. It is an indictment of the shallowness of an instrumental means–ends form of reasoning in management academia that it is unwilling or unable to engage meaningfully with an alternative logic and form of understanding despite their commitment to scholarship. In my view, poststructuralist thinking resonates with the rich tradition of Heraclitus in the West and Lao Tzu and Chuang Tzu in the East.

Learned ignorance teaches us that an innocent childlike naivety in engaging with the world of affairs may be ultimately more fruitful than a mind stuffed with facts and formal learning. For Ruskin, Matsushita, and many others who have attained mastery in whatever field of endeavour they have chosen, an effortless attainment of outcomes is intimately linked to the capacity to cleanse the mind from a reliance on artificial conceptual categories and distinctions.

UPSTREAM THINKING: FROM BEING TO BECOMING

> How *an actual entity* becomes *constitutes* what *that actual entity* is*;*
> *so that the two descriptions of an actual entity are not independent. Its "being"*
> *is constituted by its "becoming."*
> —Whitehead, 1929, p. 31

If we take a walk along the bank of a river we soon realize that what makes a river recognizable as such is the existence of a stretch of identifiable flowing water framed by the contours of the river bank. Time and the continuous passing movement of water have etched out a distinctive passage along which the river now flows. The further we proceed downstream, the more well-grooved and clearly defined are the river banks. On the other hand, as we venture upstream, we find it increasingly difficult to identify the river as a singularity, nor are its features as well defined and easily identifiable. The further up the mountain we go the more we find a multitude of rivulets, streams, and pools of water which feed into that self-same entity called a river that we readily recognize further downstream. We discover that the river originates from a multitude of sources: the nooks, crevices, and crannies high up in the mountains containing and channelling accumulated rainwater, which gradually trickles down these narrow pathways of least resistance to form increasingly recognizable streams and rivulets along the mountain side. Here, in venturing towards the origins that eventually make up that unity with its all-too-familiar features, we begin to realize and appreciate the diversity, arbitrariness, serendipity, and multiplicity of its sources. We move from self-evident simplicity and self-identity to underlying complexity in our appreciation of phenomena in the world.

Much of what I call "upstream thinking" follows the same tendency in moving us, almost inexorably, towards the as-yet-unformed and the not-yet-known: the deeper sources of our understanding and comprehension. Multiple and oftentimes loosely connected traces of past patterns of thought constrain and help shape the possibilities for future ways of thinking so much so that it is only through persistent interrogation of our habits of thought that we can begin to intellectually grow and develop into a proper Management Education Scholar. This, however, is no easy task. Our habits of thought, including our knowledge in science, are shaped by powerful and invisible formative social forces, which require a determined effort on our part to access, as the philosopher Alfred North Whitehead astutely noted:

> No science can be more secure than the unconscious metaphysics which tacitly it presupposes....Our co-ordinated knowledge...is formed by the meeting of two orders of experience....We inherit an observational order, namely the types of things which we do in fact discriminate; and we inherit a conceptual order, namely a rough system of ideas in terms of which we do in fact interpret. We can point to no epoch in human history, or even in animal history, at which this interplay began....Observational discrimination is not dictated by the impartial facts. It selects and it discards, and what it retains is rearranged in a subjective order of prominence. (Whitehead, 1933, p. 183)

Our dominant habits of thought are acquired through the process of socialization so much so that they become all too self-evident and often unquestionable. They serve as powerful formative influences in the academic production of knowledge. Until and unless we become aware of such powerful tendencies influencing our thinking, our thoughts, like the overly familiar contours of the river bed, stand in danger of becoming more and more dogmatic rather than genuinely revealing. Downstream thinking takes as given the pre-existence of an already-constituted world that we subsequently apprehend. It leads to "a denial or 'forgetting' of the constituted nature of the object of study" (Chia, 1996, pp. 2–6) and to assuming that facts are transparent and impartial and hence speak for themselves. There is a forgetting that the origin of the word 'fact' derives from two Latin roots, *factum* and *facere*, both of which mean to 'fabricate': facts are products of *fabrications!*

Moving upstream in our thinking implies exploring the inherited assumptions: the "unconscious metaphysics" informing our modes of thought. Instead of focusing attention on the downstream state of things—their spectacular manifestation that draws our attention, their clear-cut recognizable features and characteristics, the observable aspects readily accessible to us, the overt impact they engender—we redirect our attention to the historically shaped process of emergence, to the background understanding that is implied rather than stated, to what is covert rather than overt, to what is submerged, nuanced, and invisible rather than manifest. We move our ontological orientation from one of *being* to *becoming*. By this is meant a distinctive intellectual disposition or bent that treats process rather than fact as the ultimate feature of reality.

Process thinking does not deny substances, but sees them as momentary effects or "stabilized manifestations" of underlying processes. It rejects the "Process Reducibility Thesis" (Rescher, 1996, p. 27), which presupposes that all processes are ontologically secondary to substances and hence reducible to the actions of things. Rescher (1996, p. 31) identifies four priorities inherent in a process-theoretical approach to analysis. First, it places activity over substance: As we have noted, substances are deemed to be momentary effects of processes. Second, it places process over product: Outcomes are merely convenient "ar-resting points" in a ceaselessly fluxing reality. Third, it gives preference to change over persistence and stability: Change is not an exception or transitional stage and stability the norm; rather, the opposite is true. And, finally, it gives preference to the ceaseless generation of novelty over continuity: reality renews itself endlessly so that each event is a never-to-be-repeated occurrence. Thus, contingency, emergence, novelty, and creativity are the fundamental axioms of a becoming ontology.

What this "becoming" ontology implies is that social reality, in particular, is not somehow ready-made—easily accessible and apprehending us in all its completeness. Rather, like a piece of unfinished quilt-work, social reality is always in-the-making. Organizations, institutions and social systems are multifarious human strategies for arresting, fixing and stabilizing an otherwise superfluous and fluxing reality which always threatens to overflow our limited conceptualizations. Reality, in the rawness of our pre-conceptual lived experiences is nothing less than a 'big blooming buzzing confusion, as free from contradiction in its "much-at-onceness" as it is alive and evidently there' (James, 1911/1996, p. 50). James colorfully likens empirical reality to be like "one of those dried human heads with which the Dyaks of Borneo deck their lodges. The skull forms a solid nucleus; but innumerable feathers, leaves, strings, beads, and loose appendices of every description float and dangle from it, and, save that they terminate in it, seem to have nothing to do with one another" (James, 1912/1996, p. 46). And, it is out of this "aboriginal sensible muchness" that our attention works to carve out objects of awareness:

"in the sky 'constellations', on the earth 'beach', 'sea', 'cliff', 'bushes', 'grass'. Out of time we cut out 'days' and 'nights', 'summers' and 'winters'... and all these abstract *whats* are concepts" (James, 1911/1996, p. 50).

Upstream thinking moves us to question the comfortable and familiar assumptions of systemicity, orderliness, pattern, and predictability existing in nature itself and to realize that language, human consciousness, and awareness have a large part to play in the seemingly structured nature of things. It is to draw attention to our immanently constructive role in the production of meaning and order in the universe. As Whitehead, again, reminds us:

> But the mind, in apprehending, also experiences sensations, which properly speaking, are qualities of the mind alone. These sensations are projected by the mind so as to clothe appropriate bodies in external nature. Thus the bodies are perceived as with qualities which in reality do not belong to them, qualities which in fact are purely the offspring of the mind. Thus, nature gets credit which should in truth be reserved for ourselves: the rose for its scent: the nightingale for his song: and the sun for his radiance. The poets are entirely mistaken. They should address their lyrics to themselves, and should turn them into odes of self-congratulation on the excellency of the human mind. Nature is a dull affair, soundless, scentless, colourless; merely the hurrying of material, endlessly meaninglessly. (Whitehead, 1926/1985, p. 68)

For Whitehead, many of the apparent paradoxes of life exist primarily because "we have mistaken our abstractions for concrete reality" (Whitehead, 1926/1985, p. 69). Moving upstream implies abandoning the familiarity of the well-trodden pathway of thought and venturing on the "road less travelled." It implies embracing ambiguity, chaos, and uncertainty, not as an inevitable problem that has to be dealt with and contained, but as the fecund pro-generative source of potentiality inviting our active intervention and ordering.

What are the implications of this "becoming" approach to understanding the practice of management and of management education scholarship? In a previous article reviewing Henry Mintzberg's (2004) *Managers Not MBAs*, I wrote that the practice of management (and indeed in the management of management education) is essentially about "becoming aware, attending to, sorting out, and prioritizing an inherently messy, fluxing, chaotic world of competing demands that are placed on a manager's attention.... Active perceptual organization and the astute allocation of attention is a central feature of the managerial task" (Chia, 2005, p. 1092). The task of managing begins with the messiness and ill-defined nature of problem situations and with creating coherence and some sense of order from the ambiguity and chaos that one is confronted with.

Adopting an upstream approach towards management practice implies developing an acute sensitivity for the hidden, the obscured, the unstated, the implied, and the repressed. Human situations, in particular, do not always lend themselves to straightforward interpretation; the hidden meanings of behaviors and actions have to be carefully teased out from what is actually said or expressed. What is said is not always what is meant. Nor is what is meant always said. Sensitivity to the background shaping human behavior and inclinations is a crucial aspect of effective management. Whether in the practice of management itself or as an effective Management Education Scholar, this implies foregoing first impressions (downstream thinking) and being always prepared to dig deeper into the complex causal connections.

It is not always self-evident how situation become what they are. Oftentimes, chance and serendipity play a key role in bringing about a particular propensity in things and situations. Subjectivity and sentiment play a far more crucial role in human affairs than we are prepared to acknowledge and their sources of initiation, like the source of a river, are almost impossible to trace. Choosing how things "become" over their manifest states, moving upstream to the multifarious sources that engender an outcome downstream, allows us to begin to appreciate the more subtle aspects of mental shaping and influencing in the act of education. That insight is invaluable to the committed management education scholar.

As a factory manager in the mid-1980s, I ran a two-piece can manufacturing plant in Singapore that operated on a continuous 24/7 basis, running on what we called at that time a "continental shift system." One early morning upon arriving at work, I was confronted by the local union general secretary and told that the printers and technicians in the printing section, who had just finished their night shift that morning, were planning not to return later that evening. When I probed further, I was told that some of them had seen a "ghost" on the shop-floor and were too frightened to return. The union secretary insisted that we called in a Chinese Taoist priest to perform an appeasement ceremony for the ghosts so that they would not harm our staff; otherwise workers would not return for the night shift for fear of their safety. My initial instinct was to dismiss this as absurd. However, there were genuine concerns on the part of our printers given the background of this situation. Firstly, it was the month of August, and in the Chinese calendar it is the month of the dead when many Chinese believed that the ghosts of the dead rise and roam the world in search of victims; this historically often coincided with the rise of accident rates in the factory. Second, the company had recently cut down a large jackfruit tree to clear an adjacent area for building a new warehouse, without first making offerings and praying for permission to the tree gods—again something that had raised concern amongst the more traditional amongst our employees. To make the situation seem more justifiable, the reader must be told that the factory was built just after the Second World War and was located near the causeway joining Singapore to Malaysia and built on grounds where a massacre by the Japanese invading forces had taken place during that fateful fall of the island state. Since then, there had always been claims of sightings of ghosts ever so often.

I managed to get hold of one of the printers who swore he had seen the ghost and tried to establish the facts of the situation. It transpired that he had seen this old, gaunt figure dressed in white wondering around the machinery and had even called to the "ghost" from a distance, being too frightened to approach the figure before it disappeared out of the factory door into the night. It was clear that the printer was petrified by the experience and no amount of coaxing would get him and his co-workers back that night. In desperation, my assistant and I decided to conduct further investigations. Without going into much detail, we remembered that there was an old age home (a hospice of sorts) nearby and wondered if it may have been one of the inmates, but we could not figure out how he could have got in to the factory premises, which was well fenced and brick-walled in parts. Nor could we imagine how any inmate would have got out at that time of the night. Nevertheless, we made inquiries at the home and it was subsequently confirmed that there was indeed an inmate who had had the habit of getting up in the middle of the night and wandering around the premises. But we still could not figure how he managed to get into the factory. Then we remembered that due to the construction work going on in erecting our new warehouse, access had to be made from behind the factory and the rear fencing had been removed during the day to aid the movement of vehicles but was temporarily put back and held together loosely in the evenings so that it was therefore possible for a small person to get through the gaps in the fencing. This was not the end of the story, however. When we informed the union and the printers that we had found their ghost and that it was a real person, we were met with disbelief. It was not until we actually physically brought the inmate to the factory cafeteria during lunch hour that day to parade him in front of the workers did the printers eventually realize that their 'ghost' was indeed a very real person. This is the kind of unusual circumstance not infrequently faced by practicing managers who have to learn to deal with situations that do not conform to stereotypes or paradigmatic expectations.

CONCLUSION

Becoming an effective management education scholar requires immersion and exposure to a rich variety of encounters and experiences followed by sustained and rigorous reflection on the lessons to be learned from life. Such a combination is rarely found in business schools for reasons I have previously articulated. Not only are budding management scholars often limited in their life experiences, they are also discouraged from intellectually exploring boldly and widely the world of ideas because of the still-entrenched disciplinary divides that define academic scholarship. For those more intellectually adventurous it is always an "upstream" task: There is always the need to justify the immediacy of the relevance of their interest in other disciplines to management and organization studies. But the word "relevance" suggests a black and white either/or mentality: Either it is relevant or it is not. This, however, is not the way to think about the world of ideas or experience. I propose we adopt an alternative word, "relevate," meaning to make relevant that which, in the first instance, appears irrelevant. If we accept this way of thinking then everything is potentially relevant and the task is one of establishing relations: of making the connections between ideas and experiences more visible and manifest.

In this way a young aspiring management academic even without much of life experiences can still enrich his or her understanding of the human predicament and become an effective management educator through such novel weaving, experimentation, and conjecturing with the world of ideas. The adoption of such a bold and venturesome approach and a cultivated curiosity for the surprising, the unusual, and the unexpected can help to generate a deeper and more acute awareness of the necessarily arbitrary, yet socially effective, character of the structure of modern lives including especially the underlying structure of modern business. Reading widely and extensively about other worlds and other lives helps stretch the imagination and expand our horizons of understanding. Travelling, both intellectually and physically, not in privileged situations, but through "roughing it" also helps cultivate a propensity for greater intimacy with the everyday world of ordinary individuals. In her very perceptive and insightful book *Peripheral Visions*, Mary Catherine Bateson, daughter of Gregory Bateson, the one-time maverick social anthropologist, writes:

> Adaptation comes out of encounters with novelty that may seem chaotic. In trying to adapt, we may need to deviate from cherished values, behaving in ways that we have barely glimpsed, seizing on fragmentary clues.... Ambiguity is the warp of life, not something to be eliminated.... I have often chosen to go into unfamiliar settings in spite of the discomfort involved, gaining a sense of perspective in my life that has a very different kind of value from the production of books and articles... Arriving in a new place, you start from

an acknowledgement of strangeness, a disciplined use of discomfort and surprise...Having made as much use as possible of the sense that everything is totally alien, you begin to experience, through increased familiarity, the way in which everything makes sense within a new logic. (Bateson, 1994: 8–27)

In my own encounters of foreignness, there is much to compare between the strangeness of the 'logic of supplementarity' that Derrida propounds as a plausible alternative to Aristotelian logic and the actual experience I had spending time with the Muso tribe in the mountainous regions of the province of Yunnan in South West China: possibly one of the last few remaining matriarchal societies where women played the dominant role in social life. In both cases the contrast of intellectual and/or social priorities with what we have come to normally expected could not have been more stark.

Seeking out the "difference that makes a difference" constitutes the unending and interminable search for a deeper and richer appreciation of the structure of modern human existence and how that affects our overall attitude towards social life, the environment, business, and economic prosperity. When these concerns and interests are all brought together in the context of a business school to illuminate business tendencies and to reflect on the future of capitalism, the management academic can be said to be working towards the attainment of the necessary wisdom and foresight that defines an effective Management Education Scholar.

REFERENCES

Aristotle. (1998). *Metaphysics.* H. Lawson-Tancred (Trans.). London: Penguin.

Bateson, G. (1972). *Steps to an ecology of mind.* New York: Ballantine.

Bateson, M. C. (1994). *Peripheral visions.* New York: Harper Collins.

Bennis, W. G., & O'Toole, J. (2005). How business schools lost their way. *Harvard Business Review, 83*(5), 96–104, 154.

Berger, J. (1972). *Ways of seeing.* London: Penguin.

Bourdieu, P. (1990). *The logic of practice.* Cambridge: Polity Press.

Chan, W. T. (1963). *A source book of Chinese philosophy.* Princeton, NJ: Princeton University Press.

Chia, R. (1996). *Organizational analysis as deconstructive practice.* Berlin: Walter de Gruyter.

Chia, R. (2005). The aim of management education: Reflections on Mintzberg's "Managers not MBAs." *Organization Studies, 26*(7), 1090–1092

Frost, R. (1993). *The road not taken and other poems.* London: Dover Publications. (Original work published 1916)

Herrigel, E. (1985). *Zen in the art of archery.* London: Arkana. (Original work published 1953)

James, W. (1996). *Essays in Radical Empiricism.* Lincoln and London: University of Nebraska Press. (Original work published 1912)

James, W. (1996). *Some problems of philosophy*. Lincoln and London: University of Nebraska Press. (Original work published 1911)

Johnson, B. (1989). *A world of difference*. Baltimore, MD: Johns Hopkins University Press.

Jullien, F. (2000). *Detour and access: Strategies of meaning in China and Greece*. New York: Zone Books

Jullien, F. (2004). *A treatise on efficacy: Between Western and Chinese thinking*. Honolulu, HI: University of Hawaii Press.

Keats, J. (1817). Letters to G. and T. Keats, 21st December 1817. In G. F. Scott (Ed.), *Selected Letters of John Keats*. Cambridge, MA: Harvard University Press.

Law, J. (1992). *Notes on the theory of the actor-network: Ordering, strategy and heterogeneity*. Unpublished manuscript, Dept of Social Anthropology, Keele University, Staffordshire, UK.

Lacan, J. (1977), *The four fundamental concepts of psycho-analysis*. A. Sheridan (Trans.). New York: Penguin Books.

March, J. G. (1996). Exploration and exploitation in organizational life. *Organization Science, 2*, 71–87.

March, J. G. (2003). A scholar's quest. *Journal of Management Inquiry, 12*(3), 205–207.

March, J. G. & Weil, T. (2005). *On Leadership*. Oxford: Blackwell.

Marcuse, H. (1964). *One dimensional man*. London: Routledge.

Matsushita, K. (2002). *The heart of management*. New York: PHP Institute Inc.

Matsushita, K. (1978). *My management philosophy*. National Productivity Board, Singapore (Trans.). Tokyo: PHP Institute.

Mintzberg, H. (2004). *Managers not MBAs*. Upper Saddle River, NJ: Prentice Hall

Nicholas of Cusa. (1996). *Idiota de sapienta*. J. Hopkins (Trans.). Minneapolis, MN: Arthur J. Banning Press.

Nishida, K. (1990). *An inquiry into the good*. M. Abe and C. Ives (Trans.). New Haven: Yale University Press. (Original work published 1921)

Rescher, N. (1996). *Process metaphysics*. New York: State University of New York Press.

Ruskin, J. (1927). *The complete works*. London: Nicholson & Weidenfeld.

Ruskin, J. (1903–1912/1996). Modern painters volume IV. In E. T. Cook & A. Wedderburn (Eds.), *The works of John Ruskin: Library edition* (vol. VI, p. 11). Cambridge, MA: Cambridge University Press.

Sartre, J-P. (1966). *Being and nothingness*. New York: Pocket Books.

Smith, A. (1776/1976). *An inquiry into the wealth of nations*. R. H. Campbell & A. S. Skinner (Eds.). Oxford: Clarendon Press.

Taleb, N. N. (2004). *Fooled by randomness: The hidden role of chance in life and in the markets*. London: Penguin.

Taleb, N. N. (2007). *The black swan: The impact of the highly improbable*. London: Allen Lane.

Whitehead, A. N. (1985). *Science and the modern world*. London: Free Association Books. (Original work published in 1926)

Whitehead, A. N. (1929). *Process and reality*. New York: MacMillan.

Whitehead, A. N. (1932). *The aims of education*. London: Williams and Norgate.

Whitehead, A. N. (1933). *Adventures of ideas*. Harmondsworth: Penguin.

CHAPTER 3

DESIGN AND DEVELOPMENT

A Narrative of the Founding, Launch, and Early History of the *Academy of Management Learning & Education*

James R. Bailey, William P. Ferris, Roy J. Lewicki and David A. Whetten[1]

ABSTRACT

This chapter provides a narrative of the decisions that were made during the founding, launch, and the proceeding few years that shaped the *Academy of Management Learning & Education*, offering insight into both what was done and why it was done. It first describes the period of 1996–2000, during which the Academy of Management elected to launch the journal, and then recounts the intentional design decisions of the original editor and editorial team. The chapter then describes some of the journal's major early outputs in the form of notable articles, and concludes by summarizing the state of the journal and its overall impact on the field.

Being and Becoming a Management Education Scholar, pages 43–57

INTRODUCTION

Start-up ventures are consequential and complex undertakings fraught with substantive challenges. Surviving and thriving hinge on a series of key, early decisions that furnish a foundation for sustainable progress. This was especially true for one recent and successful new venture, the *Academy of Management Learning & Education* (also referred to herein as *AMLE*). The fact that there were already hundreds of academic management journals—many with august histories and powerful reputations—meant that a new entry needed to intellectually and operationally prove its worth almost immediately. More importantly, though, *AMLE* reflected a fundamental departure from traditional research orientations by arguing that rigorous research into management learning and education and its attendant instructional implications was an endeavor worthy of the field's time and talent. This novel value proposition would confront long and deeply held beliefs about what constitutes legitimate scholarship, encouraging a collective cognitive shift of priorities for the management professoriate.

The purpose of this chapter is not to offer a scholarly treatment of how empirically and theoretically verified entrepreneurial success factors translate to starting academic journals. Instead, the purpose here is to provide a narrative of the myriad decisions that were made during the founding, launch, and the proceeding few years, that shaped this unique outlet. It offers insight not just into *what* was done, but crucially, *why* it was done. This narrative takes four parts. The first describes the period of 1996–2000, during which the Academy of Management elected to launch the journal after long deliberations of its relation to their other intellectual products and a thorough documentation of the needs and desires of its large constituency. The second section recounts the intentional design decisions of the original editor and editorial team. These decisions distinguished *AMLE* from existing scholarly outlets and, ultimately, formed the character of the journal. The third describes some of the journal's major early outputs, which largely cemented its reputation as a valuable place to publish, and as one that was willing to engage primary controversy. The fourth and final section explains the current state of the journal and reflects on the power of its unique mission and value proposition within the broader context of management education and research.

FIVE YEARS OF DELIBERATIONS: THE DECISION TO FOUND

In conjunction with the Academy of Management (also referred to herein as the Academy) conference in August, 1996, the Board of Governors—under the leadership of President Steve Kerr—asked attendees their opinions about a series of strategic issues. The board members were also invited to participate in one of the "Vision Task Forces" assigned to study each of these issues, following the conference. One of these groups examined ways the Academy could enhance its support for teaching. Chief among their recommendations was the formation of a new journal, tentatively entitled *Academy of Management Teaching*. This group foresaw the new journal having a strong familial resemblance to the Academy's other journals, in that it would use scholarship to advance the practice of management education. The principle justification offered for the Academy sponsoring a teaching journal was that there were a large number of members who identified closely with the teaching component of their professorial duties and who perceived that the Academy's programs and services, including its journals, had little to say about teaching. It was further argued that inasmuch as the Academy had been highly successful in legitimating the importance of high-quality "management research" in business schools, it was now time that it did the same thing for high-quality "management teaching." In their report the group recommended that the Board of Governors systematically examine the feasibility of launching an Academy-sponsored teaching journal.

In line with this recommendation, President Michael Hitt organized the New Journal on Learning Task Force in June of 1997, chaired by Michelle Kacmar. Late in 1997, the Task Force surveyed Academy members, seeking an indication of their support for a new teaching journal. Roughly 80% of the respondents supported the proposal. Consistent with this broad expression of support from the membership, in their March 1998 report to President William Starbuck, the Task Force formally recommended the formation of a fourth Academy of Management journal focusing on learning, teaching, and education. The report also included several recommendations regarding the new journal, including:

- The journal should not only be a top-level outlet for research and conceptual articles on learning, teaching, and education, but also as an outlet for high-quality, practical materials designed to help management educators become better teachers.
- Decisions about the design and content of the journal should communicate the message that the new journal is an integral component of the Academy's mission.
- The journal should not be created in partnership with any existing journals—that is, it should be a new and independent journal.

The report also contained information about the pros and cons of adopting an electronic-only format. The principal benefit of adopting this format highlighted a substantial cost savings (70% less than a paper-only format). In terms of negatives, they expressed concern about the cognitive and behavioral paradigm shift that would be required for an electronic-only journal to be accepted by the Academy membership. Also, they noted that not all Academy members would have access to an online-only journal (recall, this was over a decade prior to the writing of the chapter, when online access was not widely available), which could possibly lead to perceptions of inequity among the teaching-oriented members of the Academy. In addition, they reported that only a small minority of survey respondents expressed a preference for an electronic-only journal.

It is noteworthy that the Task Force asked the editors of the *Journal of Management Education, ASTD Journal, Management Learning, Simulation and Gaming*, and *Case Research Journal* for their opinions on the new journal and whether a partnership might be possible. Most editors responded that they were already experiencing shortages of quality submissions, which would be further complicated by a new journal sponsored by a large, influential professional association like the Academy. In addition, most of the editors indicated that their journal's contractual arrangements with publishing firms for production and distribution would make a partnership with the Academy difficult.

At the August 1999 Board of Governors meeting, the proposal to establish a new journal was approved. Following this decision, a committee was appointed by Anne Huff, President, to outline the duties and qualifications of the journal's editor, and to nominate individuals to serve as the first editor. The committee was chaired by Randy Dunham. At their April 2000 meeting, the Board of Governors reviewed the selection committee's report, containing the names of several candidates who had been nominated by Academy members for the position, and the committee's recommendations. This report also raised concerns about the feasibility of a new teaching journal being able to attract a sufficient number of high-quality submissions. It thus included an analysis of the pros and cons of beginning the journal as a section of an existing Academy journal.

During the summer of 2000, President David Whetten invited Roy Lewicki to serve as the founding editor of the new journal. It is noteworthy that Roy, in turn, invited James Bailey to assist him as Associate Editor. Roy and James, the journal's second editor, formed the core of the editorial team that guided *AMLE* through its first eight years. At the December 2000 Board meeting, Lewicki proposed that the journal be titled *Academy of Management Learning and Education*. It was agreed that this title signaled that it would not be a "teaching journal," but rather a "learning and education journal," with articles that are "learner-focused." The Board's approval of the journal's name and an accompanying preliminary mission statement culminated a five-year planning process.

FROM COLOR TO CHARACTER:
DESIGNING A UNIQUE ACADEMIC JOURNAL

Although the leadership team reports being initially overwhelmed by the magnitude of the task and the sheer number of decisions to be made, they had received strong guidance from the Academy Board of Governors about its vision for the journal, as well as the previously mentioned work of the several previous Academy task forces and grass roots committees. They also believed that since the journal would need to receive the strong support and backing of the Academy's formal and informal leadership, it would be important to solicit their views on the form, shape, and direction of the journal early on. They therefore constructed a draft mission statement and questionnaire about possible future directions, which was distributed to a number of senior Academy members, including the current Board of Governors, whose careers had demonstrated a strong commitment to learning and education. This feedback guided focus groups at the 2000 Academy meeting. The key points that arose, and the early decisions that resulted, are as follows.

First, the journal should focus on learning and education, broadly conceived. It should address questions of learning and education in terms of research, challenges to existing practice, and intellectual debates about educational forms that should be sustained or changed. Specifically noted was that the learning, teaching, and education side of business schools received little or no attention in any professional publications, outside of a small group of journals that were predominantly focused on teaching techniques and methodologies.

Second, *AMLE* should establish a reputation of quality and professionalism that matched that of the other Academy journals, *Academy of Management Review, Academy of Management Journal,* and *Academy of Management Executive.* The leadership team actively consulted with the editors of these journals to explain *AMLE*'s intentions and seek their advice. They were invaluable in providing guidance on many dimensions, from structuring and managing editorial policy for a journal to details such as erecting and managing back-office operations.

Third, the journal should be provocative and stimulate discussion and debate. Although there was a strong commitment to publishing traditional refereed articles, the journal also wanted to intentionally solicit challenges, critiques, and opinion pieces from thought leaders throughout and beyond the Academy. Soliciting such provocation was not a primary interest of the existing Academy journals, leading to the common criticism that many people skimmed the incoming issues but seldom read any of the articles in a given issue. The leadership team began to envision distinct sections of the journal. The first would be Research & Reviews, which focused on more traditional empirical and theoretical submissions. The second was Exemplary Contributions. This was designed as an invited section, intended to engage some of the field's most respected thinkers who would not necessarily write for a journal on learning and education, but who clearly would have some interesting and important things to say on the topic. The third was the Essays, Dialogues, and Interviews section, which would publish carefully reasoned opinion, exchanges, and insights from thought leaders. Finally, there was the Book and Resource Review section. This was expanded beyond the normal bounds of just books to include other resources such as software, exercises, and instructional manuals that could inform the learning and education process.

Fourth, *AMLE* should not directly compete with existing journals. It did not want to do so, or appear to do so, especially in regards to manuscripts and publication identity. Because several quality outlets already addressed teaching tools and methodologies, *AMLE* decided to drop a focus on these kinds of articles. Editors of these similarly themed journals were sought out to establish cooperative relationships. *AMLE* also reached out to groups that focused on management education and learning, including the Management Education Division of the Academy, the Academy Teaching Committee, the Organizational Behavior Teaching Society, and the Association for Business Simulation and Experiential Learning.

Fifth, this new journal was indeed fortunate to know that it would be widely distributed to all Academy members. While this solved one problem—that it would not have to worry about securing a publisher and successfully enrolling enough subscribers to be profitable—it created a different one, which was that it would have a great deal of immediate visibility, and thus have to establish practices that would assure a strong, positive, and credible image from the beginning.

Sixth, it was decided to proceed as a paper journal. Electronic journals were becoming popular in the late 1990s. The advantages of an electronic format appeared to be the increasingly interactive nature of the web, the ability to use the journal to stimulate ongoing discussion and debate on something more frequently than a quarterly publication, and the cost savings that could be achieved relative to the printing and distribution of a paper journal. In contrast, the leadership team felt that an electronic format did not put the journal directly in readers' hands, and that readers who might not necessarily seek out and attend to a learning and education journal on the web might be more enticed to examine it if it actually arrived in a clear plastic wrapper in their mailbox. It proceeded as a paper journal, with the possibility of supplementing articles and commentary with a web-based premise.

The interviews, conversations, and focus groups were critical to reaching the above conclusions. Taken together, they secured excellent ideas about members' vision for the journal and their preferences for its content. In the process, many had suggestions for articles, themes, and topics to be addressed. Many offered to write for the journal, or to serve on its editorial board. Finally, the editor assigned James Bailey as Associate Editor of the Exemplary Contributions section; Allen Bluedorn as Associate Editor of the Essays, Dialogues, and Interviews section; and Barry Armandi as Associate Editor in charge of the Book & Resource Reviews section. All three of these associate editors have a record of achievement in relevant domains. After the first year of operation, due to the dramatic increase in submitted manuscripts, Cynthia Fukami was added as an Associate Editor at large. Fukami had been very active in the American Association of Higher Education's initiative on quality pedagogy and the development of the Scholarship of Teaching initiative. Steven Stenner, a former program director with Executive Education at the Fisher College of Business, Ohio State University, became the journal's first managing editor.

At the 2001 Academy, a slide presentation that reflected this orientation and these decisions was offered to an invited group of new editorial board members, the Academy Board of Governors, and other interested relevant professional associations and societies. Active promotion of the journal to Academy members and encouragement for them to submit manuscripts began in earnest. This process included advertising the journal in newsletters and professional meetings, targeting authors and manuscripts at national and regional Academy meetings, and widely promoting the journal's launch. The editorial board was rounded out, particularly to reach beyond the boundaries of the Academy membership in order to extend into other domains of management education.

Finally, as *AMLE* moved toward the publication launch in the Fall of 2002—a date picked based on a reasonable estimate of the time required to gather enough quality material to publish—screening and reviewing of articles began. Much of the insight offered by other journal editors proved to be astute. For instance, many submissions had little to do with the mission and purpose of the journal. Further, most suitable submissions required significant editorial guidance and revisions. The editor and associate editors found themselves wondering if they would have enough articles in the pipeline in any of the sections to sustain a high-quality publication. This concern produces what is widely known as "white page fever," or the fear that some issues would be half blank just to get it out on time. The opportunities for special issues, and special issue editors to oversee their development, began to emerge. Finally, the team began to cement editorial policies and practices, including journal look, style, and format; manuscript review processes; processes for establishing reviewer competencies and managing reviewers; and the like.

Issue 1, Volume 1 appeared in September 2002, but advance copies were available for the Editorial Board meeting at the August 2002 Academy meetings. The first issue contained a collection of articles on the meaning of 9-11 for management education, edited by Cindy Fukami; an interview with distinguished management thinker Russell Ackoff; a new approach to management education being advocated by Henry Mintzberg; and a collection of excellent essays and resource reviews. But the signature piece turned out to be from the Exemplary Contributions section, solicited by James Bailey. This was a critique of management education prepared by Jeffrey Pfeffer and Christina Fong, "The End of Business Schools: Less Success than Meets the Eye," which roundly criticized the business school community for falling behind in many aspects of their primary education mission. This article attracted much attention in the national media, and leveraged *AMLE* into quick national visibility.

AMLE now existed, in tangible form. The next challenge was to realize the promise the journal had extended by publishing papers that reflected its mission and that provoked the broader field to more carefully examine the process and potential of management learning and education.

ESTABLISHING A REPUTATION: KEY ARTICLES IN *AMLE*'S FIRST YEARS

AMLE was fortunate to publish several significant articles during the first five years leading up to its inclusion in the SSCI/ISI Thompson database as a highly cited source for those publishing in the field of management. By 2008, AMLE had risen to be virtually tied for 5th place in frequency of citation among all journals dealing with the study of management. The company in fifth place included *Administrative Science Quarterly* and *Strategic Management Journal.*

What were some of the key articles that helped *AMLE* achieve this distinction? Each year, the Editors and Editorial Board decide upon one article that is deemed the most outstanding of the year to receive the Best Paper Award. This decision revolves not only around the excellence of the writing and the contribution to the management education field of the article, but also the likely impact on the field of management, generally. The articles winning the annual award for the first five years appear in Table 3.1 below. Each article actually appeared in the year (or year and a half, in the case of 2004) before it earned the award. In addition, three other articles have actually achieved the distinction of being among the top five *AMLE* articles cited in Google Scholar as of this writing.

As mentioned earlier, the Pfeffer and Fong article, published in the first issue, was an editorial victory in that it had an immediate impact not only in

TABLE 3.1 Eight Outstanding Articles, AMLE, 2002–2007

Year	Authors	Title	Citation
2004 Best Paper Winner Google(2)	Jeffrey Pfeffer Christina T. Fong	*The End of Business Schools? Less Success than Meets the Eye*	*1*(5), 78–95 (2002)
2005 Best Paper Winner	Neng Liang Jiaquian Wang	*Implicit Mental Models in teaching Cases: An Empirical Study of Popular MBA Cases in the United States and China*	*3*(4), 397–413 (2004)
2006 Best Paper Winner Google(1) SCOPUS(1)	Sumantra Ghoshal	*Bad Management Theories Are Destroying Good Management Practices*	*4*(1), 75–91 (2005)
2007 Best Paper Winner	Donald L. McCabe Kenneth D. Butterfield Linda Klebe Trevino	*Academic Dishonesty in Graduate Business Programs: Prevalence, Causes, and Proposed Action*	*5*(3), 294–305 (2006)
2008 Best Paper Winner	Denise M. Rousseau Sharon McCarthy	*Educating Managers from an Evidence-Based Perspective*	*6*(1), 84–101 (2007)
2002 Google(3)	Henry Mintzberg Jonathan Gosling	*Educating Managers Beyond Borders*	*1*(1), 64–76 (2002)
2002 Google(5)	D. Christopher Kayes	*Experiential Learning and its Critics: Preserving the Role of Experience in Management, Learning and Education*	*1*(2), 137–149 (2002)
2005 Google(5)	Alice Y. Kolb David A. Kolb	*Learning Styles and Learning Spaces: Enhancing Experiential Learning in Higher Education*	*4*(2), 193–212 (2005)

the management field, but also in the national and international business press. Especially fortuitous was its appearance at the annual international meeting of the Academy in August of 2002, just a month before its official publication date in the initial issue, September, 2002. This meeting of over 6,000 management members and scholars was already being covered by the press for reasons that had little to do with *AMLE*, but *AMLE* saw itself thrust center stage in controversy with Pfeffer and Fong's criticism of management education's effectiveness in terms both of individual student success and overall relevance in the business world. That the lead author, Jeffrey Pfeffer, was a highly respected management scholar and theorist from Stanford only raised the prominence of the journal. From its early Task Force beginnings, Academy members had sought to encourage a journal that dealt with important issues and to stimulate dialogue among subscribers and readers on topics of the highest global significance in the field. The Pfeffer and Fong piece was made to order and helped *AMLE* fulfill that section of its mission, which was to critique any relevant part of the educational process.

Although the 2002 Pfeffer and Fong article was cited second-most among all Google Scholar *AMLE* articles by 2009, a later article, provocatively entitled "Bad Management Theories Are Destroying Good Management Practices" by Sumantra Ghoshal (2005), has had even more impact on the field of management. Ghoshal, who was a professor of strategic and international management at the London Business School as well as founding Dean of the Indian School of Business at Hyderabad and an Overseer of Harvard Business School, tragically died just before publication of his article. Not only did it win the 2006 Best Paper award, but it also is first in Google Scholar *AMLE* citations, and even more significantly, first overall in SCOPUS citations in the entire business/management/accounting field.[2] The article calls into question the very management theories that professors of management establish in their research and go on to teach. At a time when practicing managers have begun to find themselves increasingly in the middle of ethical and questionable practices, Ghoshal (2005) suggested that management researchers and professors might look to themselves for much of the blame. Too often, according to Ghoshal (2005), the field has focused on a shareholder first mentality instead of a stakeholder model. It has advanced theories of human behavior as if they had more science behind them than they actually do (the "pretense of science"), while suggesting it is possible to achieve the status of the laws of physics without regard for the difference of human intentionality that attends behavior. It has propagated "amoral theories," freeing our students "from any sense of moral responsibility." And he decries the "ideology-based gloomy vision" of the field's existing theories with their "negative assumptions about people and institutions." The article is extremely richly referenced, but coming in for special critique are the Chicago School of Economics and Social Sciences with its focus on a model of people as "rational self-interest maximizers" as well as Porter and most other strategists' model of "value appropriation rather than value creation" among firms. Ghoshal (2005) finds hope in the advent of Positive Organizational Scholarship as championed by Dutton and Cameron, and he further cites experiments such as the "ultimatum game" studies, in which people in negotiations consistently display a sense of fairness despite the opportunity to exploit their negotiation partners with little chance of being discovered. The mere existence of the Peace Corps is also discussed for the benefits it provides entire communities, benefits unpredicted by our theories. Interestingly, as much as Pfeffer and Fong (2002) think the field has little impact, Ghoshal (2005) thinks it has great impact, most of it unintentionally negative. He closes with the hope that members of the Academy, his readers, will be able to lead junior members through the jungle of tenure, in which rewards come from maintaining the negative and erroneous theories, to a new place where senior members can mentor junior members to help students become desirous of leading society to become better than it was when they entered it. This article, so widely cited and discussed, has become almost a signature of the best *AMLE* has stimulated in its first five years. Written by the author of several award-winning books, it is reflective, provocative, significant, and highly read by all members of the management professorate.

The other six articles in Table 3.1 are also worthy of note. Both D. Christopher Kayes (2002) and Alice and David Kolb (2005) add significantly to how the field considers experiential education. Kayes focuses on the importance of defining experience within the context of language and social action while Kolb and Kolb discuss how university settings can narrowly reinforce student-preferred learning styles instead of helping students "learn in regions that are uncomfortable for them" unless deans and professors become more careful in how they structure learning opportunities. Mintzberg and Gosling (2002) take their criticism of business education to a brand new place with the design of a non-traditional quasi part-time MBA program for groups of students, most of whom work for just a few large organizations; it requires completion in five separate places around the globe and also requires intercontinental student exchanges and innovative reflection papers in between each of five two-week modules. Liang and Wang (2004) compare the "implicit mental models" of typical U.S. business cases to Chinese cases and discover that both are written assuming a rationalistic environment that doesn't take into account multiple distractions, underrepresents politics, and perpetuates a mental model that overemphasizes the degree to which top management actually originates strategic decisions versus the roles of others within the firm; they find the Chinese cases' structure actually mimics the familiar Harvard Business School case style to its detriment and, yes, they do suggest remedies. McCabe, Butterfield, and Trevino (2006) studied the motivation to cheat of 5,000 graduate students at 32 U.S. and Canadian business schools, sadly rediscovering that business students cheat more than their non-business school peers, but learning for the first time that perceived severity of penalties had no effect on incidence of cheating and that perceptions that others were cheating or that they would not be caught stimulated even more cheating; the authors suggest several remedies, including that "professors and administrators work with faculty and students to develop broader programmatic efforts based upon notions of ethical community building." The 2008 Best Paper by Rousseau and McCarthy (2007) sounds the gong for bringing evidence-based management (EBM) into the classroom such that, where the science is clear, it should be advanced to future managers as how to make the most informed decisions possible rather than continuing to make decisions by whim and hunch and tradition and precedent. The authors cover the many obstacles to EBM in current classrooms and propose the prototype of an evidence-based management community, a model whose appeal has translated into a fledgling interest group within the Academy.

The foregoing summary of some of *AMLE's* best articles is merely a sample of the quality work that has appeared in its pages over the early years. In addition to Exemplary Contributions and Research & Reviews articles that invited controversy, like those just covered, many have theoretically or empirically advanced established theories of individual learning and the educational context in more traditional fashion. *AMLE* has also published essays and dialogues to generate a meaningful exchange, and interviews of important figures in the broader educational community. The Books and Resource Review section has also been a highlight by focusing on the usefulness of material for classroom application.

ELEMENTS AND ASPIRATIONS: REALIZING THE IDEA

Academy of Management Learning & Education was founded, designed, and launched with several elements in mind. The first was that the academic management community has considerable theoretical and technical prowess, but those skill sets were not, generally, applied to the educational context and process. This is despite the fact that almost all Academy members cite education as a major component of their professional activities. Second, with critical attention toward higher education—including business schools—mounting, and with a strong and prestigious international association as sponsor, *AMLE* was well situated to capitalize on a considerable talent pool and broadly increasing interest in and relevance of the topic.

In these ways *AMLE* represented an exhilarating and unique value proposition. Specifically stated, the resources of management as a *science* should be deployed to better comprehend and direct management education as a *practice*. In this way, *AMLE* provided a venue by which academic management could study itself, with special emphasis on the knowledge dissemination component of the professorial calling. The hope was that this value proposition would manifest in two ways.

One was the systematic study of individual learning and the educational process within the management domain. Examples of the kinds of questions this entails include whether the content of management curriculum is aligned with established practitioner competencies, if international students have different learning preferences or styles than domestic students, and whether assessment centers could be deployed as valid and relevant platforms for documenting student progress. The idea was not to replicate "teaching" research that might focus on the development and introduction of an instructional technique or integration of a business case within a given module. As noted previously, that important area was well covered by other outlets such as the *Journal of Management Education.* Instead, the intent was to examine management learning and education in a manner similar to reputable journals like *Harvard Educational Review, American Journal of Education,* and *Journal of Education Research.* The assumption was that the academic management community possessed the proper theoretical, methodological, and statistical skill to conduct such research, but had lacked a primary outlet though which to pursue publication.

Another version of this value proposition was applying existing topical domains within the field to the dynamics of higher education. For instance, organizational culture is a much-studied area. Examining culture within business schools could shed light on the wider context in which management education is delivered, including things like a school's dominant pedagogical approach. Similarly, the literature on job satisfaction would find testable hypotheses within the halls of academia. Does a satisfied faculty predict a satisfied student body? The point here was not to study such issues purely for scientific purposes. Rather, it was to study them with high concern for instructional practice and educational process. A primary mission of management academics is to investigate firms and industries in order to improve them. This version of the value proposition refracted the focus internally, thus arguing that business schools were valid subjects, with an aim toward making them better at what they do.

Realizing this value proposition required overcoming the twin challenges of legitimacy and respectability. In this case, legitimacy is a discipline-level construct that refers to the extent that the field as a whole endorses scholarship into learning and education. It is not uncommon that, when a novel field of inquiry emerges, a probationary period of sorts ensues as ideas are evaluated in intellectual marketplace. For *AMLE,* legitimacy was immensely facilitated by being sponsored by the Academy of Management. Equally as important was the Academy's "reach." That is, its large membership was to receive this journal, in paper form, quarterly, just as it did the Academy's other, more established journals. Additionally, the 1990s saw a great deal of popular press attention fixed on higher education, business educational included. By and large this attention was negative, questioning the value of educational institutions to meet the changing dynamics of economics and needs of society. Legitimacy, then, was fairly well secured at the outset.

Respectability, however, is a different matter altogether. For these purposes, respectability is an individual-level construct that refers to the extent that scholars believe research into learning and education is respectable enough to command their energies. Just as with any profession, professors make calculated decisions about what areas of research to pursue. Although part of that calculation is surely intrinsic interest, another part is surely based on potential status and reward.

AMLE intentionally included the Exemplary Contributions section to overcome this challenge. Exemplary Contributions invited papers from well-known and prestigious scholars, not only to provide a platform for their astute reasoning, but also to send a clear signal to the field that writing in this arena is a respectable activity.

In the final analysis, though, respectability is rooted in a sustained record of high-quality, high-impact publications. As the previous section describes, *AMLE* was fortunate to have published a series of extraordinary papers that demonstrated the careful examination of the issues surrounding management learning and education was a respectable career commitment. This, of course, is reinforced by the very high-Thompson-ISI Impact Factor, ranking *AMLE* among the most cited of academic management journals.

In conclusion, *AMLE* has surmounted all of the hurdles endemic to a start-up endeavor among academic journals as it has capitalized on all of its inherent advantages. It had the financial and moral support of the large and influential Academy of Management. It rooted its intellectual product in a broad sample of its constituents' interests. It made a series of design decisions that facilitated rigorous, traditional research while also encouraging responsible exploration and provocation. It enlisted leadership teams that adeptly managed the review and publication process and enthusiastically promoted the mission. Finally, and perhaps most importantly, it offered the promise of a novel intellectual space that allowed management academics an outlet to examine the issues that are at the heart of the professorial mission.

NOTES

1. Authors are listed solely on the basis of alphabetical order, and extend their sincere thanks to the many people who helped to make *AMLE* a success.
2. SCOPUS (www.scopus.com) maintains the world's largest abstract and citation database of research articles.

REFERENCES

Ghoshal, S. (2005). Bad management theories are destroying good management practices. *Academy of Management Learning & Education, 4*(1), 75–91.

Kayes, D. (2002). Experiential learning and its critics: Preserving the role of experience in management learning and education. *Academy of Management Learning & Education, 1*(2), 137–149.

Kolb, A., & Kolb, D. (2005). Learning styles and learning spaces: enhancing experiential learning in higher education. *Academy of Management Learning & Education, 4*(2), 193–212.

Liang, N., & Wang, J. (2004). Implicit mental models in teaching cases: An empirical study of popular MBA cases in the United States and China. *Academy of Management Learning & Education, 3*(4), 397–413.

McCabe, D. L., Butterfield, K. D., & Treviño, L. K., (2006). Academic dishonesty in graduate business programs: Prevalence, causes and proposed action. *Academy of Management Learning & Education, 5*(3), 294–305.

Mintzberg, H., & Gosling, J. (2002). Educating managers beyond borders. *Academy of Management Learning & Education, 1*(1), 64–76.

Pfeffer, J., & Fong, C. (2002). The end of business schools? Less success than meets the eye. *Academy of Management Learning & Education, 1*(1), 78–95.

Rousseau, D., & McCarthy, S. (2007). Educating managers from an evidence-based perspective. *Academy of Management Learning and Education, 6*(1), 84–101.

CHAPTER 4

I GET BY WITH A LOT OF HELP FROM MY FRIENDS

Reflections of an Accidental Management Education Scholar

J. B. Arbaugh

ABSTRACT

In this chapter, I chronicle my career migration from that of a marginal strategy/entrepreneurship scholar to that of a less marginal management education scholar. The migration took almost a decade to fully complete, and became more intentional as I became more familiar with and experienced increasing professional and personal benefits from pursuing management education as a field of study. It should be readily evident is that this was not a solitary or self-made journey; I have had and continue to have plenty of help along the way. While from my perspective this journey seems somewhat idiosyncratic, I conclude the chapter with some suggestions based upon my experiences for emerging management education scholars.

Being and Becoming a Management Education Scholar, pages 59–70

INTRODUCTION

I teach an MBA course in Personal and Professional Development where I help students develop a plan to help them acquire the qualifications and skills necessary to identify, pursue, and secure their dream job. When I consider my own career development I sometimes wonder whether I'm being a hypocrite because I certainly wouldn't have constructed a development plan to wind up at this destination, but it is a much better place than where I would have ended up had I charted a course.

As is probably the case with most who become management education scholars, I did not set out to become one. However, with a mix of location, personal interests, support from colleagues, and in my opinion no small amount of divine intervention, I may be the person who has benefited the most dramatically by becoming a management education scholar. In this essay, I reflect on my experiences and some of the things I have learned along the way in hopes that it will encourage others to enter the field and encourage those already in the field to continue to persevere—because if the things that have happened for me professionally and personally by pursuing management education research can happen to me, they can happen to any management scholar.

MY BEGINNINGS AS A MANAGEMENT
EDUCATION SCHOLAR

My start as a Management Education scholar was in late 1996, although I didn't realize it at the time. The University of Wisconsin–Oshkosh's MBA Program Director (Gordon Badovick, now Dean of the business school at the University of La Verne) began discussing plans for us to offer MBA courses via the internet. Given the conversation at the time of how online courses were THE wave of the future, as a relatively young Assistant Professor I concluded that I couldn't afford not to be part of this. So I volunteered to teach one of the two online courses we were planning to offer during the summer of 1997. It just so happened that I was teaching a classroom version of the same course during spring 1997, and it dawned on me that perhaps comparing student performance differences between online and classroom offerings of the same course might make for an interesting study. So when I asked my Dean (Al Hartman) about pursuing this research, he encouraged me to pursue a grant to fund the research through the University's Faculty Development Program. I didn't realize it at the time, but Al's other significant contribution to the development of this research was that he suggested ways for structuring the study as a quasi-experimental design so that I could collect data on class participation and student performance more rigorously. Little did I know how much this emphasis on methodology would pay off down the road.

So I conducted the study, wrote up the results, and submitted the paper to the MED Division for the 1998 Academy of Management meetings. Considering that by this time I already was a marginal strategy/entrepreneurship researcher, news that this paper had been selected for inclusion in the conference *Proceedings* was something that I'd never expected to receive regarding one of my papers. This good fortune got me thinking that perhaps I should continue to collect data on our online courses once they resumed during the fall 1998 semester. That round of data collection resulted in a 1999 Academy *Proceedings* paper, so I thought that continuing to collect data on future online courses probably would be a good idea.

And so collect data I did—for twelve semesters! I had no idea that this was not a common practice in Management Education research; I just did it because I enjoyed collecting the data, writing the papers, and having some success with the end results. Those first two Academy papers eventually became *Journal of Management Education* articles, one appearing in a special issue on Challenges and Frontiers for the 21st Century (Arbaugh, 2000a) and the other winning the 2001 Roethlisberger Award (Arbaugh, 2000b). During this time I also was getting articles published in outlets such as *Management Learning* and *Business Communication Quarterly*.

THE EMERGENCE OF MANAGEMENT EDUCATION AS MY FIRST RESEARCH PRIORITY

While this level of success certainly exceeded my expectations, there were at least three events that happened during the 2002–2003 timeframe that greatly accelerated my development to the point that I decided that I was a Management Education scholar first and a Strategy/Entrepreneurship scholar second. First, I was invited by Roxanne Hiltz to participate in a workshop held in April of 2002 sponsored by the Sloan-C Consortium and NJIT for researchers of Asynchronous Learning Networks to help define the field of research and establish some direction for future online learning scholars. Along with works by Maryam Alavi (Alavi, Yoo, & Vogel, 1997), Ray Dumont (1996), and Dorothy Leidner and Sirkka Jarvenpaa (1995), Roxanne was one of the first scholars of technology-mediated learning whose work I became aware of (Hiltz, Johnson, & Turoff, 1986; Hiltz & Wellman, 1997), so I was most humbled to be invited to this workshop. This workshop was significant for me for at least two reasons. The gathering of general education and information systems researchers (scholars such as Maryam Alavi, Chuck Dziuban, Karen Swan, and Peter Shea) helped me see that there was a much broader community of scholars studying online learning than I had realized, and what these folks were doing certainly held some implications for online management education research. Also, while at this workshop I got to interact with Raquel Benbunan-Fich, beginning what has been a most mutually beneficial collaboration. The benefits of this collaboration were demonstrated in part by the fact that some research I had developed that had been rejected for presentation at the 2002 Academy meetings became the 2003 Best Paper in Management Learning and eventually articles in *Academy of Management Learning & Education (AMLE)*, *Information & Management*, and *Decision Support Systems* (Arbaugh & Benbunan-Fich, 2006, 2007; Benbunan-Fich & Arbaugh, 2006) largely due to Raquel's involvement.

The second significant event that happened around this time was my invitation to the MED executive committee and eventual election as an MED officer. I find it particularly interesting that right before being invited to run for program chair-elect in early 2003 (by one of the editors of this book) I had scheduled a meeting with my Dean to discuss future leadership opportunities within our college. Needless to say, that meeting turned out to be a very different conversation than I originally intended. Al's advice to me was that process director (our Associate Dean equivalents) positions are always going to be around, but not many get the chance to run for an Academy division officer position, so he strongly encouraged me to do so. As a result of that decision and the good fortune of winning the MED election, I've gotten to see that the world of management education research is much broader than I first thought, and I have had the opportunity to develop collaborations and friendships with people from all over the world, such as Alvin Hwang, Regina Bento, Leigh Stelzer, Elena Antonacopoulou, Steve Armstrong, Lisa Burke, Laurie Milton, Katherine Karl, Bill Ferris, and this book's editors.

The third thing that began during this time was my involvement in writing book reviews for *AMLE*. Unlike much of what had happened in my adventures as a management education scholar to date, I was somewhat intentional about getting involved with *AMLE*. I even remember at the 2002 Academy meetings sitting outside the room where the *AMLE* board meeting was held, hoping to meet some board members and looking particularly for the now late Barry Armandi. Earlier in the year I had responded to Barry's call for book reviewers thinking this might allow me to get involved with reviewing research manuscripts for *AMLE*, and I recently had completed my first book review (Arbaugh, 2002). Barry was happy to meet me and quite pleased with my review, which suggested there would be the opportunity to do more of them. As it turned out, I liked writing book reviews as much if not better than reviewing manuscripts, and my work on book reviews has had at least as much to do with my subsequent involvement with *AMLE* as have any articles I've written.

MANAGEMENT EDUCATION RESEARCH
AS MY SOLE PRIORITY

With the abundance of opportunities generated by my subsequent involvement in leadership of management education research in editorial and organizational capacities, I recently made the decision that management education-related research will be my exclusive focus. In addition to my study of online management education, a research collaboration with Alvin Hwang and Regina Bento that has been generously supported by GMAC's Management Education Research Institute (MERI) has shown me that there are more than enough opportunities to focus on research in management education if one chooses to do so. MERI's exhaustive databases of annual surveys of MBA students from multiple institutions will provide future management education scholars the opportunity to provide new insights regarding the nature of graduate management education. If the attention that preliminary manuscripts from this research have received at conferences through awards and nominations for awards is any indication (Arbaugh, Bento, & Hwang, 2007; Hwang, Bento, & Arbaugh, 2007), this should be a fruitful stream of research for years to come. In 2009, I got to experience the culmination of my research interests in online teaching and graduate management education by being selected as an MERI Faculty Fellow. I am humbled by this honor for two reasons. First, it represents a strong endorsement of my collective body of work. Second, given the selection criteria for this award, as much as I don't want to be getting older, I guess I'm now officially a senior scholar.

Something that particularly excites me as a now "senior" management education scholar is the opportunity to encourage a new generation of emerging management education scholars such as Joy Beatty, Scott DeRue, Erich Dierdorff, Ruey-Lin Hsiao, Luigi Proserpio, Bob Rubin, and Christine Quinn Trank. I have been able to do this both informally through reviewing drafts of manuscripts and formally through my involvement in editorial activities with each of the major management education research journals, particularly *AMLE* (Lewicki & Bailey, 2008). One of the things I most appreciate about working with *AMLE* editor James Bailey is his willingness to share the spotlight of that position with his editorial team, thereby letting those of us who need some more development have the opportunity to do so. It's in part through his example that I now look for opportunities to support and encourage emerging management education scholars. Other members of the *AMLE* editorial team have helped me adopt a more senior orientation as well, particularly Rich Klimoski and David Waldman. Rich regularly talks about how merely having one's work cited is not the most important thing about your research; it is the ways in which the work is cited that is of primary importance in the field. Now that I'm starting to get over the novelty of actually having articles that are cited by others, I increasingly see the wisdom of Rich's remarks. Through collaborating with David Waldman to organize the *AMLE* Writers Workshop, I was able to see that we can approach the development of research articles on management education with the same level of forethought and rigor that is more commonly associated with discipline-based management research. While some institutional biases against management education research still exist, perceptions and external expectations of this research are changing to the point that it is attracting younger scholars, and the prospect that these researchers will far exceed anything that's been done in this area of research to date should bring great excitement to us all.

SO, WHAT HAVE I LEARNED?

When this book's editors invited me to write an essay, one of the questions they asked was "Was the journey planned, accidental, or opportunistic?" As I reflect on my experiences, I see elements of each. My entry into the field was almost entirely by accident, and then fueled initially by the opportunities generated by my early unexpected successes. These days the journey seems much more planned, particularly as I have learned more about education research in general. I just hope that this increased knowledge doesn't prevent me from making useful contributions to the field in the future.

The editors also asked me to share some lessons I've learned in my development as a management education scholar. In a sense, that is difficult because expectations for management education research already have risen so dramatically that today I don't think it would be possible for someone to pursue a path similar to the one I did. For example, I essentially knew none of the literature on online learning before I began studying it, and now there already is such a body of work in this area specific to management education that one cannot ignore it like I could and expect to get published. The "online vs. classroom" issue certainly has been studied thoroughly in a relatively short time period (Sitzmann, Kraiger, Stewart, & Wisher, 2006; Zhao, Lei, Yan, Lai, & Tan, 2005). However, there are some things that I have learned along the way that may be helpful to other current or emerging management education scholars, which I have noted below:

1. There are no "self-made" management education researchers—at least not any really good ones.

   While I did have several solo-authored publications in my earlier days, it should be evident from this essay that even then I had significant input from others on my work. In addition to the advice I received from my Dean, my colleagues at UW–Oshkosh certainly were instrumental in my development. Had they not allowed me to survey the students in their online courses, my research probably would have stopped shortly after my initial online vs. classroom study. Also, I've had the good fortune to have had Cindi Fukami happen to be the action editor for three of my articles, one published in *JME* (Arbaugh, 2000b) and two published in *AMLE* (Arbaugh, 2005a; 2005b). Cindi was particularly instrumental in helping me stretch my thinking, with the eventual results being much stronger that the originally submitted. Having now served as an *AMLE* associate editor myself, I can say that Cindi certainly was more patient with me than I might have been.

Even with this level of support, I don't think I would have developed to the extent that I have without collaborating with other authors. I think it's interesting that I didn't win an MED best paper award until I found a co-author to work with, the first being Rebecca Duray from the University of Colorado–Colorado Springs (Arbaugh & Duray, 2001). Besides being a potential source of additional data, co-authors often bring different perspectives that can refine or enhance your own ideas. In recent years I've also had the benefit of working with people who are clearly better than I am in at least one area. Raquel Benbunan-Fich is a better conceptual thinker. Alvin Hwang is a better statistician. Regina Bento is a better writer. Barb Rau is a better methodologist. While my initial work might have facilitated the development of these collaborations, the subsequent results have far exceeded what I could have done by myself. Therefore, I heartily encourage those interested in management education research to rigorously seek potential collaborators who at least partially share your interests.

2. Bringing the tools of traditional research to management education research makes for better management education researchers.

   I remember then-*AMLE* editor Roy Lewicki make a comment during a PDW at the 2004 Academy meetings regarding how astounded he was by how many people who had been rigorously trained in theoretical development, research design, and methodology seemed to forget all of that training when they conducted management education research. Having now reviewed numerous manuscripts myself, I find myself agreeing with this assessment more often than I'd like. I think the fact that someone like me is able to comment legitimately on the methodological state of affairs of a body of research is evidence alone that there's a lot of room for improvement in this area (Arbaugh & Hiltz, 2005). We can do a lot better regarding methodological issues such as the use of appropriate controls, valid and reliable measures of our variables, and statistically powerful sample sizes. While there has been improvement in recent years, we also can do a much better job of examining prior literature in order to better frame our studies regarding how they build upon prior research. Finally, while it may be a by-product of my disciplinary upbringing, we can also do more to make our research findings more generalizable through the use of multi-course, multi-discipline, and multi-institutional studies.

3. The disciplinary lens through which we view the world can provide interesting management education research questions.

    This lesson underscores the importance of us bringing our disciplinary training and socialization to our management education research. In studying online management education, I have been struck by the differences in how management researchers and information systems researchers view this phenomenon. I remember seeing an article published in *JME* by some information systems scholars and being concerned that they considered surveying students in the same course multiple times to be a "longitudinal" study (Yoo, Kanawattanachai, & Citurs, 2002). Then I went to an OCIS session at the 2003 Academy meetings where I discovered that this is a common methodological approach used by that community to examine organizational settings. This experience got me thinking about how my own training has influenced how I study management education. With strategy as my background, is it all that surprising that I am interested in course- and discipline-level effects on online learning?

    I would even argue that our home disciplines can be immensely helpful for us to frame our studies. In 2002 I started thinking about how subject matter might influence online course outcomes. To me, this seemed to be an obvious question that almost no one was asking empirically at the time. But I didn't know how I should frame such a study. Then while walking down the hall of the floor where my office was located soon after returning from the 2002 Academy meetings, a burst of what I would call divine inspiration struck: "How much does 'subject matter' matter?" The subsequent attempt of developing this study and conceptualizing it based upon Rumelt's (1991) classic work on industry- and firm-level effects eventually through the assistance of Cindi Fukami and others became an *AMLE* article of which I am most proud (Arbaugh, 2005a). Therefore, I say embrace your discipline rather than try escaping from it while doing management education research (Arbaugh, 2008).

4. Good management education research is harder to do than most management researchers think.

    Such encouragement to embrace our disciplines may sound ironic since oftentimes our disciplines may not want to embrace us or our research. I remember getting counsel from some of my colleagues that I shouldn't be doing educational research but rather should focus on work in the discipline. I've since found it interesting how things like Best Paper and Best Article Awards tend to silence such counsel. I'm convinced that if one does management education research well, it often will be more rigorous and will be better than most of the "discipline-based" research done by our colleagues at our home institutions. In fact, given emerging institutional and external pressures for more accountability for learning outcomes, our research is likely to be increasingly welcomed and encouraged. Therefore, while a b-school professor certainly would not want to completely ignore conducting discipline-based research, this expectation should not be used to dissuade them from conducting management education research if they wish to.

While the best management discipline-based research presently is likely more rigorous than management education research, there is one aspect of conducting well-done management education research that is more difficult: the breadth of literature that should be considered. In most management-related disciplines, for most researchers in those disciplines there are now probably 5–10 journals in each of those fields that contain the key research, and nearly all who are doing good research in those areas know what journals are in that group. Conversely, while there is an emerging grouping of management education journals, good and relevant work related to education can come from myriad directions. Even today I continue to encounter scholars and works from other fields that should have been influencing my work. In addition to *AMLE, JME, Management Learning, DSJIE* and other journals explicitly devoted to management education, education-related journals from other disciplines as well as general education journals often have significant theoretical, methodological, and analytical insights that have relevance to our research and should be brought to the attention to our community. Therefore, to be truly effective, management education researchers likely will have to read much more broadly than do their more discipline-based colleagues.

Typically, when the term boundary spanning has been used to describe journals such as *AMLE*, it refers to manuscripts that could fit with more than one of the Academy's journals (Bailey, 2005). I would like to extend the idea of boundary spanning for management education research journals to include the introduction of theories and concepts from educational research into research on management learning and education. Because almost no management professors are trained to be educational researchers during their doctoral education, such a state of affairs certainly is understandable. Therefore, I believe that authors who can clearly and rigorously introduce theoretical frameworks and methodological approaches developed in education and other disciplines do the rest of us a tremendous service. I'm finding that I gain an increasing proportion of my intellectual stimulation from the relationships that I've forged with education researchers, and expect these relationships to be a primary source of my research production as I assume the role of AMLE's next editor (Dziuban, Shea, & Arbaugh, 2005; Garrison & Arbaugh, 2007).

CONCLUSION

It's not often that one gets the opportunity to publicly reflect on his development and subsequent contributions to a field, particularly at a relatively young age. I'm most flattered that Bob and Charlie have extended me this opportunity. I'll be curious to see if others determine that this history is as accurate as I remember it. While it seems like I'm a lot busier now than when I first began this journey, it has been a very good trip. As a result of taking this path, I have a lot more friends in the field and am much better connected than I ever expected to be. While I've mentioned many of those who have helped along the way, I'm sure I forgotten the contributions of some, for which I apologize. I just hope that my thoughts and experiences and those of others included in this volume will encourage and motivate others to build upon this foundation.

REFERENCES

Alavi, M., Yoo, Y., & Vogel, D. R. (1997). Using information technology to add value to management education. *Academy of Management Journal, 40,* 1310–1333.

Arbaugh, J. B. (2000a). Virtual classroom characteristics and student satisfaction in internet-based MBA courses. *Journal of Management Education, 24,* 32–54.

Arbaugh, J. B. (2000b). Virtual classrooms versus physical classrooms: An exploratory study of class discussion patterns and student learning in an asynchronous internet-based MBA course. *Journal of Management Education, 24,* 213–233.

Arbaugh, J. B. (2002). Review of "Beyond Change Management: Advanced Strategies for Today's Transformational Leaders." *Academy of Management Learning & Education, 1,* 221–223.

Arbaugh, J. B. (2005a). How much does "subject matter" matter? A study of disciplinary effects in on-line MBA courses. *Academy of Management Learning & Education, 4,* 57–73.

Arbaugh, J. B. (2005b). Is there an optimal design for on-line MBA courses? *Academy of Management Learning & Education, 4*, 135–149.

Arbaugh, J. B. (2008). From the editor: Starting the long march to legitimacy. *Academy of Management Learning & Education, 7*, 5–8.

Arbaugh, J. B., & Benbunan-Fich, R. (2006). An investigation of epistemological and social dimensions of teaching in online learning environments. *Academy of Management Learning & Education, 5*, 435–447.

Arbaugh, J. B., & Benbunan-Fich, R. (2007). Examining the influence of participant interaction modes in web-based learning environments. *Decision Support Systems, 43*, 853–865.

Arbaugh, J. B., Bento, R. F., & Hwang, A. (2007). An exploratory study of regional effects on MBA student career preparation. Manuscript presented at the 67th annual meetings of the Academy of Management, Philadelphia, PA.

Arbaugh, J. B., & Duray, R. (2001). Class section size, perceived classroom characteristics, instructor experience, and student learning and satisfaction with web-based courses: A study and comparison of two on-line MBA programs. In D. Nagao (Ed.), *Academy of Management Best Papers Proceedings*, MED A1–A6.

Arbaugh, J. B., & Hiltz, S. R. (2005). Improving quantitative research on ALNs. In S. R. Hiltz & R. Goldman (Eds.), *Learning Together Online: Research on Asynchronous Learning Networks* (81–102). Mahwah, NJ: Lawrence Erlbaum Associates.

Bailey, J. R. (2005). The next four years. *Academy of Management Learning & Education, 4*, 133–134.

Benbunan-Fich, R., & Arbaugh, J. B. (2006). Separating the effects of knowledge construction and group collaboration in outcomes of web-based MBA courses. *Information & Management, 43*, 778–793.

Dumont, R. A. (1996). Teaching and learning in cyberspace. *IEEE Transactions on Professional Communication, 39*(4), 192–204.

Dziuban, C., Shea, P., & Arbaugh, J. B. (2005). Faculty roles and satisfaction in ALNs. In S. R. Hiltz & R. Goldman, (Eds.), *Learning together online: Research on asynchronous learning networks* (pp. 169–190). Mahwah, NJ: Lawrence Erlbaum Associates.

Garrison, D. R., & Arbaugh, J. B. (2007). Researching the community of inquiry framework: Review, issues and future directions. *The Internet and Higher Education, 10*(3), 157–172.

Hiltz, S. R., Johnson, K.D., & Turoff, M. (1986). Experiments in group decision making: Communication process and outcome in face-to-face versus computerized conferences. *Human Communication Research, 13*, 225–252.

Hiltz, S. R., & Wellman, B. (1997). Asynchronous learning networks as a virtual classroom. *Communications of the ACM, 40*(9), 44–52.

Hwang, A., Bento, R. F., & Arbaugh, J. B. (2007). Does the MBA experience support diversity? Regional and demographic effects on MBA program satisfaction. Manuscript presented at the 38th annual meeting of the Decision Sciences Institute, Phoenix, AZ.

Leidner, D. E., & Jarvenpaa, S. L. (1995). The use of information technology to enhance management school education: A theoretical view. *MIS Quarterly, 19*, 265–291.

Lewicki, R. J., & Bailey, J. R. (In press). Scholarly Outlets and Scholarly Identity: A Narrative of the Founding of the *Academy of Management Learning & Education*. In C. Wankel & R. DeFillippi (Eds.) *Being and Becoming a Management Education Scholar*. Charlotte, NC: Information Age.

Rumelt, R. P. (1991). How much does industry matter? *Strategic Management Journal, 12*, 167–185.

Sitzmann, T., Kraiger, K., Stewart, D., & Wisher, R. (2006). The comparative effectiveness of web-based and classroom instruction: A meta-analysis. *Personnel Psychology, 59*, 623–664.

Yoo, Y., Kanawattanachai, P., & Citurs, A. (2002). Forging into the wired wilderness: A case study of a technology-mediated distributed discussion-based class. *Journal of Management Education, 26*, 139–163.

Zhao, Y., Lei, J., Yan, B., Lai, C., & Tan, H. S. (2005). What makes the difference? A practical analysis of research on the effectiveness of distance education. *Teachers College Record, 107*(8), 1836–1884.

CHAPTER 5

WHEN LEGITIMIZING TEACHING METHODS BECOMES AN OPPORTUNITY TO DEVELOP MANAGEMENT EDUCATION SCHOLARSHIP—BRINGING IT INTO ACTION

The Narrative of a French Business School Professor's Experience

Laurence de Carlo

ABSTRACT

The Business School environment is generally constrained in terms of introducing new ideas and changes in management education. In such a constrained environment, I have developed a non-classical way of teaching negotiation in complex decision processes and have been responsible for creating several innovative pedagogical projects. The obligation to legitimize

Being and Becoming a Management Education Scholar, pages 71–94
Copyright © 2010 by Information Age Publishing

this non-classical way of teaching gave me the opportunity to reflect upon my pedagogical methods through research. After describing such an evolution, the chapter will show the role played by several institutional forces in the development of this type of management education scholarship. Finally, several key elements of this experience will be presented, which may be considered critical for young colleagues. Personal conviction and motivation seemed to be essential in recognizing opportunities in what otherwise would have appeared only as external and internal constraints.

INTRODUCTION

This chapter describes the personal experience of an everyday professor at ESSEC Business School, near Paris, France. The business school environment is generally constrained in terms of introducing new ideas and changes to management education. In such a constrained environment, and as a member of the faculty, I have successfully been able to (1) offer courses as well as individual and collective tutoring geared towards students' needs; (2) lead or co-lead and be responsible for several institutional pedagogical projects; and (3) conduct research and publish in the field of management education. This narrative—an individual's experience in management education and development—illustrates the use of non-classical theoretical backgrounds in research. Legitimizing these non-classical teaching methods and ways of coaching to students and participants in continuing education courses has given me the opportunity to reflect upon my pedagogical methods. Further research led to a deeper understanding of the proposed teaching process and then to publication. It is argued that in certain institutional contexts, and within specific conditions, it is possible to develop management education scholarship in a way that can be defined as creative (Amabile, 2001; Amabile, Barsade Sigal, Mueller, & Staw, 2005; Winnicott, 1986).

This chapter, given in the form of a narrative, is based on personal and professional experience. Although it may pose methodological problems (i.e., an individual experience that cannot be proved scientifically) the content has been qualified as "straight, honest, and true" by more experienced colleagues in the same institution. This individual experience may be of interest to younger colleagues as one example of many different ways one can become a management education scholar.

Firstly, my way of teaching negotiation and collective decision processes and of practicing individual and collective coaching in the French cultural context will be defined. These pedagogical choices will also be compared to other ones. Secondly, I will describe the management education projects dealt with in my institution over a 13-year period. The research I then began resulted from the need for legitimization of these choices and projects.

Later, I will describe the role played, from my point of view, by several institutional forces in the development of this type of management education scholarship. Finally, several key elements of this experience will be presented, which may be considered as critical for young colleagues—the most important element being the conviction that the professor's personal investment will be useful for students. Personal convictions and motivation allowed me to recognize an opportunity to develop creative management education scholarship in what otherwise may have been considered as external and internal constraints, originating both inside and outside of the classroom. We will see that such constructive perceptions may not always be developed in all institutional environments.

TEACHING METHODS, INDIVIDUAL AND COLLECTIVE COACHING PRACTICES DEVELOPED AT ESSEC BUSINESS SCHOOL, FRANCE

Management students will work or are working in complex environments. These environments are qualified as complex ones based on many factors. Among the most important factors of complexity are the uncertainty of the decision contexts and the number and diversity of persons and groups involved in decision processes. Dealing with these factors of complexity obliges one to negotiate with others and be creative in order to reach satisfying agreements and make collective decisions that can be implemented. To understand and participate in collective decisions in such environments, students need to experiment self-reflective or double-loop learning processes. A double-loop learning process or a self-reflective one signifies bringing into question the basis of our usual rationale and habits, which restrains our way of thinking and does not allow for decision making in a satisfying way (Argyris & Schön, 1978; Argyris, 1982). This questioning permits creativity. Creativity emerges from the dynamics of students and the professor in the classroom setting; the professor, in such a way of teaching, has to continually adapt herself to a new class dynamic making different choices and new decisions inspired by this dynamic.

According to Winnicott, psychoanalyst and pediatrician, there are two types of creativity:

> I must make clear the distinction between creative living and being artistically creative. In creative living you or I find that everything we do strengthens the feeling that we are alive, that we are ourselves. One can look at a tree (not necessarily a picture) and look creatively. . . . Although allied to creative living, the active creations of letter writers, writers, poets, artists, sculptors, architects, musicians, are different. You will agree that if someone is engaged

in artistic creation, we hope he or she can call on some special talent. But for creative living we need no special talent. (1986, pp. 43–44)

Here, we are addressing the creativity each individual can develop under certain conditions in his or her everyday life. In an organizational context, Amabile, et al. define creativity as "coming up with fresh ideas for changing products, services, and processes so as to better achieve the organization's goals" (2005, p. 367). In Amabile's model, the three components of creativity are: "*domain-relevant skills*, competencies and talents applicable to the domain or domains in which the individual is working; *creativity-relevant processes*, the personality characteristics, cognitive styles and work habits that promote creativity in any domain; and *intrinsic task motivation*, an internally driven involvement in the task at hand, which can be influenced significantly by the social environment." (2001, p. 333).

Regarding the professor's creativity, we can say that professors in Business schools are recruited according to their competencies in at least one domain; an artistic-like talent is not required. The dimensions of creativity-relevant processes and intrinsic task motivation regarding the professor will be discussed later in this chapter.

The conviction of the importance of helping students and participants in developing self-reflective processes and creativity stems from a personal interest in Freudian psychoanalysis. Freudian psychoanalytical therapy consists of a type of self-reflective process that improves one's autonomy, self-awareness, and creativity. It also helps in accepting the unconscious residual part of one's behavior and discourse, which is not accessible for conscious self-reflexivity. The consequence, in complex situations, is to improve one's capacity to create and decide either alone or within groups. Greater self-awareness and a greater acceptance of unconscious phenomena allow for a greater open-mindedness to others in a variety of circumstances—whether working with participants in a negotiation, or working with colleagues coming from another country, or just from next door.

In the psychoanalytical process, this self-awareness comes from bringing into question the patient's rationale and habits established in childhood. In the classroom, we do not go back to the students' childhood; however, students are offered a safe environment and are engaged in developing a "here and now" self-reflection process concerning the ways they analyze and act in this environment. The safe environment has several dimensions, one of the most important being the framework defined by the professor at the beginning of the course—that is, a set of rules to be respected in the classroom during the course. These rules emanate from the professor (type of evaluation, for example) or are defined at an institutional level (attendance sheets, for example). They are a major tool against the fusional illusion that there would be a coincidence between the students' demand of training and the professor's offer. The distance maintained is the impetus of the training and of the work it requires. The rules play the role of a "third entity" that guarantees that the students are neither alienated nor destroyed by fusional illusion (Kaës, Anzieu, et al., 1997, p. 72). During the course, the students grow progressively more aware of themselves and they more readily accept their own and their classmates' apparently irrational behaviors. Thus they develop their flexibility and their capacity of understanding others, as well as their ability to create solutions with others to the problems they face together.

In analogy with the psychoanalytical process, the classroom is conceived as a psychic container of which the professor is a part. When psychically contained, students feel free to express themselves, and at the same time are made to feel secure by the limits placed. Limits include those specified by the professor such as the rules of the course, those expressed by the professor including those of the institution in order to respect the course frame, and limits put into practice by the professor's own behavior (as an example) including the respect of others and the acceptance of emotional expression (Kaës, Anzieu, et al., 1997). In such conditions, students are less afraid of engaging themselves in a self-reflective process.

In the role of an individual coach, my office is also conceived as a psychic container. Students are free to discuss their difficulties in choosing a specialty, or in particular, feelings of not performing well enough compared to other students. They do so because they know their emotions will be accepted and not judged. Their emotions are then used as a personal knowledge tool in helping them discover their own desires, interests, and goals—what they "really want to do"—in view of their own strengths and abilities, and especially learning to avoid comparison with other students. I coach approximately 20 students each year. The initiative of the relationship is theirs, often after having taken one of my courses. As a collective tutor, working with groups of students and executives involved with business partners, the classroom is equally considered as a psychic container. In this context, the ideas of each student or executive are reformulated, showing the specific interest of each idea, making links between the different interventions. I also am directly involved in helping to solve conflicts between the students or executives when they occur in collective discussions.

Very often, participants are encouraged not to immediately answer a question asked by a business partner, but instead are asked to try to understand his or her rationale and underlying objectives, all the while knowing that they may not intellectually master all the elements of the given situation. In doing so, students and executives learn to accept greater uncertainty—that is, the uncertainty of not understanding all the questions the business partner has in mind and consequently not being able to answer all of them. Paradoxically, if they accept this uncertainty, they are afterwards more able to listen carefully to their business partner, can better understand their own underlying and real demands, and finally are better able to answer them. Even when doubts are expressed during the pedagogical process, by the end of the project, the students or executives understand the methods used, especially in view of the results attained.

Since my arrival at ESSEC in 1994, I have created several courses that encourage double-loop learning processes at different levels (undergraduate, graduate, specialized masters, executive programs) and on different subjects (negotiation in planning and environment, seminars in the field with local authorities, and learning-by-doing research seminars). I have also coached teams (projects with firms for undergraduates and executives) and undergraduate and graduate students individually (tutored during the course of their studies) using the same pedagogical philosophy. Courses of this nature and coaching are not a usual part of the French pedagogical tradition.

THE CONSTRAINT OF THE FRENCH
PEDAGOGICAL CONTEXT

There are two institutional systems for undergraduate and graduate studies in France. The first is the university system; the second is constituted by the "grandes écoles" (higher education establishments), only found in the business and the engineering fields. ESSEC is a Grande École of Business. The specificity of the Grandes Écoles of Business is that they are schools in which one can enter only after passing very competitive entrance exams following two years of study in preparatory classes between the ages of 18 and 20; alternately, students can also enter directly in the second year of Business school after obtaining another diploma (doctor, engineer, etc). French Grandes Écoles of Business are independent from universities. They are semi-private organizations with an independent status as ESSEC has, or they are owned by a local chamber of commerce. Their diplomas are recognized (except for the lowest ranking schools) by the State, which as a result controls the quality of the studies. Students coming from Grandes Écoles of Business very easily find jobs in the international marketplace, whereas it is much more difficult for students coming from the university system. The University of Dauphine in Paris is an exception, as it is well recognized by the job market. The top rankings in France are largely occupied by the grandes écoles. The top business schools are referred to as "the three Parisians," among them ESSEC, and this tradition is translated into the rankings.

As with all French grandes écoles students, ESSEC students are chosen and recognized as part of the French elite for their very high level of abstract knowledge. As a result, they define themselves from their earliest academic experience (first grade) by this knowledge, acquired and to be acquired.

In France students work from the beginning of their academic experience, gaining privilege based on the amount of abstract knowledge they memorize. The source of this knowledge is given by a professor whose legitimacy comes from her presupposed omniscience, at least in her academic domain. Students are usually not conscious of their other potentials and capacities, such as being open to others, listening, being empathetic, understanding contradictory visions of reality, being creative, etc. However, in order to develop self-reflection and soft skills such as negotiation and group decision capacities, they must draw upon these potentials. Often French students are neither sure they possess these skills nor aware if they have the ability to develop them. As a result, not only do many of them feel vulnerable, but some are not sure enough of themselves (as individuals) to let it be known that they are not invulnerable. This is a feeling they do not appreciate, which can result in some students reacting defensively when they are asked to work on these and other abilities. For example, some students may refuse to "play the game" of the course and remain by themselves, or they may act aggressively towards the professor and/or other students.

In order to begin what will be a new experience for them, students have to understand why these learning processes and skills are important for both their future career in management and for their personal development. They have also to be told that nobody possesses these skills completely from the first day—we are all in a learning process. Verbalizing this fact decreases defensive reactions caused by the novelty of the learning objectives. Thus ways have to be found to help the students understand this information and feel secure in the classroom—that is, finding ways to legitimize my teaching methods and pedagogical objectives with reference to the students themselves. For some courses, seminars, or collective coaching processes, this legitimacy was found through "real-world" links students or executives may have with organizations, firms, or local government entities. When carrying out real projects successfully, they legitimize the pedagogy used to achieve this success, despite the feeling that the work they were asked to do was both demanding and difficult to thoroughly understand during the project process.

This process is made more difficult if there are no connections with business organizations in a course. Lack of time is often the reason these courses have no links with "real projects," rendering the process all the more difficult because the methodology practiced needs time to be understood and appreciated.

In this case, the students can legitimize the pedagogy used when comparing their results with ones they had before the course in similar situations. Some do it successfully. But this comparison in itself requires a distance some of the students may not have developed yet at the end of the course. Thus, throughout the course, I try to regularly explain my way of teaching and how it may differ from their own experience, as well as how understanding this new experience will be useful to them in their future real-world jobs.

Legitimacy is not a given. It has to be continually sought out and attained. It also has to be demonstrated to peers in our own institutions.

THE CONSTRAINT OF CHOOSING A SPECIFIC WAY OF TEACHING NEGOTIATION

Among my courses, I teach one concerning negotiation in public decision processes in planning and environment, called "Negotiation and Local Democracy." Negotiation can be taught without requiring a self-reflective process from the students. However, concepts and methods of negotiation presented as abstract knowledge often do not reflect the complexity of real-life circumstances. Therefore, students participating in a course may have the delusion of acquiring real negotiation skills while interacting with one another and with the professor while in fact they are simply using new tools to reproduce classical power relations with which they are already familiar. And, naturally, at the end of such a course, students and executives appreciate feeling more powerful through the use of "new tools" without having had to fundamentally change their way of interacting (i.e., in power relations). Thinking they will succeed in each new negotiation following the course, they will be deluded into feelings of omnipotence. Teaching methods that rely on the delusion of omnipotence, as may also be seen in the dynamics of certain organizations (Vidaillet, 2007), reactivate the infantile roots of people's behavior, favoring their narcissism and unconsciously promising them an impossible wholeness. This type of negotiation course is often tremendously successful with students and executives seduced by both the delusional learning process and the narcissistic mirror. Thus, courses taught in this delusional framework obtain very good evaluations from all the students. Yet, as with all courses teaching soft skills and involving students' behaviors in addition to their knowledge (and as is often the case with overwhelming political majorities) an overwhelming majority of all "good" course evaluations from its students should be regarded as symptomatic of the delusional learning process. For if each participant is respected in her individuality and considered as a subject in a social psychological sense, there should, at least in the short term, be some students who give poor course evaluations. When this does not occur, it may signify that one is running the risk (more often unconscious than conscious) of manipulation, once again creating delusional circumstances.

In a social psychological sense, the subject is ". . . a human being [who is] named, situated in space and time, original and singular, complex and conflictual, pretending to produce herself in a cohesive unity and in a coherent continuity, eager for pleasure, and confronted with suffering, revindicating recognition and sharing, [the subject is] responsible and alienated" (Ardoino & Barus-Michel, 2006, p. 258; translation by author).

The subject is characterized by her divisions and contradictions and internal and external conflicts. The subject has complex relationships with others, including unconscious behaviors. Such subjects do not always readily accept the course structure proposed by the professor. They can express criticisms in the framework of the classroom as long as they respect its rules. Kaës, Anzieu et al. write: "To form oneself is to loose a social and relational code, often the fact of being part of a group, in order to try to acquire another supposedly more adequate code. The moment between the two stages that characterizes the passage of one code and one structure of a relationship to other codes and to other relationship structures is conflictual and it must be conflictualized in order to go beyond this passage " (2001, p. 74; translation by author).

As for me, I did not want to employ a delusional pedagogy. Thus I needed to find a way to legitimize my teaching method, which, if successful, will and should receive a few negative evaluations, in contrast with courses using more popular teaching methods.

In this context, I propose different courses, for which the majority of students give positive evaluations by the end of the course period and others at a later time, as they tell me when I see them months or years afterwards. However, there are a few students who do not want, or who cannot for their own reasons, enter into the course dynamics. They tend to adopt a defensive attitude, either consciously or not. Importantly, this attitude is part of their individual freedom. So, their attitude is respected, as guaranteed to them by the course conceived as a psychic container, insofar as they express it in a way that does not impede the others' learning process. These few students will negatively evaluate the course. As a result, the comparison of student evaluations at the end of the course does not show this teaching method in a favorable light, which additionally explains why this teaching method must be legitimized at the institutional level.

My tutorship approach can also be compared with other coaching methods that favor the students' narcissism. These methods confirm the coachees in their delusions of omnipotence and mastering, reinforcing their egos (Vidaillet, 2007), instead of allowing them to realistically develop a professional project in accordance with their own personality, desire, and potential. In these methods, tutors unknowingly use students in order to reward their own narcissism, unconsciously desiring to achieve a guru-like status, as opposed to actively participating and nourishing a real relationship with the student as a subject, that is, taking into account the limitations of the student's potentials as well as the limitations of the tutor's capacities.

The relationship between the tutor and the student lasts for several years. In a constructive tutelage, the student and the tutor will have the time to thoroughly evaluate the work accomplished together and see the results of the method used applied to real-life circumstances, at school and in internships. At the end of their academic career, students very often express their gratitude for this experience in a moving way. The expression of sincere gratitude in itself shows that the students, at the end of the interaction, are able to accept that they have been responsible and yet dependent on someone to make their professional choices. Therefore, they no longer have the delusion of omnipotence but have experienced and integrated the reality of individual responsibility and human interdependency, with which they will experiment first-hand, particularly in their first professional experience.

Reflection on my own pedagogical methods came from the need to build legitimacy and grew into an opportunity to begin research in pedagogy. Pedagogy then became a center of interest for me, and these reflections evolved into fresh ideas for the creation of institutional pedagogical projects and new courses.

The search for legitimacy is a focus point in this chapter as it allows links to be made between the evolution of career choices and the evolving institutional context. Without institutional legitimacy, the different projects, courses, and products presented here could not have come into being. While the search for legitimacy may be seen as an obsession, in this case, such an obsession meant perseverance in wanting projects to be realized. Additionally it allowed me to deal with non-classical courses and projects in the school (Amabile, 2001).

If the main objective of enhancing students' self-reflective creative capacities had not been attained, I would not have tried to legitimize these teaching methods. In each class of the course "Negotiation and Local Democracy," students are divided in two universes, role-playing the same deliberation at the same time. At one phase of the deliberation, they must overcome the constraints of the simulation—that is, the given instructions—in order to find a mutually satisfying agreement. In doing so, they create a new option. In most of the classes, one of the two groups is able to achieve this goal, while the second group progressively moves forward without daring to circumvent the imposed constraints. Afterwards, a collective discussion allows the students to share and analyze what happened in each universe. The students' individual results on the final exam, based in part on their individual logbook, show that more than 80% of the students learned from this experience in terms of feeling and understanding through their own experience and through collective discussions about what it means for themselves and for their colleagues to participate in a creative process.

Regarding projects with organizations, 80% of the recommendations are found to be pertinent and original by the business partners and professors.

Regarding the individual tutorship, an open, qualitative evaluation completed two years ago by all of my tutored students showed that they felt the process to be both challenging and reassuring in terms of developing individual ideas and reflections. Additionally, they were conscious of being in a process where they were making their own choices and not those desired by their professors, parents, or their friends.

INSTITUTIONAL PROJECTS

I have been directly involved with several pedagogical projects in my institution. In particular, between 1995 and 1998, I conceived a CD-ROM with a colleague to teach negotiation in planning and environment: a very large simulation of a real public decision process on a highway project. Today this CD-ROM remains the largest and most realistic simulation tool available in the field and at the international level (de Carlo, 2005, 2007a). From my point of view, this CD-ROM was conceived because I felt the necessity of using a tool adapted to my method of teaching negotiation in planning and environment. First, the simulation had to take place in the field and in France in order to give students the particular flavor and complexity of real public decision processes occurring in France. Regarding the concept of Common Interest ("l'Intéret Général"), the pedagogical tool had to take into account the French historical, cultural, and institutional context. Second, the teaching tool also had to propose a simulation of the complexity of many decision processes in the field at the international level—that is, intractability (Gray, 1997). For example, at one phase, students have to be creative enough not to follow the CD-ROM's instructions if they want to come to an agreement on a highway route.

In 2000, I was responsible for bringing pedagogical reform into action for the first-year or undergraduate program (370 students). The principles of this reform were defined the preceding year and concerned the coherence and organization of the entire year's courses. The reform's implementation was begun in 1999. The school director then asked me to carry through the implementation process in 2000, and I accepted. This mission offered me the opportunity to organize and participate in discussions about management education with colleagues from all departments and services in the institution, and then to put the results of these discussions into action. A project like this constitutes a great constraint in terms of time and energy investment. Additionally, while engaged in such a reform, one can neither conduct research nor publish as we would like—that is, we are not able to advance our careers. But, at the same time, our vision of management education is enriched, and we can more accurately understand the stakes and constraints of the various disciplines as they are practiced. In particular, this experience helped me afterward to legitimize my own way of teaching: I realized that through my courses I offered soft skills that were not available in many other courses—skills that the students would need as early as their first year of studies in order to participate in their first group project with a business partner.

This experience also helps build constructive representations in management education; that is, we can transform new management education ideas into action, and although not an easy task, it can be done if a clear and fair collective process is defined. Therefore, being involved in such a mission allows us to develop and implement new ideas in management education that we can see come to fruition.

This reform implied in particular two new courses with active pedagogy, one of which I created with three colleagues. In this course, first-year students working in groups approach a societal subject of reflection through the use of multiple sources and references in order to understand the subject's multidimensionality and complexity, as well as accepting the project's inherent uncertainties. In this way, they experiment with a research process, learning by doing. They then make recommendations on the chosen subject based on their understanding of it. This course is followed by the students' first experience with a business partner. In carrying out a real business project for an organization in groups, they apply the research methods acquired in the precedent course. When preparing the students prior to working for an organization, we wanted to help them add real value to a project. In particular, we wanted to help students develop the capacity to accurately understand the demands of their business partner in reference to the organization's context, in order to redefine the problem itself, if necessary, and finally, drawing their conclusions and giving their recommendations.

In 2005–2006, I was responsible for tutor training, involving 118 tutors tutoring 1288 students. This training was provided to tutors to more precisely define the role of the tutors and give them the opportunity to improve their listening skills in relation to their students with the goal of improving the help they give to students in their professional and personal choices. In order to achieve this goal, the training team decided to first provide the tutors with information concerning the way students deal with reality at their phase of personal development—that is, young adults searching for their identity in a very competitive world. Second, we underlined the role of framing the relationship between the tutor and the student. Finally, the tutors listened to varied case types of coaching situations and ways of communicating with students. Our aim was to realize a tutoring based on listening and understanding the students, as this is an essential base for both respectful and effective exchanges and for giving advice. We did not want to develop a tutorship based on delusion, unrealistically favoring the students' egos, nor an equally unrealistic coaching based on the projection of the tutors' own ambition on their students. This training was largely successful among the tutors who, for the greater part, spontaneously communicated their congratulations and appreciation for what they perceived to be useful knowledge.

RELATED RESEARCH PROJECTS AND PUBLICATIONS

After a few years of teaching, involvement with institutional projects in management education, and research in my disciplinary field, I began to do research in management education. The resulting publications have been published in books and journals, both in France and in the U.S. I began in 1999 by reflecting, with a colleague, on our tutoring methods (de Carlo & Chevrier, 1999). Tutorship appeared at ESSEC as early as 1994 with the creation of an apprenticeship system where students alternate between their studies and business internships. Each apprentice was obligated to have a tutor inside the teaching institution as well as a hierarchical referent inside the company. I have volunteered to be a tutor from the very beginning of this new system. Now all students have individual tutors.

Afterwards, I worked with another colleague in order to better understand the French management educational system. During the course of a year we operated within the framework of a European community workshop on management education and then published a chapter in the workshop's collective book (Takagi & de Carlo, 2003). We chose to analyze the evolution, choices, and constraints of principal French higher education management institutions from the 1970s to the present. As newcomers to the French management field (I first trained in engineering and did my Ph.D. work at the University of Montreal, and my colleague is Japanese and did her own Ph.D. work at Stanford), this historical research allowed us to better understand the ways our own school functioned within its historical and institutional context. Then I began to write about and publish work on my courses.

For an international audience of negotiators and professors of negotiation, I explained the way I use the CD-ROM I developed in order to favor joint agreements among the students through collaboration and creativity (de Carlo, 2005). The results of graduate seminars with local authorities were also conceptualized. The originality of the seminars comes from the fact that the results were obtained through interviews and analyses carried out by young adults studying in the concerned local communities and not by confirmed researchers with no link to these communities (de Carlo, 2002a).

For a French audience of high-level public decision makers and professors, the way the CD-ROM is used was discussed: in the interest of reaching pedagogical goals, thus submitted to students to be used only as an information tool, and not as an interactive device whose central interest is the full use of the technology, as could also be the case (de Carlo & Choulet, 2003; de Carlo, 2002b).

These publications treat different dimensions of management education, yet they have a point in common: They were guided by a search to give more meaning to a personal experience and conceptualizing it, whether in an institution at large or in an experience as a professor and tutor. This search can often be highly motivating, inspiring one to begin research in management education: It can be directly related to our experience, improving it by allowing us to enter into a learning process.

My other publications are in the field of environmental and planning conflicts and conflict resolution. These two research domains have been developed in parallel. Studying real conflicts in public decision processes through research helped in making pedagogical choices. For example, in my courses I now increasingly insist on the concept of paradox.

Suzuki, Fromm, and de Martino (1998, p. 114) define paradoxical logic as one that establishes that both A and non A can be equal to X. Such a logic that accepts that a thing and its contrary can coexist opposes itself to Aristotelian logic. As for the concept of ambivalence defined by Freud (Laplanche & Pontalis, 1998) the originality of a paradox is firstly that the thing and its contrary are simultaneous and indissociable and secondly that the opposition is not dialectic—that is, there is no way to get around it. Winnicott vindicates a paradoxical logic in apprehending human phenomena: "It seems silly, but we are dealing with human nature, and in matters of human growth and development we need to be able to accept paradoxes.... Paradoxes are not meant to be resolved; they are meant to be observed" (1986, p. 148).

Now, in courses and tutorship, I try to heighten students' awareness to the paradoxical dimension of phenomena (i.e., reality is paradoxical). I help them develop a rationale authorizing paradox. The more students have the opportunity to deal with paradox, the more they will be able to understand complex decision processes and be able to handle their intractable conflicts, for participants and situations are often paradoxical (de Carlo 2007b; Henriksen, 2007). The importance of paradoxes in today's public decision processes has been discussed (de Carlo, 2006, 2007b) and then imported into courses and tutorship, to finally use it in management education research (de Carlo, 2007a).

At another level, conducting research in a disciplinary field gives a professor greater legitimacy in his or her institution. Thus, it seems pertinent to first begin with research in one's own discipline and then in parallel to begin research in management education. Naturally, these choices should take into account one's specific institutional environment.

INSTITUTIONAL CONSTRAINTS AND OPPORTUNITIES

Institutional forces were shown to be constraining at the organizational level in French business schools (Takagi & Cerdin, 2004; Takagi & de Carlo, 2003). These forces include research-funding sources such as, in my case, the French State and ESSEC Research Center, the school evaluation policy, and, to a smaller extent, the AACSB accrediting agency. Consequently, these institutional forces could also be considered as constraining for each professor at the individual level. Yet in my case, after 13 years of experience, they played a double role: both as a constraint and an agent of incentive and recognition. This paradox will be explained, for each institutional constraint.

Usually, the main objective for a course in a business school is the acquisition of knowledge and skills; the majority of research is conducted in the management disciplines. The type of teaching presented here deals not only with knowledge and skills but also with *savoir-être* (understanding "how to be") and notably self-awareness in order to better negotiate and make decisions with others. Additionally, part of my research is concerned with and about the pedagogy of management, an area that is not a mainstream research subject in management schools. As a result, the constraint of my institution's evaluation procedure played the overall role of a test for my conviction of what was important for me to teach and research.

The easiest way to be promoted quickly would have been to teach negotiation without promoting double-loop learning processes. Promoting only single-loop learning processes (i.e., the acquisition of methods and concepts) would have satisfied the students in the short run and rewarded my own ego, but students would not have been better able to negotiate in real-life circumstances afterwards. I had to make do with the evaluation procedure constraint, knowing that I had to convince my colleagues where the interest of my pedagogical choices lies.

Luckily, the ESSEC evaluation procedure allows for a long-term analysis of a professor's pedagogical activity, as it considers the logic and coherence of a professor's activity over a given period (usually a few years). In my case, this made the evaluation procedure not just a constraint, but also an opportunity to show the evaluation committees the interest of my method. Additionally, as for all colleagues, the procedure forces us to improve our courses over time. Thus it worked as a constraint and an opportunity.

This experience in self-assertion encouraged me to pursue research in pedagogy. And so, in this circumstance, it worked as an opportunity. Publishing articles and book chapters about this teaching experience helped me to rationalize my ideas and intuitions, giving me the opportunity to create relationships with colleagues interested by similar pedagogical issues.

It should be noted that other institutions may employ similar evaluation procedures but may only concentrate on the quantitative results of each professor in predefined categories, without analyzing the professor's entire activity or the reasoning behind their teaching methods.

THE AACSB ACCREDITING AGENCY OPPORTUNITY

In 1997, ESSEC was the first non-North American institution to be accredited by the AACSB; it was reaccredited in 2007. Accreditation processes in themselves are constraining. They require quotas and precise data that are carefully examined by neutral evaluators. Thus they make up part of the constraining forces at an institutional level. Yet, as Mottis and Thévenet (2003) mentioned, the accreditation process can also be used creatively by the concerned institutions. For the authors, the accreditation process should not only be seen as a normative constraint; the way individual institutions use this process should also be examined.

From my individual point of view, the ESSEC accreditation team understood the accreditation process not only to be a constraining force, but also an opportunity for creativity for actors inside the institution. For example, this accreditation process was an opportunity to shed light on parts of my work, knowing that I work in a small department, giving courses that are non-classical in terms of content and method. The seminar I run dealing with local government entities has been noted in the first AACSB accreditation report as innovative. And the tutors' training program I organize with a team of colleagues has been cited in the second AACSB accreditation report. As a result, for a professor who is interested in implementing non-classical projects, accreditation processes, if well exploited, can be considered as an opportunity for gaining institutional recognition.

A STATE FUNDING OPPORTUNITY

In 1996, when I began to work on the CD-ROM tool, I progressively started to understand that the depth and means needed to pursue the project would require a tremendous amount of resources—particularly in terms of employing professional assistants to help us put it into place. In short: We needed money. I turned to a very important research fund on transportation, which depended upon several ministers, PREDIT. The project was accepted because of the indicated intention of afterwards producing research about the use of this pedagogical tool. In this case, wanting to do research in management education has been an opportunity.

THE ESSEC RESEARCH POLICY CONSTRAINT
AND OPPORTUNITY

In all business schools in the international market, publications in well-known English-languate journals are preferred. As a result, French professors in all disciplines need to publish more often in these English-language journals than in French journals or books, even if they are well recognized. As is the case with many researchers from outside the U.S., we have to thus accustom ourselves to the Anglo rationale and way of presenting research and writing articles. These constraints influence our publication strategy.

Moreover, I wanted to also publish in the field of management education without proposing articles to journals specialized in education, in order to stay in the management field. So, I had to find, among these recognized international journals, those that would accept articles on this subject using non-classical theoretical backgrounds.

ESSEC has its own list of privileged journals that are ranked. The professors' evaluation depends on the ranking of the journals in which he or she publishes. This institutional list includes the classical international journals, but also other publications that accept pedagogical articles with non-classical theoretical backgrounds. This means, firstly, that the composition of the list is very strategic in order to guarantee a diversity of research in the institution. Secondly, it means that professors can progress in their own careers by publishing articles in journals appearing on this open list. Yet there is a price to pay.

The price to pay for choosing to do research in management education, and applying a non-classical theoretical background, is that the professor will not progress as quickly as if he or she had published in the few international journals considered as the very best ones in the field of management (i.e., those that appear on all publication lists). This may be considered as fair only if the difference in career progression between professors making different choices is not too large—that is, if we, as researchers in management education (among other domains), consider the difference as not overly penalizing to our careers.

In this context, I decided to publish also in French supports (i.e., books and journals) in order to have a voice in the French pedagogical debate, as, from my point of view, this field in France greatly needs to evolve. However, I knew that these publications would not be recognized for my career.

The ESSEC scientific committee not only establishes the publications list but also manages a research budget that professors can use based on calls for research projects twice a year. The members of the scientific committee, all professors, accept different types of research, theoretical backgrounds, and methodologies. Once having obtained an initial budget, if it is used as announced and if there is a publication at the end of the research project, obtaining another budget is made easier, based on the trust that has been established with the scientific committee members. Original research themes can then be proposed, and among them, management education.

Thus we can see concretely how the institution research policy plays the role of both a constraint and an opportunity in the evolution of a professor's research choices.

DISCUSSION AND CRITICAL REQUIREMENTS

Personal Conviction

It was clear from the very beginning of my career as a professor that the critical requirement to make my management education projects "real" was the conviction that this pedagogical work would be useful to students—especially for their personal and professional development. Thus, the major motivation has been personal. This is consistent with Amabile's componential theory of creativity in which intrinsic task motivation plays a major role; intrinsic task motivation is "the motivation to do something primarily because it is interesting, challenging, or enjoyable," whereas extrinsic task motivation is "the motivation to do something primarily to meet some socially imposed extrinsic constraint, such as a deadline or a promised reward" (Hennessey & Amabile, 1988, pp. 236–237).

Personal convictions and motivation have been determinant in the development of these projects for several reasons: firstly, in order to look at institutional constraining factors in a more complex and constructive way (i.e., seeing them as both constraints and opportunities); and secondly, because creative pedagogy surprises or even frightens students, who can become defensive, I had to find creative ways of legitimizing my pedagogy to them. I had to sufficiently and thoroughly explain my objectives and methods in order to be understood by the students and to motivate them. Such a legitimization process requires energy that is motivated by personal convictions. This second point has been essential, as in itself it became an incentive to do more research and publishing in management education.

Another opportunity arose out of a constraint. Personal convictions shape the way we represent reality, which helps us to implement our ideas.

Personal convictions also make us aware of ancillary rewards defined at an individual level. For me, one of them is succeeding in linking research and action in everyday activities. Another one is to acknowledge the learning process realized by students. It is highly rewarding, at the end of a course, when students show that they are truly able to listen to others and create new options to reach an agreement—when they "think out of the box." It is also highly rewarding to see the evolution of students in tutorship and to accompany them through the choice of a first job which really suits them.

But personal convictions cannot be realized in all institutional contexts.

Choice of Institution

The choice of an institution seems critical when striving to develop scholarship in management education. I do not know many institutions from the inside, nor have I had a long period of observation in many institutions other than my own and a few others. However, based on my experience, a criterion that can be useful in choosing an institution is the faculty dynamics and, in particular, internal conflicts concerning the various ways research is valued and how the work of the professors is valued in general.

If the conflicts are strong and lively, they are a good indication of open-mindedness and of the acceptance of variety and diversity in terms of different types of contributions from the professors. This is not evident when experiencing these conflicts in one's day-to-day professional life. It could be concluded that conflict is a waste of time and is not efficient. But in fact, these conflicts are the proof that different ways of defining and valuing research have a voice in the institution. In such institutions they are also opportunities to value non-mainstream types of research, through different measures and decisions, depending upon the results of the discussions and power relations at the time. Diversity can be objectified in particular through the concerned institutions' publications list. If there are no internal conflicts, there is a greater chance of the institution having a sole vision of research, and it is likely that this vision will not favor management education scholarship, or only if it is mainstream. These conflicts have another advantage. They are a guarantee that there are colleagues who are involved in their institution and who want to do their job in a meaningful way. As Simmel (1995) mentioned, conflicts are signs of human interaction, as opposed to indifference, which does not create social ties.

Taking the Time to Acquire Experience and Work with Real Projects

It seems to me that it would be difficult in our international and institutional contexts and constraints to develop management education scholarship at the beginning of one's career. This scholarship can be developed parallel to a disciplinary scholarship and over time, while acquiring experience in the pedagogy of one's own field, gathering further knowledge in the way the institution functions as well as implicit principles regarding education. Thus one piece of advice could be: Be patient and take your time. The time before doing research in management education can be applied to projects in management education.

These projects help deepen our reflections and give us more ideas for research afterwards. Moreover, these projects can help make one's own perspective of management education understandable in one's own institution, through concrete realizations and results, more so than articles could have done. And this understanding can informally, and perhaps partly unconsciously, help us implement new management education projects and begin new research projects in this field.

This time may also be used to develop trust.

Let Trust Grow

This chapter relates formal processes in particular, addressing formal institutional constraints and potentialities. But each procedure can be put into action in different ways, depending on individual ethics and the institutional culture shared by those persons in charge. Looking at the past with greater distance and reflection, I can tell that I benefited from the trust of certain colleagues who played an important role in my career. I think now it was both fair and logical to receive financial support in order to begin my research and implement my institutional projects on pedagogy. Yet, at the time when the scientific committee members chose these research projects, perhaps reliability played an important role—that is, trust. Trust can compensate for what can be seen as "off beat" or "bizarre" ideas. This could be analyzed in cultural terms. France, as a European country, is often seen as more conservative than the U.S. France is generally perceived as less enthusiastic towards new ideas. On a larger scale, this perception is verified by the number of young French researchers who expatriate to develop their projects in the U.S. But on a smaller scale, you can count on trust to develop new ideas.

Trust takes years to build. But once we have demonstrated our reliability, we can take risks and receive support from our colleagues who are in charge of funding research or pedagogical programs, even if we have ideas that are not in the mainstream. This phenomenon is very informal and non-verbally expressed. Perhaps it could also be explained by the French culture of conflict: We commonly have combative relationships and we do not hesitate to openly criticize someone's point of view or project. Positive opinions have a greater chance of remaining unexpressed in France, more so than in other cultures.

ESSEC no longer has an entirely French faculty, as many colleagues come from a diverse range of countries. They bring their own cultures to the institution. However, at this point in time, this factor does not seem to change the importance given to reliability and trust by institutional committees.

The Paradox of Accepting a Slow Evolution in Our Careers While Acting in Order to Value Management Education Scholarship in Our Institution

We have to accept that we will not be promoted quickly while we could be conducting other types of research and be involved in other choices. But acceptance is not the key to success in acquiring scholarship in management education. It is rather a way of not spending psychic energy on delusion but keeping one's energy for real projects. Accepting a different career pace is not a given. The difference must stay reasonable according to each person and compensated by an environment that allows creativity.

While accepting that management education pedagogy is a non-mainstream domain, we can at the same time be involved in our institution and take on responsibilities that allow us to develop management education scholarship and result in management education being better recognized as a serious field.

This paradoxical posture of accepting the situation and taking initiatives to change it seems to be a key to pursing one's objectives in the field, and perhaps in every non-classical domain of activity. Management education in itself is not mainstream and this fact needs to be accepted because it is a reality. Once it is accepted, we can find open-minded institutions and colleagues. And in doing so, we will be rewarded with professional satisfaction. But we will only have this satisfaction if we are very sure of our convictions, knowing that they are the key in allowing us to accept (within reasonable limits) a career orientation that may not be classical.

We have to recognize our desire in terms of research and activity domains for currently, management education scholarship is not a domain that will allow a researcher to become quickly known in the academic community.

CONCLUSION

This chapter gave me the opportunity to reflect on my professional choices. It has been written as the narrative of an ordinary professor's experience in management education in a French business school. It goes without saying that it is not the aim of this chapter to represent the typical experience of a professor wanting to develop scholarship in management education. The narrative speaks for itself. Nevertheless, based on this case example, several factors in enabling a professor to develop scholarship in management education have been identified.

It is necessary to choose an institution through its open-mindedness regarding management education. Once an open-minded school or university has been chosen, institutional forces are not a strong enough deterrent, at least in France, to impede one's development in management education scholarship.

But fundamentally we, as professors, must above all be convinced of the interests of studying and acting in the field of management education. We must have the personal conviction that our work will be useful to our students and for the field in general. Such convictions allow us to consider students' difficulties in understanding our way of teaching as opportunities to legitimize and develop our vision of management education through research. They allow us to look at institutional forces not only as constraints but also as opportunities.

Such convictions are not required in all fields. But they will be as soon as we want to operate outside the mainstream. They help us represent our environment in a constructive way, i.e. not only as a field of constraints but also as a set of opportunities. In doing so, we can succeed.

In Amabile's terms, the professor's intrinsic motivation is a key factor for being creative in management education, with his or her domain-relevant skills (knowledge and experience) and his or her creativity-relevant skills (styles of thinking and working) (Hennessey & Amabile, 1988, pp. 236–237). The role played here by the institutional environment can also be expressed in Amabile's words: "Certain extrinsic motivators, which support competence development and deep involvement in the work, can add to intrinsic motivation and creativity through a process of 'motivational synergy'" (Amabile, 2001, p. 334).

Nevertheless, it would be illusory to tell a young professor that he or she can invest in management education and have the same career evolution, in terms of speed in particular, as one who chooses to invest in classical management disciplinary research. This would be unrealistic and delusional. In the current conditions of reality, and as I have tried to illustrate here, it is possible to reflect on and implement new pedagogy while pursuing an interesting and meaningful career in management.

REFERENCES

Amabile, T. M. (2001). Beyond talent: John Irving and the passionate craft of creativity. *American Psychologist, 56*(4), 334–356.

Amabile, T. M., Barsade Sigal, G., Mueller, J., & Staw, B. M. (2005). Affect and creativity at work. *Administrative Science Quarterly, 50*(3), 367–403.

Ardoino, J., & Barus-Michel, J. (2006). Sujet. In J. Barus-Michel, E. Enriquez, & A. Levy, (Eds.), *Vocabulaire de la psychosociologie* (pp. 258–265). Paris: Eres.

Argyris, C. (1982). *Reasoning, learning and action: Individual and organizational.* San Francisco: Jossey-Bass.

Argyris, C., & Schön, D. (1978). *Organizational learning: A theory of action perspective.* Reading, MA: Addison-Wesley.

De Carlo, L. (2002a). A proposal to use mediation and night correspondents to curb urban violence in Cergy, France. *Negotiation Journal, 18*(2), 163–175.

De Carlo, L. (2002b). La Francilienne: Un outil multimedia de formation à la concertation. *Metropolis, 108/109,* 91–94.

De Carlo, L. (2005). Accepting conflict and experiencing creativity: Teaching "Concertation" using La Francilienne CD-ROM. *Negotiation Journal, 21*(1), 85–103.

De Carlo, L. (2006). The French high-speed Méditerranée train decision process: A large-scale public decision case study. *Conflict Resolution Quarterly, 24*(1), 3–30.

De Carlo, L. (2007a, June). *The classroom as a potential space: Teaching negotiation through paradox* (ESSEC Research Document no. 07017). Paper presented at the International Society for the Psychoanalytic Study of Organizations (ISPSO) conference, Stockholm, Sweden.

De Carlo, L. (2007b, July). *To negotiate or not to negotiate: Doing it without telling: A French public decision process in planning.* Communication presented at the International Association for Conflict Management (IACM) conference, Budapest, Hungary.

De Carlo, L., & Chevrier, S. (1999). Comment former quels entrepreneurs? *Proceedings of the Conference Entrepreneurial et Enseignement: Rôle des institutions de formation, programmes, méthodes et outil* (pp. 141–157). Lille, France: Pôle Universitaire Lille Nord-Pas-de-Calais.

De Carlo, L., & Choulet, J. P. (2003). Quelle place pour le multimedia dans la formation à la concertation? In R. Billé & L. Mermet (Eds.), *Concertations, Décision et Environnement, Regards Croisés - 2* (pp. 77–96). Paris: La Documentation Française.

Gray, B. (1997). Framing and reframing of intractable environmental disputes. In R. J. Lewicki, B. H. Sheppard, & R. Bies (Eds.), *Research on negotiation in organizations* (pp. 163–188). Greenwich, CT: JAI Press.

Hennessey, B. A., & Amabile, T. M. (1988). Story-telling: A method for assessing children's creativity. *Journal of Creative Behavior, 22*(4), 235–246.

Henriksen, H. J. (2007, June). *To live with paradoxes in a temporary organization—Social learning and reframing using Bayesian belief networks.* Communication presented at the international Conference on Multi-Organizational Partnerships, Alliances and Networks (MOPAN), Leuven, Belgium.

Kaës, R., Anzieu, D. et al. (1997). *Fantasme et formation.* Paris: Dunod.

Laplanche, J., & Pontalis, J. B. (1998). Ambivalence. *Vocabulaire de la psychanalyse.* (pp. 19–21). Paris: PUF.

Mottis, N., & Thévenet, M. (2003). Faut-il faire crédit à l'accréditation ? *Revue Française de gestion, 6*(147), 213–218.

Simmel, G. (1995). *Le conflit.* Paris: Circé.

Suzuki, D. T., Fromm, E., & de Martino, R. (1998). *Bouddhisme, Zen et Psychanalyse.* Paris: PUF.

Takagi, J., & Cerdin, J. L. (2004). Internationalizing French management education: A contextual analysis of strategies in French business schools. In G. Wankel & R. DeFillippi (Eds.), *The cutting edge of international management education* (pp. 37–62). Greenwich, CT: Information Age.

Takagi, J., & De Carlo, L. (2003). The ephemeral national model of management education: A comparative study of five management programs in France. In R. P. Amdam, R. Kvalshangen, & E. Larsen (Eds.), *Inside the business schools* (pp. 29–57). Oslo, Malmö, Copenhagen: Abstrackt, Liber, Copenhagen Business School Press.

Vidaillet, B. (2007). *Les ravages de l'envie au travail.* Paris: Editions Eyrolles.

Winnicott, D. W. (1986). *Home is where we start from.* New York: W.W. Norton and Company.

CHAPTER 6

FROM "GOOD TEACHING" TO "SCHOLARLY TEACHING"

Legitimizing Management Education and Learning Scholarship

Gordon E. Dehler, Joy E. Beatty and Jennifer S. A. Leigh

ABSTRACT

This chapter distinguishes between good teaching, scholarly teaching, and teaching as scholarship to advance two related positions. First, the standard of "good teaching" is not sufficient to meet today's student needs. Rather, management educators must raise their instruction to the level of "scholarly teaching," which shifts the focus from the teacher to student learning. Second, meeting this challenge is imperative for the scholarly domain of management education and learning to achieve legitimacy in the academic community. Legitimizing the scholarship of teaching and learning is attainable only if management instruction moves beyond "teaching-as-technique" to the realm of "scholarly practice," which is the required antecedent for those engaged in the domain of "teaching as scholarship." When teaching is viewed narrowly as technique, practice is commoditized and cannot achieve the credibility required to be a legitimate scholarly domain within organization and management studies.

Being and Becoming a Management Education Scholar, pages 95–118
Copyright © 2010 by Information Age Publishing

95

For what Plato so clearly saw was that education in the true sense
of the term is the process through which people acquire that kind
of philosophical enlightenment that will emancipate them from the
dictates of ignorance, dogma and superstition.

—Carr (1995, p. x)

INTRODUCTION

Teaching occupies a central place in our academic lives, and along with research and service comprises a significant part of the scholarly triumvirate. For many faculty, it was the prospect of teaching that led them to the academic profession. Yet, at the end of the day, the teaching component takes a back seat to the conduct of research. The first priority becomes maintaining currency in their discipline and contributing to it through scholarly endeavors. Since time might be the most precious resource, research and teaching have traditionally competed for the academic's time and attention (Rice, 1991). Junior faculty are advised not to invest too much time in their teaching practice because the key to career success and legitimacy lies in the publication of disciplinary research (Wilson, 2001). Later, senior faculty understand that establishing a scholarly reputation in their discipline is the route to opportunity. For both junior and senior faculty, research productivity leads to the benefits of academia: recognition, status, and rewards.

While teaching aspirations may attract many to an academic career, doctoral education is designed for students to learn how to conduct rigorous research that contributes to the discipline's base of scholarly knowledge—not training teachers (Forray, 1996; Fukami, 2007). Through such apprenticeship programs, "students" emerge as "scholars." Consequently, doctoral students may complete their programs with meager experience running their own class. Finding one's way in the classroom subsequently becomes a personal experiential learning process.

Comprehensive universities typically promote a balanced view of research and teaching through a teacher–scholar model, yet research productivity still carries disproportionate weight in advancement decisions. Even in lower-tier institutions that emphasize teaching, accreditation and marketing pressures shape requirements for research productivity—often despite lacking sufficient resources and infrastructure to support substantive research and creative endeavors. In essence, research simply adds one more priority without reducing teaching loads or service demands.

Certainly, it may be entirely possible to have a satisfying career based solely on the act of teaching; however, since most institutions now base their hiring and retention decisions on research potential and productivity, security and long-term career success become increasingly risky prospects for those entering the profession hoping to focus explicitly on the teaching aspect. Shapiro (2006) dramatically depicts the normative privileging of research over teaching through the construction of two hypothetical scenarios drawn from personal accounts of promotion and tenure reviews. On one side, the high-impact researcher with a lackluster teaching record receives accolades and tenure. On the other, the candidate with an excellent teaching portfolio is denied tenure because research was not published in quality journals and did not garner strong support from external referees. The absence of tenure and status can be costly for teachers relegated to the role of adjunct. Higher education now employs a half-million adjunct instructors who are paid approximately 64% less per hour than their full-time counterparts, and lack both benefits and job security (Hoeller, 2006).

The preceding commentary on teaching as a meaningful component of our professional lives provides entree into the central topic: the actual conduct of teaching practice. This chapter explicitly addresses the practice of teaching in the context of management education and learning (MEL). Its basic argument proposes that "good teaching" is essential, yet *not adequate* in satisfying the requirements of business schools and their constituents today. That is, good teaching is necessary but not sufficient to meet the demands of the "accountability triangle": public, academic, and market needs (Burke, 2005). The challenge is to raise MEL instruction to a higher level: beyond good teaching to teaching as scholarly practice. As will be evident, this is a difficult and likely controversial call to action for management educators—some will concur with our argument and critique while others will object. We contend that this is imperative, however, in order for the MEL domain to establish scholarly legitimacy. Our intent is to subject management education to critical scrutiny, thereby promoting conversation and debate among management faculty.

The chapter unfolds in this way: Drawing from the education literature, we first take a brief look at the context of education more broadly, including the evolving expectations of contemporary students, and then the demand for more innovative and productive instructional approaches. Next, we develop our argument by elaborating three related modes of instruction: good teaching, scholarly teaching, and the scholarship of teaching and learning (e.g., McKinney, 2007). The key to our argument is the distinction between teaching as technique, teaching as a scholarly practice, and teaching as scholarship. Our contention is that good teaching is no longer good enough; that scholarly teaching is the emergent standard in management curricula; and that greater legitimacy needs to be earned and justified by rigorous scholarship in the MEL domain within the academy. We conclude with some suggestions for a way forward that accomplishes scholarly teaching as the aspirational state for management educators, and that for some, career progress can be punctuated by locating one's scholarly interests in the MEL domain.

THE NEW EDUCATIONAL LANDSCAPE, CHANGING STUDENT NEEDS AND THE IMPERATIVE FOR INSTRUCTIONAL TRANSFORMATION

The "massification" of education in the last century democratized access to institutions of higher learning. But while the social efficiency principles derived from the industrial revolution allowed for scale in making education widely available, they also perpetuated the application of Taylorist principles in its delivery. More recently, the notion of education as a public good, fostering the ideals of democracy and a critical citizenry, was replaced by a market logic of capitalism and technocratic rationality (Kanpol, 1997; Welsh & Dehler, 2007). That is, education is now increasingly construed as a personal investment, thereby legitimizing resource reductions from public sources, as *state-supported* education becomes *state-assisted*, with the consumer–students bearing a greater cost burden under the auspices of "user fees." The misalignment between the ideal of public education as a social good and the private investment market model is becoming readily apparent. Yet students, as the consumers of learning, have been lost in this "McDonaldization" of education, merely there to be "burgered" (Hayes & Wynyard, 2002) in the managerialist McUniversity (Parker & Jary, 1995).

Today's students require more complex learning abilities to meet the needs of their disciplines, professions, workplace, and society. Specifically, Huber and Hutchings (2004) highlight the value of pedagogy to increase students' capacity to achieve *for themselves* connected learning across contexts; more integrative learning (see Martin, 2007); the ability to see problems from multiple perspectives; and ultimately to engage in *intentional learning*, where learning is the goal rather than an incidental outcome (see Bereiter & Scardamalia, 1989; Dehler, 1996).

The import of these evolving demands is that traditional approaches to instruction, what we label teaching-as-technique, are ineffective in meeting the learning needs and life situations of today's college students. They are inadequate in preparing them for the dramatically evolving global context characterized by uncertainty (Lueddeke, 2003; Weimer, 2003). Yet former Harvard president and longtime commentator on higher education Derek Bok (2006, p. 32) laments that college faculty feel "no compelling necessity" for reform in instruction or to experiment with new pedagogic methods "to help students accomplish more." This neglect of pedagogy, he notes, is caused in large part by institutional failure to meet the learning needs of students. He reports one survey in which only eight percent of teachers surveyed acknowledged taking any account of scholarly research on teaching and learning in preparing their classes (p. 50).

Shapiro (2006) contends that in spite of two decades of reform, faculty and administrators still have not redirected their attention from teaching to a learning culture. For business schools the problem is similarly structural as institutional logics perpetuate the shift from "education as professionalism" to "education as business" (Welsh & Dehler, 2007). The challenge at the level of the management educator, then, is to build on and extend the existing MEL scholarly foundation to foster transformation from reliance on teaching-as-technique to achieve "good teaching" to a focus on scholarly teaching to achieve "good learning." Realizing this transformation would then create more legitimate career opportunities for the teacher–scholar who pursues an instructional orientation over the traditional disciplinary orientation through teaching scholarship. The following sections address those three arenas.

GOOD TEACHING: TEACHING-AS-TECHNIQUE

To be clear at the outset, we acknowledge the inherently positive aspects of good teaching, but we argue that this is a desirable *minimum condition* of effective instruction. The overwhelming majority of management educators are no doubt good teachers. McKinney (2007) points out that good teaching promotes student learning and has been operationalized in numerous ways, including student satisfaction ratings (i.e., course evaluations), peer classroom observation, and personal reflection. Good teaching supports institutional missions and goals. Our contention, however, is that good teaching as a standard in MEL is no longer satisfactory in developing the next generation of organizational leaders or in moving the MEL domain forward. Our critique focuses on four related attributes of good teaching: (1) a limited construction of teaching-as-technique; (2) a fundamental orientation in the teaching paradigm—particularly transmission-based pedagogies such as lecture—that takes student learning for granted; (3) a narrow definition of "learning" itself; and 4) a disconnect between teaching practice and educational scholarship.

First, many of us received our introduction to the practical side of "skillful teaching" through the treatises of educational icons such as McKeachie (1986), Lowman (1995), and Brookfield (1990). Perusal of these works reveals a wealth of helpful "teaching tips" for beginning and accomplished teachers alike. But the topics are narrowly focused on the practical: meeting the first class, classroom dynamics, developing interpersonal skills and teaching style, planning course content, techniques to enhance student interest, giving helpful evaluations, organizing effective discussions, lecturing creatively—essentially a technician's view of an educator's competencies as a mechanistic "toolbox" (Arbaugh, 2006).

While these concerns are highly pragmatic, the fundamental problem is that employing a "technique" is explicitly teacher-centered, myopically focused on the teacher's behaviors. This reinforces Britzman's (1991, in Brookfield, 2005, p. 5) lament that "everything depends on the teacher" and a "teacher as Atlas" view that the instructor shoulders the entire burden of learning (Matthews, 1996, p. 105).

Grey (2004, p. 181) argues that management education fails to meet the needs of managers in part because of its dependence on "reliable techniques" that promise something "illusory." Yet effective teaching is not merely a matter of acquiring a set of teaching competencies or applying general principles according to rule (Biggs, 1999). Lowman (1995) himself identifies the shortcomings of a relentless application of techniques in all contexts whether or not they are called for. A management example might be the advent of business process reengineering in the 1990s. In principle, it had potential, yet was too often implemented merely as a technique without consideration of its philosophical underpinnings with quite adverse consequences (e.g., mindless downsizing).

Second, rigid adherence to technique and over-reliance on the teacher are consistent with the tenets of the teaching paradigm, which has a familiar history so its attributes will be touched on just briefly here. Barr and Tagg (1995) provide the most comprehensive account of its distinction from the learning paradigm. They identify six dimensions for comparison: mission and purposes, criteria for success, teaching/learning structures, learning theory, productivity/funding, and the nature of roles. Some criteria within these categories (sequentially to above) that relate to our discussion in this chapter include the delivery of instruction, the quality of instruction, covering material, knowledge as "out there," productivity assessed equally per student, and faculty primarily as lecturers.

The teaching paradigm focuses on the actions of teachers as the locus of the educational encounter. If teachers simply do the teaching behaviors, then student learning can be assumed to have occurred. This is exemplified by Freire's (1990) banking model of teaching, in which students are seen as empty vessels passively awaiting deposits of the teacher's expert knowledge for later withdrawal, which captures the essence of the teaching paradigm. The university represents a place where we teach rather than one where learning is produced. The teaching paradigm perpetuates "conceptions of teaching that are increasingly recognized as ineffective" (Barr & Tagg, 1995, p. 13).

Weimer (2002, 2003) posits that these traditional instructional approaches or techniques are unresponsive to students' learning needs. She is especially critical of the use of lecture to "cover" content and instruction that generates only surface learning (e.g., memorizing facts, focusing on discrete elements of readings, and failure to differentiate between evidence and information). Surface learners (Ramsden, 1992) characterize students who focus on the parts—separate words or sentences in an article rather than on deriving meaning and understanding based on the larger point. Their intention is merely to complete the requirements of the assignment—that is, learning is equated with their work product, not their engagement in the process of *doing* the task. A preponderance of studies point to the limitations of this pedagogy (Lueddeke, 2003). Lecture fosters a content orientation that provides students with lower-level surface learning of propositional knowledge sufficient for students to pass objective examinations—but it does not foster *understanding* (Ramsden, 1992). Students master test-taking but lack the capacity to invoke useful knowledge when confronted with practical dilemmas, and recall is notoriously limited. A transmission approach to teaching is one of *the* major sources of the problem with education generally, and specifically regarding management education. This overemphasis on teaching "is an impoverished method" (Gosling & Mintzberg, 2006, p. 421), based on the notion that management knowledge resides in instructors' heads to be "delivered by teacherly engagements' (p. 424).

Now, at this point we acknowledge that lecture persists as "the oldest teaching method and still the most widely used in American colleges and universities" (McKeachie, 1986, p. 69). In a survey of faculty across disciplines, 76% listed lecture as their primary instructional method (Weimer, 2007), while another study found that nearly 50% of class time was spent lecturing (Lammers & Murphy, 2002). To be sure, there are determined defenders of lecture (e.g., Burgan, 2006), and institutional resource considerations virtually demand its use in large-class venues. Yet of "all the methods of college teaching, the lecture is probably the most frequently abused" because it is authoritarian and teacher-centered (Brookfield, 1990, p. 71). Invoking Freire's recognition that not all lecturing is banking education, Brookfield acknowledges that both students and teachers have "strong expectations that lecturing will be a major educational method.... The challenge we face as teachers is to make our lectures as enlivening and critically stimulating as possible" (1990, p. 72). Improving lecturing technique can enhance teaching performance. Thus, since we all employ lecture, the issue is a matter of extent and purpose (see Brookfield, 1990, ch. 6).

Third, how we define learning also raises another point for debate. Simplistically, transmission models of teaching presume that if information is moved from the professor's head to students' heads, mediated by textbooks and filled notebooks, and regurgitated via objective tests, then learning has occurred. Teaching-centered approaches are generally content-oriented and tend to foster lower-level learning. Learning is equated with students' "possession" of information, usually short term in order to pass exams, and requires cues to retrieve relevant knowledge to do so—rather than the ability to learn intentionally. Students lack the ability to apply knowledge in novel ways to cope with practical dilemmas (Barr & Tagg, 1995; Ramsden, 1992).

Sotto (1994), who provides a compelling account of the teaching-learning process, contends that "didactic teaching seldom results in significant learning" (p. 60). Didactic telling, rote learning, and drill-and-practice may help students remember, but "learning is not the same as remembering [and] remembering is not the same as understanding" (p. 51). "Learning, real learning, isn't what happens when we are fed information. Learning is what happens when we realize we don't know something which we consider worth knowing, form a hunch about it, and test that hunch actively" (p. 50). Fourth, narrowly addressing techniques and behaviors associated with good teaching reflects a disconnect between action and mindful practice; that is, practice grounded in a sound conceptual foundation. Just as the development of a personal teaching philosophy needs to be located in educational philosophy (Beatty, Leigh & Lund Dean, 2009), the conduct of teaching similarly needs to be underpinned and legitimized by pedagogical scholarship. The ad hoc creation of teaching heuristics can unfold through experience, but replicating "what works" remains superficial and unreflective without framing practice in the educational and pedagogical knowledge base for fostering continuous improvement.

Narrow attention to techniques on the *teaching* side of practice overshadows the more important process of *learning* as an outcome of informed *scholarly initiatives* that build students' learning capabilities. As Menges and Weimer (1996, p. xvi) argue, "the focus of pedagogical literature has been too much on the teacher." Sotto posits provocatively, that "teaching must often stop before learning can begin. The converse is surely true: it does not follow that anybody is learning because somebody is teaching, even teaching well" (1994, p. 144). When teaching shifts from the teacher to the student, becomes learning-centered and informed by scholarship, then practice begins to take on the appearance of scholarly teaching. This is addressed next.

SCHOLARLY TEACHING:
PRACTICE INFORMED BY SCHOLARSHIP

Turning from good teaching to scholarly teaching raises the bar for management educators. But scholarly teaching is not as readily defined in the literature as good teaching, due in part to its more recent conceptualization. McKinney (2007) links scholarly teaching to reflective practice (e.g., Brookfield, 1990; Schon, 1983), whereby teachers are critically reflective

(Lueddeke, 2003) and informed by the disciplinary literature on teaching and learning appropriate to their field (Shulman, 2000)—that is, MEL in our case. McKinney briefly describes it as taking "a scholarly approach to teaching just as we would take a scholarly approach to other areas of knowledge and practice" (2007, p. 9).

In order to undertake a more in-depth explication of scholarly teaching, the following discussion is organized along the same four attributes addressed in good teaching: (1) scholarly teaching as a broader construction of the instructional role; (2) a fundamental orientation in the learning paradigm; (3) a broader definition of "learning" itself; and (4) drawing explicit linkages between teaching practice and educational scholarship.

First, reiterating our earlier point, Smith (2001) notes that one can be an excellent teacher without being a scholarly teacher or making a contribution to teaching scholarship. But a distinguishing feature of academics is the expectation that they will conduct their work in a "scholarly" manner. Embracing scholarly teaching requires knowledge about teaching and learning, pedagogy and andragogy, instructional design, learning styles, and assessment methods. Beyond knowledge, being scholarly refers to the approaches we employ—preparation, methodology, and reflective critique. Looking past these contextual aspects that shape teacher behaviors, however, there is an explicit shift of emphasis from the teaching process to the learning process, and the re-orientation of the role of the student-as-learner.

The teacher-as-expert of good teaching possesses answers and pursues a right-answer orientation. On the other hand, the scholarly teacher poses questions and facilitates learning by guiding and collaborating with students in the process of sense making and creating meaning. But instead of making problems easier, the teacher makes them more complex, involving and stimulating—artfully complicating the situation, thereby challenging students to think harder (Kohn, 1999, p. 135). This approach resists the temptation to create a false simplicity incongruous with a complex world, instead increasing students' tolerance for ambiguity and enhancing their level of complicatedness (e.g., Dehler & Welsh, 1993; Dehler, Welsh & Lewis, 2001). Coping with complexity calls for more complex problem-solving skills.

Students cannot adopt a passive stance, but must accept responsibility for learning— "let students be the heavyweights" (Menges & Weimer, 1996, p. xvi). Learning implies change, and change can be difficult. Yet "there is no such thing as significant learning without considerable difficulty" (Sotto, 1994, p. 14). In other words, learning entails engaging in a *struggle*, and true learning "only comes about when we have had an appropriate experience. And the more we have to struggle during that experience, the more powerful is our learning likely to be" (p. 60). The challenge for the student-centered teacher, then, is to create the conditions that enable students to learn. Creating a learning context relates to the learning paradigm.

Second, the aim of the learning paradigm is to move students to the center of the learning process—in essence, shifting the focus from the teacher to the student. Student-centered learning alters many of the taken-for-granted beliefs of traditional education. (Table 6.1 provides an overview that contrasts student-centered learning with teaching-centered instruction.) For example, the goal of promoting student learning disrupts traditional views of power and authority. This de-emphasizes notions of teaching techniques and methods, recasting focus on learning facilitation (Weimer, 2002). In the pursuit of deep learning, the learning facilitator seeks to legitimize students' interaction with course content—especially in relation to their own experience.

Deep learning (Ramsden, 1992) challenges students to relate previous knowledge to new knowledge, incorporate knowledge from different courses, connect theoretical ideas to practical experience, distinguish evidence and argument, and organize and structure content into an idiosyncratic coherent integrative whole. This goes beyond memorizing for purposes of assessment and associating facts and ideas unreflectively. In other words, students need to create knowledge structures that connect ideas in a manner that makes sense to them—that is, knowledge transformation rather than mere knowledge telling (Dehler, 1996). In the process of inquiry, students engage their tasks as intentional learning; that is, they invest effort in learning beyond that required to complete the task (Bereiter & Scardamalia, 1987) and are on their way to becoming life-long learners (Huber & Hutchings, 2004). Knowledge becomes the means rather than the end of the learning process (Dehler, 1996) that seeks to construct meaning and understanding. If learners actively construct their own knowledge rather than passively receive it from teachers and textbooks, then questions arise about the meaning of learning itself.

The third aspect of scholarly teaching relates to how learning is defined. Sotto (1994, p. 30) suggests that learning is the ability to do something that one could not do before. Learning becomes "a process of the active construction of meaning" (Stage, Muller, Kinzie & Simmons, 1998, p. 37) as the teacher promotes active dialog with students, and among students. Students begin to connect new knowledge to previous learning, thereby building individual knowledge structures (e.g., Dehler, 1996) from which they begin to create meaning and derive understanding. This suggests, then, that knowledge itself is constructed (Kohn, 1999). When students construct their own meanings, inquiry becomes a problem-solving endeavor with teachers aiding student development and fostering their reflection on constructed solutions. Students are encouraged to ask their own questions and voice their own views. For

TABLE 6.1 Juxtaposition of Traditional Instruction and Student-Centered Instruction

Instruction	Student-Centered Learning Environments
transmission, acquisition	interpretation, construction
mastery, performance	meaning making
external reality	internal reality
dualism, absolutism	cultural relativism, perspectival
abstract, symbolic	contextualized, authentic, experiential
individually interpreted	socially negotiated, co-constructed
mind-centered	community-based, culturally mediated
directed	intentional
reductionistic	complex, self-organizing
individual	collaborative
idealist, rational	pragmatist
encoding, retention, retrieval	articulation and reflection
internal, mental	social
receptive, reproductive	constructive
symbolic reasoning	situated learning
psychology	anthropology, sociology, ethnography
laboratory	in situ
theoretical	everyday
central processing architecture	distributed architecture
objective, modelable	experiential, interpretive
symbol processor	symbol builder
disembodied	experiential
conceptual, memorial	perceptual
atomistic, decomposable	gestalt
independent	emergent
possessed	distributed
objective, stable, fixed	subjective, contextualized, fluid
well-structured	ill-structured
decontextualized	embedded in experience
compliant	self-regulated

Source: Jonassen & Land, 2000, p. viii

example, students might identify a contradiction between the maximizing shareholder wealth "fact" learned in their finance class when encountering the balanced scorecard or the triple bottom line. Learning, then, acquires a different look when teaching becomes more scholarly. Student-centered strategies shift responsibility for learning to the student and redirect emphasis on developing student capabilities necessary to become lifelong learners.

Finally, in contrast to good teaching, which may be technically effective, scholarly teaching demonstrates a clear line of sight to the literature on management education and learning. Weimer states the case clearly: "While we value the techniques of teaching, we deplore overemphasizing them.... Emphasis on technique trivializes the rich complexity that is the situated knowledge of teaching contexts and circumstances" (1996, p. 5). Instructional strategies in a scholarly context, based in research findings, lead to a deeper understanding of students and how they learn, and result from "notions of teaching that are grounded in philosophy and principle" (p. 5). In other words, "the *practice of instruction* needs to be informed by scholarship" (Menges & Weimer, 1996, p. xiii).

From this view, then, scholarly teaching at its core includes technique, but it is imperative that practice is informed by knowledge connected to the educational foundation. Analogous to researchers becoming conversant with the scholarly literature of research methodology in which they must ground their inquiry, we argue that management educators must similarly develop a "knowledge base on teaching and learning as a secondary discipline in which to develop expertise" (McKinney, 2007, p. 9). Using surveys, for instance, represents a technique; but it requires the researcher to legitimize and justify this technique by connecting it to the research methods arena. Richlin (2001) proposes that to "engage in the scholarly process, the teacher must justify the selection of method from what is known in the literature; it must be made explicit" (p. 60). Scholarly teaching extends beyond being a scholar in one's disciplinary field and "knowing the latest stuff" (Smith, 2001, p. 70). Ultimately, scholarly teachers reflect back on their practice in order to promote continuous improvement that enhances instructional effectiveness and student learning. This takes the teaching–learning process full circle: "The application of new knowledge about teaching and learning to the professor's practice is the end product of scholarly teaching" (Richlin, 2001, p. 61).

To this point, we have argued that traditional technique-based and teaching-centered strategies no longer suffice because they do not adequately prepare students for the challenges they face in the evolving global milieu. In distinguishing between good teaching and scholarly teaching, we propose that the latter represents the new standard in today's education environment—particularly in management education. We stop short, however, of explicitly advocating for teaching-as-scholarship as an endeavor for everyone. This is intentional, yet this topic is worth exploring for different reasons—perhaps most obviously because the large proportion of management faculty's daily life is consumed by instructional endeavors. This speaks to the imperative for legitimizing the MEL domain itself. Generating greater credibility for scholarly contributions to MEL within the academy enhances career opportunities for management educators.

TEACHING SCHOLARSHIP:
THE SCHOLARSHIP OF TEACHING AND LEARNING

The preceding argument advocates for the transition to scholarly teaching from good teaching. We now turn to the link between scholarly teaching and teaching scholarship. Our commentary begins with a basic assumption: Although the MEL domain has existed at least informally for some time, it has not achieved credibility matching the status of other management domains. Management scholars can realize *scholarly legitimacy* by conducting research in subdisciplines such as organizational behavior, strategy, entrepreneurship—but *not* via scholarship in MEL. Richlin (2001, p. 61) notes "the sad truth" that too often departments and institutions do not consider pedagogical scholarship to be recognized in terms of faculty members' scholarly accomplishments. In light of the AACSB's newfound focus on teaching, it could be argued that an academic's scholarly portfolio should include work in the area. But it is difficult to establish MEL as a core research domain because the quality of scholarship is not always considered credible. This may well be due to its origins in "good teaching"—publishing "a little teaching tip" is nice, but the larger management studies discipline rewards "real disciplinary" research in recognized subdisciplines. The MEL field itself may contribute to its contested status by the kinds of scholarship it publishes (e.g., exercises and cases) and the methods it employs (e.g., first-person reflection, action research) that may be inconsistent with more accepted traditional, positivist research.

This is the crux of the dilemma in our argument: When conceptualized as "good teaching," work in the pedagogical arena tends to be *constrained by technique rather than enriched by scholarship.* The MEL domain simply cannot achieve the academic legitimacy to which it aspires by deriving from precepts of good teaching. Opportunity, however, emerges if it derives from the notion of scholarly teaching because that is explicitly grounded in scholarship rather than merely technique. The scholarship of teaching "builds on the end product of scholarly teaching" (Richlin, 2001, p. 61). Only from this position can MEL establish the scholarly credibility required to stand on its own as a management domain worthy of serious respect in the wider academy as well as in local reward systems. So, if scholarly teaching becomes the new standard for instruction, it then serves as the antecedent for legitimizing teaching scholarship—which has its origin in the scholarship of teaching and learning (SOTL).

The SOTL movement evolved in the early 1990s from Boyer's (1990) inspired discussion of faculty priorities. He argued that the careers of faculty in higher education were limited by narrow definitions of scholarship that fail to recognize the full range of faculty endeavors. Most faculty have a clear sense of what *scholarship* means in the scholarship of discovery (i.e., traditional research), which is frequently all that matters in evaluation and advancement decisions at many institutions (highlighted by Shapiro's account earlier in this chapter). Boyer's other areas of scholarship—integration, application, and teaching—are more difficult to define. In suggesting their inclusion among academic priorities, Boyer pointed to a political and cultural environment of higher education that impedes the recognition of a broader range of scholarly activities. He makes it clear that the underlying values driving the reward system are a core issue.

Addressing values about teaching, Weimer (1997) argues that the academy holds assumptions that actually devalue teaching, which either overlook or trivialize the intellectual complexity of the activity. Many view teaching as content-driven and little more than a matter of technique; requiring little training or ongoing development; and lacking scholarly standards. In the context of our argument, these assumptions arguably might have merit *if* one distinguishes between good teaching and scholarly teaching (acknowledging the problematic nature of these assumptions). Thus, in promoting teaching-as-scholarship, proponents are seeking to "up the ante with respect to the intellectual credibility of teaching" (Weimer, 1996, p. 5).

Boyer's notion of teaching scholarship was introduced without any preconceived parameters concerning definition or operationalization. Subsequently, academics have been left to debate attributes that represent legitimate scholarship, distinguishing it from merely "good" or "scholarly" teaching (Braxton, Luckey & Helland, 2002). There is some irony here: the literature intended to advocate for the legitimacy of teaching scholarship struggles to define what it tries to defend. The term "scholarship of teaching" has fostered considerable debate regarding standards related to "scholarship" in the education domain, i.e., should teaching scholarship mirror the standards of rigor of disciplinary research?

Reviewing definitions in the SOTL literature, four recurring elements emerge that distinguish scholarship (Braxton, et al., 2002; Shulman & Hutchings, 1998; Weimer, 1996). First, teaching scholarship should inquire into student learning, as differentiated from a sole focus on teaching. Second, it needs to be grounded, building on the body of existing educational literature. Third, it should use rigorous and systematic methods of inquiry (Weimer, 1996). Finally, results of teaching scholarship must be made public and subjected to critical scrutiny via peer review. Just as in other domains, consideration of "what" constitutes scholarship leads to ongoing dialog surrounding what form of peer review is acceptable, ranging from a stricter standard of published manuscripts in peer-reviewed education journals (Richlin, 2001) to other less rigorous forms such as conference presentations (Cross, 1998). These latter concerns in particular underscore the ongoing debate surrounding education and learning in the academy broadly, and the management discipline more narrowly. We turn next to the challenge of legitimizing MEL scholarship.

LEGITIMIZING SCHOLARSHIP IN MANAGEMENT EDUCATION AND LEARNING

The central issue regarding the legitimacy of MEL scholarship relates to the fourth aspect noted above: subjecting teaching scholarship to peer review and making it public—typically through publication in recognized journals, academic and practitioner alike. (We include as practitioner journals outlets such as *Harvard Business Review* and *California Management Review*, which may speak to Boyer's scholarship of application.) There are at least two concerns related to publication: rigor, and the relation of reward systems to publication and journal quality. Our preceding discussion addressed the issue of rigor by arguing that teaching can be a scholarly activity.

The second concern has to do with the priorities of the professoriate, which are largely shaped by the promotion and tenure system and strongly influenced by the scholarship of discovery (traditional discipline-based research). Faculty productivity is usually assessed in terms of traditional scholarship, with the de facto metrics merely transferred to teaching scholarship. Insistent calls for accountability within the emerging "culture of assessment and regulation" (Evans, 2004, p. x) have further increased this reliance on historic measurement systems. We emphasize that our following discussion establishing the legitimacy of teaching scholarship is not unproblematic, but reiterate our intention to provoke dialog rather than resolve the dilemma.

The key indicator for judging the scholarship of discovery is the number of publications in peer-reviewed journals, with measures of journal quality and reputation assessed by impact factors. A variety of journal ranking studies (Coe & Weinstock, 1984; Extejt & Smith, 1990; Gomez-Mejia & Balkin, 1992; Sharplin & Mabry, 1985; Tahai & Meyer, 1999) have identified a core set of management outlets. From these published ranking lists and impact factors, some management departments have created tiered lists of acceptable publications to define and standardize their reward structure.

Published ranking studies have a homogenizing effect on acceptable outlets. Marsh and Hunt (2006) note that reducing the number of "important" sources of knowledge is likely to similarly constrain the kinds of research getting published: "Innovation that falls outside the current domain of established journals will be discouraged. The end result for the academic community as a whole may be too much research that reflects the mainstream and/or the fads of the moment and not enough research that calls into question the existing models and perspectives" (p. 310). Significantly, management education journals are not included in any of the journal ranking studies, and only two MEL journals (*Management Learning* and *Academy of Management Learning and Education*) are currently included in the journal *Factor Impact Analysis*. These omissions are significant barriers to establishing legitimacy in teaching scholarship because they imply that MEL journals are not reputable scholarly outlets.

This might suggest that the route to legitimacy is a matter of moving the management education journals into the rankings fold, but we believe this overlooks an important feature of the management education literature. Impact factors measure how often research is cited in other academic articles, implying that the metric is assessing the contribution to other researchers' work. Teaching scholarship, however, has a practical impact that is not readily captured in the citation trail of others' research. Impact also reflects classroom application, as teachers adopt new concepts and methods. Whether MEL scholarship can compete in the legitimacy game using the same institutionalized metrics of discovery scholarship is questionable and deserves greater scrutiny—and management educators should begin asking if this is even the right game to be playing.

The issue is that the metrics may push the management education field to adopt the dominant practices valued in the scholarship of discovery (e.g., positivist methods), while devaluing qualitative and interpretivist strategies that are methodologically appropriate and traditionally used in the teaching domain (e.g., first person reflection). Just as the dominant positivist paradigm in management research is being challenged by a wider range of ontological, epistemological and methodological perspectives, exploring new metrics might more accurately reflect the contribution of teaching scholarship.

The growing interest in the publication of teaching scholarship illustrates the emergence of the MEL field over the last two decades, and suggests that legitimacy is increasing. Whether this aspiration is fully embraced by promotion and tenure committees remains to be seen. The legitimacy of teaching scholarship still varies across institutions, and too often remains to be considered "less than" other kinds of research. But adopting a scholarly approach to teaching can influence this viewpoint.

THE CHALLENGE FOR MANAGEMENT EDUCATORS

Our inquiry into teaching as a scholarly endeavor is inspired by the fundamental question posed by Stefani (2006, p. 114): "Do faculty fully understand what it means to take a scholarly approach to learning and teaching?" It is not our intention here to reinvent the management education wheel, nor is it our desire to subject all management educators to accusations of reliance on mere technique unconnected to scholarship. There are abundant examples of student- and learning-centered instruction documented in MEL journals, conference presentations, as well as anecdotally, that could arguably represent scholarly teaching. Rather, we are critiquing a vital component of our professional endeavor—teaching practice—in addition to initiating a call to management educators to undertake introspective self-critique of their instructional philosophy. The next step is the ongoing pursuit of development initiatives that enhance their practice. Thus, in this final section, we attempt to enrich the conversation surrounding the evolution from teaching-as-technique to the scholarly practice of teaching and learning.

As described above, Shulman and his Carnegie colleagues have provided a starting point for defining teaching in terms of scholarship. Yet we have suggested that merely importing a template from traditional, positivist disciplinary scholarship into teaching practice is limited and insufficient. For instance, while Glassick, Huber, and Maeroff's (1997) attempt to elaborate Boyer's work did offer further insight, it still treated instruction in teaching paradigm terms (e.g., clarity of goals, preparation, effective presentation) rather than in learning terms. Stefani (2006) raises this issue explicitly, challenging traditional science-based notions of research as opposed to research paradigms employed in sociology, psychology, and philosophy. Despite the call for richer pedagogical approaches to management education, the focus on a technique-based view of teaching persists despite confronting dramatically different learning needs of today's students in an increasingly demanding global environment. Without doubt, evolving to a learning paradigm approach raises further dilemmas regarding epistemological (Schon, 1995) and ontological (Welsh & Dehler, 2007) questions, both of which are vital concerns but beyond the scope of this chapter.

Our view of teaching scholarship in the MEL context, then, extends some of these ideas and introduces others. Below, we identify five attributes intended to foster dialog on building a foundation for scholarly teaching in MEL: (1) linking instruction to scholarship in the MEL and higher education domains; (2) reflecting critically on our instructional practice; (3) adopting personal views of learning and linking them to our pedagogies; (4) exploring pedagogies that are explicitly oriented toward student learning needs; and (5) working programmatically and/or institutionally to embed learning-centered approaches in practice and socialize students to learning-centered activities.

First, in connecting extant educational scholarship to our practice, we draw a parallel with empirical research. When conducting research, it is imperative that our inquiry draws from and is grounded in documented, scholarly literature on methodology to lend credibility and legitimacy to our work. This also allows others to judge its veracity in context. Analogously, then, we suggest that management educators similarly need to ground their instructional practice in documented educational philosophy and principles. This shifts the focus on "how" from a technique standpoint to one of process (Weimer, 1996). In what way is our teaching practice informed by the literature on education and learning? Just as we expect students to ground their understanding in course material, our instruction should be explicitly connected to established educational literature in a defensible manner.

Second, teaching has been construed as a "reflective activity" (Biggs, 1999) where instructional practice is subjected to critical reflection (e.g., Glassick et al., 1997). This implies that instructors subject their pedagogical practices to personal review and scrutiny as a regular activity to keep their teaching philosophy current (Beatty et al., in press). This also needs to extend beyond mere assessment of technique to reflecting critically on our fundamental purposes in the teaching–learning enterprise. Teachers should make their underlying assumptions about learning transparent, adopting a socially situated orientation to the construction of meaning and understanding, an explicit awareness of power dynamics in the classroom, and develop cognizance of issues related to emancipation and social justice (Welsh & Dehler, 2004).

Third, we need to identify "what kind of pedagogical theory might underlie the process of learning about teaching for academics" (Rowland, 2000, p. 44). Meanings associated with "learning" are inevitably problematic. It is incumbent upon management educators to actively seek information about teaching and learning "with the intention of expanding their knowledge and applying it to their own teaching practice . . . carrying out their own action research" (Stefani, 2006, p. 120). Identifying *what* we want students to learn should be consistent with *how* we generate learning opportunities. In a sense, our teaching practice should be an ongoing action research project focused on how our practice might be improved (Whitehead, 1994).

Fourth, specific pedagogies need to be selected based on student learning needs. Strategies aimed at developing deep learning in students transcend those that are passive and minimally engage students. Biggs (1999) suggests developing teaching strategies that move students from low-level engagement (e.g., memorizing, note taking, recognizing) toward higher-level engagement (e.g., relating, applying, reflecting, theorizing). In this context, he promotes pedagogies intent on "getting the most students to use higher cognitive level processes that more academic students use spontaneously" (Biggs, 1999, p. 4). For example, he identifies problem-based learning as a potential pedagogy, which happens to be among the array of pedagogies addressed in the MEL literature under the umbrella of "social inquiry" (Coombs & Eldon, 2004). There are ample examples of these approaches in the MEL journals, including the use of action research by students (Dehler, 2006).

Finally, a barrier to learning-centered education within the management domain is the socialization of business students to more passive forms of learning in other disciplines. Management educators are in the position to engage colleagues in fostering the cultural transformation of college teaching, both internally through collegial discourse and externally through organizations such as the Academy of Management's Management Education and Development Division and the OBTS Teaching Society for Management Educators. Our knowledge of teaching derives not only from educational literature, but from personal classroom experimentation with alternative pedagogies as well. Sharing those experiences at conferences and in communities of practice leads to transforming implicit instructional knowledge into explicit teaching theories. This exchange of ideas about teaching and learning can engender creation of a teaching commons, an "emergent conceptual space for exchange and community among faculty, students, administrators, and all others committed to learning as an essential activity in contemporary democratic society" (Huber & Hutchings, 2005, p. 1). Certainly, making conversations about teaching and learning more transparent is especially relevant to the management discipline and a natural consequence of our long-standing initiatives related to the education of managers.

The above five attributes represent actionable strategies to move teaching and learning in the MEL domain beyond mere technique into the realm of scholarship. They are not proposed as a "recipe" or formula, but to engage MEL scholars in the debate about what constitutes a scholarly approach to our practice. Indeed, we need to be cautious about viewing teaching and learning as if it is generic, independent of any particular subdiscipline (Rowland, 2000). Different teachers may use the same teaching method differently, but what matters is what they focus on in their practice rather than merely any particular methods they use. Ultimately, our focus needs to be redirected onto students' experiences of learning, using the consideration of these experiences in thinking about how we organize our teaching (Ashwin, 2000).

CONCLUSION

It is clear that the legitimacy dilemma is emerging as a critical issue in establishing management education and learning as a scholarly domain (Arbaugh, 2008; Schmidt-Wilk, 2007). It is imperative that management educators adopt a more scholarly approach to teaching practice for a number of reasons, not least of which is enriching the learning experience of our students. Other meaningful reasons include management's increasingly visible role in the academy, the AACSB's growing interest in the delivery of management education, greater prominence of the teaching-and-learning process in institutional mission statements and accreditation requirements, and stakeholders' increasing demands for accountability. But to date only limited attention has been devoted to the MEL outlets or to the scholarly grounding of management education practice.

As to publication outlets, Bilimoria and Fukami (2002) describe the state of management education scholarship and the historical development of what we arguably consider the leading MEL journals: *Management Learning, Journal of Management Education (JME)*, and *Academy of Management Learning and Education (AMLE)*. They too note the domain's struggle for acceptance and legitimacy, labeling it as "somewhat marginalized as a specialized area of secondary scholarship" (Bilimoria & Fukami, 2002, p. 126). In terms of management practice, Korpiaho, Päiviö, and Räsänen (2007) reviewed these three core journals to explore various orientations in the delivery of management education. Their findings represent an important contribution by identifying five different conceptions of management education, which they explicitly connect to the scholarly foundation of the MEL domain. This is the kind of research that the MEL subdiscipline desperately needs to establish its credibility as a scholarly project.

Management faculty influence the educational experience of thousands of students annually in the United States. Therefore, it is in the long-term interest of management educators, their institutions, and society to embrace—and raise—teaching as a scholarly endeavor. This sentiment is underscored by several arguments: (1) empirical research from the broader education, SOTL, and MEL literature; (2) the support of various economic actors such as the student educational consumers and their future employers; (3) the core historical mandate for educational institutions; and (4) a proactive response to address issues of relevance, context, and transparency by political bodies at the state and federal level, as well as consumer advocacy groups. In sum, the case for legitimization of the management education and learning domain now confronts us. So, the challenge is clear and management educators have the potential to lead this initiative in business programs across the globe.

REFERENCES

Arbaugh, J.B. (2006) Introduction: Selecting and stocking the management educator's toolbox. *Academy of Management Learning & Education, 5,* 123–124.
Arbaugh, J.B. (2008) From the editor: Starting the long march to legitimacy. *Academy of Management Learning & Education, 7,* 5–8.

Ashwin, P. (2006) The development of learning and teaching in higher education: The changing context. In P. Ashwin (Ed.), *Changing higher education: The development of learning and teaching* (pp. 3–15). London: Routledge.

Barr, R.B. & Tagg, J. (1995) From teaching to learning—A new paradigm for undergraduate education. *Change, Nov/Dec*, 13–25.

Beatty, J., Leigh, J., & Lund Dean, K. (2009). Philosophy rediscovered: Exploring the connections between teaching philosophies, educational philosophies, and philosophy. *Journal of Management Education, 33*(1), 99–114.

Bereiter, C. & Scardamalia, M. (1987). An attainable version of high literacy: Approaches to teaching higher-order skills in reading and writing. *Curriculum Inquiry, 17,* 9–30.

Bereiter, C. & Scardamalia, M. (1989). Intentional learning as a goal of instruction. In L. Resnick (Ed.), *Knowing, learning and instruction: Essays in honor of Robert Glaser* (pp. 361–392). Hillsdale, NJ: Lawrence Erlbaum.

Biggs, J. (1999). *Teaching for quality learning at university: What the student does.* Buckingham, UK: Society for Research into Higher Education and Open University Press.

Bilimoria, D. & Fukami, C. (2002). The scholarship of teaching and learning in the management sciences: Disciplinary style and content. In M.T. Huber & S.P. Morreale (Eds.), *Disciplinary styles in the scholarship of teaching and learning: Exploring common ground* (pp. 125–142). Washington, DC: American Association for Higher Education.

Bok, D. (2006). *Our underachieving colleges: A candid look at how much students learn and why they should be learning more.* Princeton: Princeton University Press.

Boyer, E.L. (1990) *Scholarship reconsidered: Priorities of the professorate.* Princeton: The Carnegie Foundation for the Advancement of Teaching.

Braxton, J.M., Luckey, W., & Helland, P. (2002). Institutionalizing a broader view of scholarship through Boyer's four domains. *ASHE-ERIC Higher Education Report, 29*(2).

Britzman, D.P. (1991). *Practice makes practice: A critical study of learning to teach.* Albany: State University of New York Press.

Brookfield, S.D. (1990). *The skillful teacher.* San Francisco: Jossey-Bass.

Brookfield, S.D. (2005). *The power of critical theory: Liberating adult learning and teaching.* San Francisco: Jossey-Bass.

Burgan, M. (2006). In defense of lecturing. *Change, Nov/Dec,* 30–34.

Burke, J.C. & Associates. (2005). *Achieving accountability in higher education: Balancing public, academic, and market demands.* San Francisco: Jossey-Bass.

Carr, W. (1995). *For education: Towards critical educational inquiry.* Buckingham, UK: Open University Press.

Coe, R., & Weinstock, I. (1984). Evaluating the management journals: A second look. *Academy of Management Journal, 27,* 660–666.

Coombs, G. & Elden, M. (2004). Introduction to the special issue: Problem-based learning as social inquiry—PBL and management education. *Journal of Management Education, 28,* 523–535.

Cross, K.P. (1998). Classroom research: Implementing the scholarship of teaching. In T. Angelo (Ed.), *New directions for teaching and learning* (pp. 5–12). San Francisco: Jossey-Bass.

Dehler, G.E. (1996). Management education as intentional learning: A knowledge transforming approach to written communication. *Journal of Management Education, 20*(2), 221–235.

Dehler, G.E. (2006). Using action research to connect practice to learning: A course project for working management students. *Journal of Management Education, 30*, 636–669.

Dehler, G.E. & Welsh, M.A. (1993). Dialectical inquiry as an instructional heuristic in organization theory and design. *Journal of Management Education, 17*, 79–89.

Dehler, G.E., Welsh, M.A., & Lewis, M.W. (2001). Critical pedagogy in the "new paradigm": Raising complicated understanding in management learning. *Management Learning, 32*, 493–511.

Evans, M. (2004). *Killing thinking.* London: Continuum.

Extcjt, M.M. & Smith, J.E. (1990). The behavioral sciences and management: An evaluation of relevant journals. *Journal of Management, 16*, 539–551.

Forray, J. (1996). Doctoral education and the teaching mission: A dialogue with Jean Bartunek, Lee Burke, Craig Lundberg, Jane Giacobbe Miller, Pushkala Prasad, and Chris Roberts. *Journal of Management Education, 20*, 60–69.

Freire, P. (1990). *Pedagogy of the oppressed.* New York: Continuum.

Fukami, C. (2007). The third road. *Journal of Management Education, 31*, 358–364.

Glassick, C.E., Huber, M.T., & Maeroff, G.I. (1997). *Scholarship assessed: Evaluation of the Professoriate.* San Francisco: Jossey-Bass.

Gomez-Mejia, L.R. & Balkin, D.B. (1992). Determinants of faculty pay: An agency theory perspective. *Academy of Management Journal, 35*, 921–955.

Gosling, J. & Mintzberg, H. (2006). Management education as if both mattered. *Management Learning, 37*, 419–428.

Grey, C. (2004). Reinventing business schools: The contribution of critical management education. *Academy of Management Learning & Education, 3*, 178–186.

Hayes, D. & Wynyard, R. (2002). *The McDonaldization of higher education.* Westport, CT: Bergin & Garvey.

Hoeller, K. (2006). The proper advocates for adjuncts. *The Chronicle of Higher Education.* June 16.

Huber, M.T. & Hutchings, P. (2004). *Integrative learning: Mapping the terrain.* Washington, DC: Assn. of American Colleges and Universities, and the Carnegie Foundation for the Advancement of Teaching.

Huber, M.T. & Hutchings, P. (2005). *The advancement of learning: Building the teaching commons.* San Francisco: Jossey-Bass.

Jonassen, D.H. & Land, S.M. (Eds.) (2000). *Theoretical foundations of learning environments.* Mahwah, NJ: L. Erlbaum & Associates.

Kanpol, B. (1997). *Issues and trends in critical pedagogy.* Cresskill, NJ: Hampton Press.

Korpiaho, K., Päiviö, H. & Räsänen, K. (2007). Anglo-American forms of management education: A practice theoretical perspective. *Scandinavian Journal of Management, 23*, 36–65.

Kohn, A. (1999). *The schools our children deserve: Moving beyond traditional classrooms and "tougher standards."* Boston: Houghton Mifflin.

Lammers, W.J. & Murphy, J.J. (2002). A profile of teaching techniques used in the university classroom. *Active Learning in Higher Education, 3*, 54–67.

Lowman, J. (1995). *Mastering the techniques of teaching* (2nd ed.). San Francisco: Jossey-Bass.

Lueddeke, G.R. (2003). Professionalizing teaching practice in higher education: a study of disciplinary variation and "teaching-scholarship." *Studies in Higher Education, 28,* 213–228.

Marsh, S.J. & Hunt, C.S. (2006). Not quite as simple as a-b-c: Reflections on one department's experiences with publication ranking. *Journal of Management Inquiry, 15,* 301–315.

Martin, R. (2007). How successful leaders think. *Harvard Business Review,* June, 60–67.

Matthews, R.S. (1996). Collaborative learning: Creating knowledge with students. In R. J. Menges, M. Weimer & Associates (Eds.), *Teaching on solid ground* (pp. 101–124). San Francisco: Jossey-Bass.

McKeachie, W.J. (1986). *Teaching tips: A guidebook for the beginning college teacher* (8th ed.). Lexington, MA: D.C. Heath.

McKinney, K. (2007). *Enhancing learning through the scholarship of teaching and learning: The challenges and joys of juggling.* Bolton, MA: Anker Publishing.

Menges, R.J., Weimer, M. & Associates (Eds.) (1996). *Teaching on solid ground.* San Francisco: Jossey-Bass.

Parker, M. & Jary, D. (1995). The McUniversity: Organization, management and academic subjectivity. *Organization, 2,* 319–338.

Ramsden, P. (1992). *Learning to teach in higher education.* London: Routledge.

Rice, R.E. (1991). The new American scholar: Scholarship and the purposes of the university. *Metropolitan Universities, 1,* 7–18.

Richlin, L. (2001). Scholarly teaching and the scholarship of teaching. In C. Kreber (Ed.), *Revisiting scholarship: Perspectives on the scholarship of teaching* (pp. 57–68). San Francisco: Jossey-Bass.

Rowland, S. (2000). *The enquiring university teacher.* Buckingham, UK: The Society for Research into Higher Education & Open University Press.

Schmidt-Wilk, J. (2007). Editor's corner: "Why should my *JME* count?" *Journal of Management Education, 31,* 439–441.

Schon, D.A. (1983). *The reflective practitioner: How professionals think in action.* New York: Basic Books.

Schon, D. (1995) The new scholarship requires a new epistemology. *Change, Nov/Dec,* 27–34.

Shapiro, H.N. (2006). Promotion & tenure & the scholarship of teaching & learning. *Change, March/April,* 38–43.

Sharplin, A.D. & Mabry, R.H. (1985). The relative importance of journals used in management research: An alternative ranking. *Human Relations, 2,* 139–149.

Shulman, L.S. (2000). From Minsk to Pinsk: Why a scholarship of teaching and learning? *The journal of scholarship of teaching and learning (JoSoTL), 1,* 48–53.

Shulman, L.S. & Hutchings, P. (1998). *About the scholarship of teaching and learning: The Pew Scholars national fellowship program.* Menlo Park, CA: The Carnegie Foundation for the Advancement of Teaching.

Smith, R. (2001). Expertise and the scholarship of teaching. In C. Kreber (Ed.), *Revisiting scholarship: Perspectives on the scholarship of teaching* (pp. 69–78). San Francisco: Jossey-Bass.

Sotto, E. (1994). *When teaching becomes learning: A theory and practice of teaching.* London: Continuum.

Stage, F.K., Muller, P.A., Kinzie, J. & Simmons, A. (1998). *Creating learning centered classrooms: What does learning theory have to say?* Washington, DC: The George Washington University, Graduate School of Education and Human Development and Association for the Study of Higher Education.

Stefani, L. (2006). Towards a shared understanding of scholarship in the classroom. In P. Ashwin (Ed.), *Changing higher education: The development of learning and teaching* (pp. 113–124). London: Routledge.

Tahai, A. & Meyer, M.J. (1999). A revealed preference study of management journals' direct influences. *Strategic Management Journal, 20,* 279–296.

Weimer, M. (1996). Why scholarship is the bedrock of good teaching. In R.J. Menges & M. Weimer (Eds.), *Teaching on solid ground: Using scholarship to improve practice* (pp. 1–20). San Francisco: Jossey-Bass.

Weimer, M. (1997). Assumptions that devalue university teaching. *International Journal for Academic Development, 2,* 52–59.

Weimer, M. (2002). *Learner-centered teaching: Five key changes to practice.* San Francisco: Jossey-Bass.

Weimer, M. (2003). Focus on learning, transform teaching. *Change, Sept/Oct,* 48–54.

Weimer, M. (2007). Letters: Do lectures really need defenders? *Change, Jan/Feb,* 4–6.

Welsh, M.A. & Dehler, G.E. (2004). P(l)aying attention: Communities of practice and organized reflection. In M. Reynolds & R. Vince (Eds.), *Organizing Reflection* (pp. 15–29). Aldershot, UK: Ashgate.

Welsh, M.A. & Dehler, G.E. (2007). Whither the MBA? Or the withering of MBAs? *Management Learning, 38,* 407–424.

Whitehead, J. (1994). How do I improve the quality of my management? A participatory action research approach. *Management Learning, 25,* 137–153.

Wilson, R. (2001). A higher bar for earning tenure. *The Chronicle of Higher Education, 47,* A12.

CHAPTER 7

THE SCHOLARSHIP OF MANAGEMENT EDUCATION AND DEVELOPMENT

State of the Art

Cynthia V. Fukami and Steven J. Armstrong

ABSTRACT

The scholarship of management teaching and learning is increasingly being recognized as a field in its own right. Believing that the time was now right to present an account of the state of the art of this discipline, the authors engaged in developing a *Handbook of Management Learning, Education and Development* to do just that. The goals of the handbook were to map out where the discipline is going and to identify what are the key debates and issues that comprise the discipline. This chapter charts the journey of the development of the Handbook, from conception to birth. We begin by introducing the research process undertaken to determine key historical, current, emerging, and future issues surrounding the field. Next, we provide an integrated summary of the contents of the entire Handbook. We then turn our attention to some of the opportunities both for achieving academic success in management education and development scholarship, and for ensuring quality and

Being and Becoming a Management Education Scholar, pages 119–133

relevance in our provision of the overall student experience. Finally, we conclude by considering some of the constraints impacting this work and some of the significant challenges facing providers and how these may be overcome.

SOTL IN MANAGEMENT TEACHING AND LEARNING

The scholarship of teaching and learning (SOTL) was introduced by Ernest Boyer, then president of the Carnegie Foundation for the Advancement of Teaching and Learning, in his seminal book, *Scholarship Reconsidered* (Boyer, 1990). In this book, Boyer identified teaching as part of the overall enterprise of scholarship, along with discovery through basic research and efforts to advance the integration and application of knowledge (Huber & Hutchings, 2005). As the *Being and Becoming a Management Scholar* volume proves, the idea that teaching can be considered as scholarly work has been receiving abundant attention in the academy in general (Bernstein & Bass, 2005), and in management teaching and learning in particular (Schmidt-Wilk & Fukami, this volume).

At its core, SOTL involves being scholarly about one's teaching. Thus, SOTL is not merely a matter of method and technique, both of which may result in excellent teaching. To engage in the scholarship of teaching implies that we investigate our teaching, and our students' learning, in much the same way we investigate an area of disciplinary concern. As Lee Shulman, current President of the Carnegie Foundation, has stated,

> Viewing teaching as scholarly work is essential. Teachers so often have to carry out their work in isolation from their colleagues, and, with notable exceptions, their practice is rarely evaluated by professional peers. The result is that those who engage in innovative acts of teaching do not have many opportunities to build upon the work of others. Through CASTL (the Carnegie Academy for the Scholarship of Teaching and Learning), we seek to render teaching public, subject to critical evaluation, and usable by others in the field and in the research community. (1999, p. 1)

Along with Boyer's work, and the work of his colleagues at the Carnegie Foundation, there have been a number of other events contributing to the rise of interest in SOTL. There has been increased pressure for effective teaching from a number of stakeholders of higher education: students, parents, administrators, and legislators. Accrediting agencies are demanding assessments and assurance of learning. Peer-reviewed journals in which to publish this work are available in abundance (Schmidt-Wilk & Fukami, this volume). In management education, there are three prominent journals: the *Journal of Management Education, Academy of Management Learning and Education,* and *Management Learning* (Korpiaho, Päiviö, & Räsänen, 2007), and a number of other print journals are available for the dissemination of teaching-related scholarly work.

At the same time, there has also been a surge of criticism of management education. Starting with Porter and McKibbin's (1988) review of the shortcomings of MBA education, and continuing to the present, Mintzberg (2004), Pfeffer and Fong (2002), Bennis and O'Toole (2005), Ghoshal (2005), and others have published thought-provoking articles on the limitations of MBA programs. They each point to different issues in business schools, but all agree that there is a lack of relevance in the MBA curriculum. For example, recent studies at *Business Week* (Lavelle, 2006) show a negative correlation between long-term corporate performance and the presence of MBAs in C-level executive positions.

In a rather upending essay, Pfeffer and Fong (2002) find that (a) there has been little assessment of the impact of business schools on either their graduates or on the profession, (b) what assessments do exist suggest that business schools are not particularly effective, and (c) there is little evidence that business schools have influenced management practice. Others have reported similar findings. One such study reported that 73% of the surveyed MBA program graduates indicated that they made little use of what they had learned in the classroom on their first assignments as managers (McCall, Lombardo, & Morrison, 1988). Students who graduate successfully from an MBA program must earn a minimum grade point average to do so, implying that they have gained a "passing" level of knowledge, yet the results listed above imply that these students were either unable or unwilling to put their knowledge into practice (Fukami, 2007).

Our current educational system contributes to this problem, because excellence is often defined as intellectual performance (Martin & Martinez de Pisón, 2005). Knowledge is a quantity of data to be possessed, and an educator is the means to obtaining these data. Higher educational systems assume that educators are the font of knowledge and our students are the sponges who soak it up, to varying degrees of effectiveness on either side. The student's performance in the classroom is traditionally evaluated on the basis of how much of this knowledge can be recalled within a very short period of time, ten to sixteen weeks, depending on the length of the term of study, and the educator's teaching performance is evaluated at least in part by how effectively she or he has conveyed this knowledge. One symptom of this situation is captured by the comment sometimes heard from those who employ our graduates, that is, that they know much but can't do anything. Perhaps as a result, many excellent companies, such as Southwest Airlines, don't recruit at leading business schools, and don't show a preference for hiring MBAs (Pfeffer and Sutton, 1999). In the handbook, we refer to this as the "how" problem, that is, that *how* we teach needs to be addressed.

With this backdrop, it appeared to us that the time was right to present an account of the state of the art of this discipline, to map out where the discipline is going, and to identify the key debates and issues that comprise the discipline. The result was the development of the *Handbook of Management Learning, Education and Development (MLED)* (Armstrong & Fukami, 2009). The remainder of this chapter will first trace the development of this handbook, from conception to birth. Next, we will provide a brief summary of the contents of the handbook. We will then present our sense of the opportunities and constraints facing those attempting to be or become a management education scholar, from our unique perspective as editors of the handbook.

RESEARCH PROCESS UNDERTAKEN TO DEVELOP THE STRUCTURE OF THE HANDBOOK

The journey of the handbook's development occurred in three phases: planning, development, and execution. We discuss each phase in more detail below.

Planning Phase

In May 2006 at the European Academy of Management meeting in Munich, Germany, Steve Armstrong was approached by an editor from Sage Publications (Kiren Shoman) and asked whether he would be interested in contributing to the series of Sage Handbooks that are recognized as benchmark volumes in their field. The subject would be management education and development, and Steve was approached because at that time he was Division Chair of the Management Education and Development (MED) Division of the U.S. Academy of Management. In the higher levels of management studies, Sage Publications saw management education as one of the most exciting and dynamic areas of research and practice. They felt that the topic had become a major subject in the U.S. over the past decade and was spreading worldwide. This was evident from the exponential growth of membership in the Academy of Management's MED Division and the launch of the Academy of Management's new journal, *Academy of Management Learning and Education (AMLE)*. As a publisher, Sage had previously dominated this area with two other competing journals, *Journal of Management Education* and *Management Learning*. They were therefore in a strong position in terms of marketing and editorial contacts for this exciting handbook project and saw a substantial and untapped market in students in post-graduate management studies, the academic community, lecturers and researchers within the wider discipline of management learning, program directors and business school leaders. In preparing this chapter we sought further clarification from Sage about what initially inspired them to want to publish such a handbook. Their response was as follows:

> Everything we do on the management list at SAGE is inextricably linked to the future of management education. Market size and strategy are obviously factors, but contributing to an understanding of the state of management education as a whole is for the long term good not just for SAGE, but for other publishers and the wider academic community. In terms of SAGE's book publishing program, Handbooks are probably the most prospective contribution we make to the literature, so this was an important opportunity, and the timing was right, to make a statement about the field in which we operate. The *MLED Handbook* addresses the building blocks of what we do, in a manner in keeping with the philosophy of reflexivity and criticality behind it. (Alan Maloney, Sage Publications, personal communication, October 21, 2008)

As someone who had spent several years in management positions in industry, then several more years in management education, Steve felt he may well be suited to the project being offered. During a period of reflection, he realized that his own passion for management education was inspired while studying as a part-time student for an MBA during a successful career as an R&D manager in the electronics industry. This was a very positive experience with student-centered learning as it focus—radically different from his previous experience as an electronic engineering degree student some 15 years earlier where didactic teaching was the norm. However, enjoyable as this experience was, he was still left with a feeling that there was a serious disconnect between management practice and the theories learned. This led to a new-found interest in management education, which he pursued when he became a senior university lecturer in a business school in 1993. Shortly afterwards, in support of this new interest, he completed a teaching certificate in higher education (1995) and soon after that became the recipient of a prestigious two-year teaching fellowship awarded on the basis of his outstanding innovations in curriculum development, teaching, and learning. Related to these interests he went on to co-found the European Learning Style Information Network (1996), served in various roles on the executive committee of the Academy of Management's MED division from 1999 (leading to the position of President) and served as Director of the Centre for Management and Organizational Learning in his own institution from 2001. After this short period of reflection Steve decided that the project offered by Sage would indeed be of significant interest to him.

Through Steve's contacts in the Academy of Management it wasn't long before he identified an equally interested person in the U.S., Cindi Fukami. Cindi also had a background well-suited to this project. Since 1978, Cindi had been a regular participant at the Organizational Behavior Teaching Conferences, and had served for five years on the Board of Directors of the Organizational Behavior Teaching Society. During two of those years, she was elected "OB-1," the society's tongue-in-cheek title for the Chair of the Board. She served on the inaugural Teaching Committee for the Academy of Management, and subsequently chaired the committee. Cindi served two terms as Associate Editor of the *Journal of Management Education*, and one term as Associate Editor of *Academy of Management Learning and Education*. She was a scholar in the Carnegie Foundation's Academy for the Scholarship of Teaching and Learning, and is a Fellow of the Carnegie Foundation. In short, recognizing, enhancing, and contributing to the scholarship of teaching and learning has been a fundamental theme in her career as a professor.

We decided that this would be a wonderful, important, and timely project on which to collaborate and made plans to meet in person at the upcoming Academy of Management Annual Meeting in Honolulu, Hawaii. On August 7, 2005, Steve, Cindi and Kiren discussed the development of a formal proposal and to agree on timescales. The seeds for the project were now set.

Development Phase

To help develop the proposal we reviewed the entire contents of four major journals in business/management education: *Academy of Management Learning and Education, Management Learning,* the *Journal of Management Education,* and the *Journal of Management Development.* Additionally, we reviewed the previous ten years' titles of all papers, symposia, and professional development workshop activities accepted by the Management Education and Development Division at the Academy of Management's annual meetings. We also referred to a previous review article from the field (Bilimoria & Fukami, 2002). This process enabled the editors to identify major themes in the literature, and names of leading authors associated with those themes. The three major themes to emerge were "management learning" from a theoretical perspective, "management education" from the perspective of a credit-based formal learning context, and "management development" from a non-credit-based non-formal learning context. From within each theme we distilled a number of major topics that were seen to recur throughout these data sources. After careful scrutiny (checking for duplications and overlaps) we reduced the number of topics to 82: 29 for management learning, 32 for management education, 21 for management development, and a number of others that represented threads that could potentially run through all three themes (e.g., management learning, history and traditions, educational reform). To continue the process of distillation we conducted telephone and email interviews with a number of well regarded experts in the field—similar to a Delphi exercise (Dalkey & Helmer, 1963). To help with our search for authors we began to categorize topics as "must have," "highly desirable," and "desirable." Our ultimate aim was to identify eight or nine chapters within each of the three major themes, in addition to an opening and closing chapter. We realized at this stage that we needed to assemble an editorial board from around the world to help steer the project and to help with the reviewing of draft chapters. Outcomes of this process culminated in an initial detailed proposal in November of 2005 and also led to the present structure of the handbook.

We determined that the focus of the handbook would be on the education and development of managers, which would necessarily embrace theoretical aspects of individual and collective learning, the delivery of formal management education, and the facilitation of management development. The volume would reflect the interdisciplinary nature of the field and would analyze, promote, and critique the role of MLED to management understanding.

According to Mintzberg (2004), management is a practice that has to blend a good deal of experience with a certain amount of insight and some analysis. It is not too difficult to imagine how analytical skills can be formally taught. It is difficult to imagine, however, how insight or the outcomes of management experience can be formally taught, but it is easier to imagine how they can derive from a developmental process. Herein lies the need for the two terms known as "management education" and "management development," and it is important to differentiate between these two processes. Within this perspective, "management education" is taken to imply formal learning that takes place under the auspices of academic institutions within credit-bearing courses to enhance managers' analytic and critical skills. This type of learning is usually provided in organized, time-bound, and structured programs. Such programs often emphasize the scientific aspects of management, but they are often criticized for spoon-feeding analysis and technique and for being rather static in nature, emphasizing memory and repetition. In contrast, non-formal learning, which is more closely associated with "management development," is believed to offer a more effective approach by emphasizing on-the-job learning that occurs experientially in culturally embedded ways, situated in communities of practice within work-based organizations. Such learning is believed to result in tacit or procedural knowledge contributing to the art and craft of management, whereas formal education is believed to result in explicit or declarative knowledge. The latter refers to knowledge about something, whereas the former is more about how to do something and is believed to be more closely associated with successful managers.

Formal and informal learning approaches, however, should not be treated as being mutually exclusive. Instead, they should be regarded as being complementary and necessary components in the overall process of management learning. With this in mind, the handbook sought to explore a variety of challenging approaches to the diverse forms of management learning, linking new ideas and developments as a way of advancing both theory and practice. It aimed to identify and examine best practices in university-based management education programs, and training and development processes in corporate, consultancy, and independent college settings. We aspired for the handbook to appeal to academics, researchers, educators, program directors, deans of business schools, advanced postgraduate students, and practitioners in corporate education.

The initial proposal was reviewed by six referees selected by the volume's editors, which led to a further revision prior to formally submitting it to Sage Publications in January, 2006 for their consideration. In March of 2006 we received detailed reviews from 14 anonymous reviewers selected by Sage. Each reviewer responded to 18 questions put forward by Sage publications. These fell into three broad categories associated with marketing (e.g., is there a gap in the market; does the proposal fill that gap; what competition is there, etc.), pricing (e.g., what is the minimum price you would pay; what price could your library afford, etc.) and details of the proposal itself. This last category had the biggest impact on shaping the final proposal. Questions were associated with strengths and weaknesses of the proposal, topics omitted, appropriateness of the structure and balance, feedback on the proposed list of potential contributors, names of potential editorial board members, and how appropriate the proposed editors were. This feedback led to a number of important changes such as: new chapters (e.g., ethics and learning); Part III of the handbook being renamed (from "Informal Learning" to "Management Development: Non credit based learning"); further names of potential authors; names of potential editorial board members; and a widening of the international spread of contributing authors. Nine of the reviewers expressed interest in contributing to the handbook themselves and specified their areas of interest. When the names of these reviewers were released to the editors, some were invited to contribute and several in fact did so. The proposal was revised in light of these reviews, resubmitted and then formally accepted by Sage in April 2006.

Execution Phase

An editorial board was assembled during May of 2006 comprising members from Australia, New Zealand, the U.S., Scandinavia, mainland Europe, and Japan. We thought it critical for the Handbook to have a global perspective, and for there to be representatives from formal and informal education (their names being duly acknowledged in the final version of the Handbook). A formal contract was issued by Sage on June 14th, 2006. We then started the hard work of identifying and contacting potential authors. Since we had already identified the topic areas for the Handbook, we needed to secure authors who could contribute in these areas. On the other hand, there were authors that we wanted to contribute to the Handbook, and we needed to be flexible so that the topics on which they wanted to write could be included in the outline. We divided the number of chapters in half, and Steve and Cindi each took editing responsibility for half of the table of contents.

The process of approaching potential authors commenced in June, 2006, and by October we had agreement from all of the present authors and the writing of chapters was initiated. We were now set to try to achieve a manuscript submission date of November 30, 2007. A significant number of draft chapters were received by July 2007 and the remainder arrived by September.

All chapters were blind reviewed by at least two reviewers (in some cases four), who were either members of our editorial board, contributing authors, or others with specific expertise in the subject area. Based on these reviews and our own reading of the material, we asked the authors to revise their chapters. Revised versions of the chapters began to arrive in October 2007 with the last few received by February or March 2008. Approximately 15% of revised chapters went through a second review and revision cycle. The final manuscript was submitted to Sage on 31st March 2008 except for chapters 1 and 29, which followed shortly afterwards. We will now turn to a brief description of the contents of the Handbook.

INTEGRATED SUMMARY OF THE HANDBOOK

The handbook is organized into three main parts. Prior to Part 1 there is an introductory chapter entitled "Past, Present and Future Perspectives of Management Learning, Education and Development." The chapter provides an introduction and theoretical overview of the field including historical context, perceptions of the present state of MED, the need for more scholarship, and future perspectives and challenges. Part 1 covers theoretical aspects of knowledge acquisition in the context of management learning. It draws on other disciplinary fields such as philosophy, education, psychology, and sociology, as well as organization theory, with a commitment to broadening and deepening our knowledge and understanding of the most relevant management theory. Specific areas covered in Part 1 include: the nature of knowledge and knowing; experiential learning theory; theory of distributed cognition in the context of collective learning; reflection, reflective practice, and organizing reflection beyond the reflective practitioner; critical management education; development and use of collaborative learning approaches and designs; ethics pedagogy and its inclusion in business school curricula; and lastly a consideration of the implications of the pervasiveness of emotion in organizations from the point of view of learning and education, with an emphasis on the role of emotions and emotional intelligence training in leadership programs.

Part 2 of the Handbook is concerned with using theory to improve practice and to promote ways of enhancing learning effectiveness in formal settings. The chapter topics in Part 2 reflect a very wide range of both traditional and innovative issues relating to the classroom (whether actual or virtual), including the use of visual, creative and performing arts, technology, distance learning, learning-centered course design, diversity, cognitive styles, teams, and problem-based and project-based learning. In addition, Part 2 contains material on issues beyond the classroom, such as mentoring PhD students, assessment and accreditation, and the nexus between research and teaching. Chapters in Part 2 explore a variety of learning and teaching phenomena including learning styles and teaching strategies, course design, teaching practice, technology in the classroom, distance learning, mentoring frameworks, culture and diversity issues, evaluation methods, problem and project based learning, team learning, and importantly, the research-teaching nexus.

Part 3 is concerned with exploring non-credit-based management development through a variety of approaches and concepts including reflexive practice, action learning, development of competencies, leadership development, coaching and mentoring, situated learning, and development of global mindsets as ways of maximizing learning effectiveness in an informal context. Part 3 explores important aspects of management development in a non-credit-based learning context. Areas covered include the importance of reflexivity in management learning; action learning and related modalities that conceive of practice as having its own epistemology; competency development related to effective managers and leaders; best practices and theoretical and empirical advances in leadership development; applications, benefits and efficacy of coaching and mentoring as forms of development intervention in organizations; interaction learning models that allow managers to learn cultures "on the fly" when engaging in multicultural assignments and interactions; a proposition to reverse the concept of a community of practice to practices of a community leading to a wider understanding of practice-based studies; and lastly a consideration of assessment, accreditation, and quality certification schemes associated with non-formal management development in the context of recurrent and lifelong learning. Part 3 concludes by considering ways of assessing these informal approaches to learning. The handbook ends with a concluding chapter that considers future perspectives of management learning, education and development and their implications in light of what has been presented in preceding chapters.

THE HANDBOOK'S CONTRIBUTION TO THE FIELD

Recent literature on the state of management education and development is replete with examples of why we should be doing this differently. Examples include Bennis and O'Toole's (2005) assertion that we are currently failing to impart useful management skills, failing to instill norms of ethical behavior, failing to prepare leaders, and failing to lead our graduates into good management careers. They also suggest that business schools are too focused on scientific research, leading them to hire professors with limited real-world experience and graduating students who are ill-equipped to wrangle with complex, unquantifiable issues so reminiscent of actual management practice. Others too believe that management education is in a perilous state (Grey, 2004), that the future of business schools is in doubt because its research and teaching missions are compromised (Starkey & Tempest, 2005), and that bad management theories are destroying good management practice (Ghoshal, 2005).

Despite these criticisms, after reviewing 28 chapters of the handbook written by committed scholars in the field, we conclude that it is absolutely possible to have business schools that provide excellent learning and opportunities for achieving academic success while ensuring quality and relevance in student experience. The group of scholars assembled to contribute to this handbook brings to bear a number of important theoretical contributions to help guide action. For example, with regard to the very nature of knowledge and knowing, one author (Chia, 2009) brings into focus the kind of knowledge taught in business schools, arguing that the over-reliance on explicit representational forms of knowledge is a mistake and that they should focus more on practical wisdom or tacit knowledge. This is supported by other theoretical contributions that demonstrate how knowledge creation can occur through the transformation of experience at multiple levels (individual, team, and organization); how collaborative learning can facilitate critical thinking and problem solving; how emotional skills may be taught to assist in the development of organizational leadership; and ways of adopting ethics pedagogy, which engages students in active learning to address the continuing global debates about recent business practice.

The handbook also offers a wide range of innovations in learning and teaching related to both actual and virtual classrooms in a formal educational setting. Examples include use of visual, creative, and performing arts as a way of providing a rich pedagogy that offers unique avenues for learning about complex behavior in organizations and for developing future leaders; use of a wide range of technology tools to facilitate effective learning in the classroom as well as distance learning and web-based instruction; concrete ways of managing diversity and facilitating diversity learning; intensive and extensive approaches to team-based learning; and problem-based learning where the learner uses theory in action, enabling the acquisition of managerial tacit knowledge through exposure and interaction with a work environment. Authors consider ways in which individual differences in students' cognitive styles can be used to manage the overall effectiveness of the learning process by adopting appropriate learning strategies on the part of the student and appropriate instructional design on the part of the teacher. Innovative ways of engaging in research supervision at doctoral level are also offered. The handbook considers this from both sides of the dyadic relationship by offering a model derived from apprenticeship and mentoring literatures. The critical topic of assessment and accreditation of management learning in business schools is also covered with helpful advice and guidance offered.

Further innovations are provided for the context of non-credit-based learning. For example, the importance of reflexive practice is put forward as a cornerstone for ethical and responsive management and is shown to be fundamentally and crucially important for both management practice and management learning. Principles and advantages of action learning arising from engagement of the learner in the solution of real-world work problems are presented together with a cluster of strategies for implementation aimed at individual and team levels. The concepts are also extended to global action learning, and it is demonstrated how working with global cross-cultural teams can lead to critical lessons in intercultural competence. In terms of developing competencies, a holistic approach is put forward using intentional change theory from a complexity perspective as one way of developing outstanding managers. Guidance is also provided on the teaching of leadership as well as ways of improving the efficacy of current and future leadership development programs in practice. Other important areas that are covered include core competencies of coaching and mentoring programs; creating a coaching and mentoring culture; measuring the impact of coaching and mentoring; an intercultural, interactive learning model for preparing global business leaders who need to interact with multiple cultures; and ways in which practical knowledge may be enabled in situated contexts of action.

We believe that the handbook discussed in this chapter will provide every reader with comprehensive and insightful reviews of core topics as well as providing alternative techniques and practices of management education and development. However, some would argue that seeking improvements in this way may lead to more effective management learning for the medium term, but that the dominant mode of management education isn't working and there is a need to break out of the existing paradigm.

IMPLICATIONS AND FUTURE DIRECTION

The handbook's concluding chapter by James O'Toole draws on a range of criticisms of management education, particularly from the chorus of business school deans. Their concerns are observed to be mutually consistent, with a call for the reconceptualization and redefinition of the very purpose of management education at the core of all their arguments. O'Toole (2009) suggests that the central problem of management education is the corrosive impact of 1950s managerialism, 1970s management science, and 1990s investment capitalism driving out the original purpose of business schools, which was to create a true profession of management similar to the law, medicine, or even theology professions. He calls for a pluralistic model of professorial excellence as one way of improving the quality of business school offerings and Boyer's (1990) vision of scholarship is recommended as one model for advancement. O'Toole is particularly critical of the apparent lack of purpose of business schools and regards this as *the* major problem. He argues that too many scholars are concerned about *how* to teach when there is little agreement about *what* to teach. For example, what does it mean to be an educated manager? What is the purpose of a management degree? What is the essential core content of its curriculum? He does acknowledge, however, that the handbook is about management learning and not about curricular reform. In this regard he concedes that its authors are quite right to have focused on alternative modes of learning within the existing dominant paradigm and that its readers will find something that is personally useful to fit every interest and bias.

In the longer term, O'Toole believes that a radical paradigm shift is needed where business school decision makers rethink their assumptions about the marriage of "the why," "the what," and "the how" of management education. However, few deans seem willing to break with established norms and take control of their own destiny by creating bold and innovative programs. Instead the majority appear to be content to continue in their quest to improve the delivery of a poor product. Some radical thinkers (e.g., Mintzberg, 2004) have argued that it is time to break down the disciplinary silos (e.g., marketing, finance, operations, etc.) in business schools and put old paradigms out to pasture. With careers now crossing boundaries of function, organization, industry, cultures, and political borders, management education needs to change accordingly, and this means redesigning the curriculum in such a way that it is organized around the key constituencies that a manager needs to engage in order to be effective.

A few management schools are showing signs of more radical reforms, such as Yale, who has moved towards a more integrated curriculum, or Kellogg & Wharton Schools of Business who is moving to more innovative educational methods such as analogically situated experiences (Houde, 2007). Unfortunately, so far there are only a few examples, but according to Lyman Porter the comfortable period for business schools is over. Almost none of the casual practices, procedures, and assumptions about what we should be doing and how we should be providing education are likely to survive the next two decades (Porter, 2000). However, institutional inertia theory suggests that universities will be slow to change given internal politics and past successes. The overall consensus is that change will come slowly given the massive infrastructure and particularly the staff incentive programs currently in place that favor scientific research over learning and teaching, which is traditionally afforded significantly lower status. Lewicki and Bailey (2009) provide a systematic examination of this relationship in the handbook, where they identify institutional pressures that serve to perpetuate the tension between these two equally important activities. They also call for a radical culture change in management education—so that research and teaching can effectively co-exist, and so that reward systems reflect the twin pillars of scholarship and education that serve as the very foundation of our existence.

REFERENCES

Armstrong, S.J. & Fukami, C. (2009). *Handbook of Management Learning, Education and Development.* London: Sage.

Bilimoria, D., & Fukami, C. (2002). The scholarship of teaching and learning in the management sciences. In M. T. Huber and S. P. Morreale (Eds.), *Disciplinary styles in the scholarship of teaching and learning: Exploring common ground* (pp. 125–142). Washington, DC: American Association for Higher Education.

Bernstein, D. & Bass, R. (2005). The scholarship of teaching and learning. *Academe, 91*(4), 37–43.

Bennis, W.G. & O'Toole, J. (2005). How business schools lost their way. *Harvard Business Review, May*, 96–104.

Boyer, E. L. (1990). *Scholarship reconsidered: Priorities of the professoriate.* Princeton, NJ: The Carnegie Foundation for the Advancement of Teaching.

Chia, R. (2009). The nature of knowledge and knowing in the context of management learning, education and development. In S.J. Armstrong & C.V. Fukami (Eds.), *Handbook of management learning, education and development* (pp. 25–41). London: Sage.

Dalkey, N.C., & Helmer, O. (1963). An experimental application of the Delphi method to the use of experts. *Management Science, 9* (3), 458–476.

Fukami, C.V. (2007). Can wisdom be taught? In E.H. Kessler & J. R. Bailey (Eds.), *Handbook of organizational wisdom.* Thousand Oaks, CA: Sage.

Ghoshal, S. (2005). Bad management theories are destroying good management practice. *Academy of Management Learning and Education, 4,* 75–91.

Grey, C. (2004). Reinventing business schools: The contribution of critical management education. *Academy of Management Learning & Education, 3*(2), 178–186.

Huber, M. & P. Hutchings (2005). *The advancement of learning: Building the teaching commons.* San Francisco, CA: Jossey-Bass/The Carnegie Foundation for the Advancement of Teaching.

Houde, J. (2007). Analogically situated experiences: Creating insight through novel contexts. *Academy of Management Learning and Education, 6*(3), 321–331.

Korpiaho, K., Päiviö, H. & Räsänen, K. (2007). Anglo-American forms of management education: A practice-theoretical perspective. *Scandinavian Management Journal, 23*(1), 36–65.

Lavelle, L. (2006, March 20). Is the MBA overrated? *Business Week,* pp. 78–79.

Lewicki, R., & Bailey, J. (2009). The research teaching nexus: Tensions and opportunities. In S.J. Armstrong & C.V. Fukami (Eds.), *Handbook of management learning, education and development* (pp. 385–402). London: Sage.

Martin, M. K. & Martinez de Pisón, R. (2005).. From knowledge to wisdom: A new challenge to the educational milieu with implications for religious education. *Religious Education, 100,* 157–173.

McCall, M.W., Jr., Lombardo, M. M., & Morrison, A. M. (1988). *The lessons of experience: how successful executives develop on the job.* Lexington, MA: Lexington Books.

Mintzberg, H. (2004). *Managers not MBAs: A hard look at the soft practice of managing and management development.* San Francisco: Barrett-Koehler Publishers.

O'Toole, J. (2009). The pluralistic future of management education. In S.J. Armstrong and C.V. Fukami (Eds.), *Handbook of Management Learning, Education and Development* (pp. 547–558). Sage: London.

Pfeffer, J., & Fong, C. (2002). The end of business schools? Less success than meets the eye. *Academy of Management Learning & Education, 1*(1), 78–95.

Pfeffer, J. & Sutton, R.I. (1999). Knowing what to do is not enough: Turning knowledge into action. *California Management Review, 42,* 83–108.

Porter, L. & McKibbin, L.E. (1988). *Management education and development: Drift or thrust in the 21st century?* New York: McGraw-Hill.

Porter, L. (2000). Observations on business education. *Selections, 16*(2), 29–30.

Schmidt-Wilk and Fukami, C. V. (in press). *The Journal of Management Education:* In search of balance between relevance and rigor. In R. DeFillippi & C. Wankel (Eds.), *Being and becoming a management scholar.* Charlotte, NC: Information Age Publishing.

Shulman, L. (1999). Carnegie Foundation launches initiative to develop the scholarship of teaching in K-12 and teacher education. Retrieved April 16, 2008 from http://carnegiefoundation.org/news/sub.asp?key=51&subkey=367

Starkey, K., & Tempest, S. (2005). The future of the business school: Knowledge, challenges and opportunities. *Human Relations, 58*(1), 61–82.

CHAPTER 8

RELEVANCE WITH RIGOR

Stories from the
Journal of Management Education

Jane Schmidt-Wilk and Cynthia Fukami

ABSTRACT

Becoming a management education scholar entails publishing in management education. This chapter explores a key issue in publishing in management education: balancing relevance and rigor, by exploring the history and contents of the peer-reviewed *Journal of Management Education (JME)*. We discuss the contribution of the scholarship of teaching and learning to management education scholarship, share insights from our roles as editors of the journal regarding the relevance and increasing rigor of its contents, and present stories of its relevance to the management education community. We discuss the current dialectic between relevance and rigor in management education scholarship and conclude with some thoughts about the future of the scholarship of teaching and learning in management education.

Being and Becoming a Management Education Scholar, pages 135–155

INTRODUCTION

Traditionally, the work of a professor in much of the world but in the United States in particular, has focused on three areas: research, teaching, and service, usually in that order. This emphasis starts in PhD programs where young scholars are indoctrinated into the professoriate. Doctoral students take course work on the literature of their discipline, and course work on research methodology. In most cases, they are not allowed to begin work on their dissertations until they pass rigorous comprehensive exams in both areas of study. Most often, especially in large research institutions, their faculty role models show a general disregard for teaching by aspiring to teach less, and by assuming that novice graduate students can do an acceptable job of teaching undergraduates in large sections of introductory courses.

Often, there is little to no preparation for teaching, and concurrent lack of awareness of a literature on teaching. From this early preparation to our time on the tenure track, it is rather obvious that teaching effectiveness takes a distant second place to our effectiveness as a researcher. We have developed elaborate measurement schemes to evaluate research effectiveness, but measure teaching effectiveness in primitive and simple ways often relying heavily on student evaluations of teaching that are neither rigorous or accurate measures. We reward research effectiveness with "release time" and reduced teaching "loads," the symbolism of which is difficult to ignore (Fukami, 2007). Tenure is awarded to those who publish, even though they may be poor teachers. Excellent teachers are not tenured, unless they are also acceptable researchers.

With this backdrop, then, it is rather remarkable that, in 1974, the Organizational Behavior Teaching Society (OBTS) was founded, long before the term "scholarship of teaching and learning" was coined. A small group of academics, concerned with the practice of innovative management education, started to meet on an annual basis. OBTS's informal voice, a hand-typed newsletter, began in 1975, dedicated to "conversation about the teaching of organizational behavior" and was distributed among colleagues at 15 institutions (Bilimoria & Fukami, 2002). It aimed to "share ideas, aspirations and disasters" about teaching in the then young field of organizational behavior. Over time, the newsletter evolved into *Exchange*, and then into the *Organizational Behavior Teaching Review*. Finally, in 1991, based on the increasing scope and focus of teaching in all management disciplines, the name of the journal was changed to the *Journal of Management Education*.

In his editorial notes announcing this name change, then-editor Larry Michaelsen (1989–90, p. iii) wrote, "A few years ago, we were a discipline that was in search of respectability and we tended to be isolated from and looked down on by many of our colleagues in the more traditional business disciplines. In my opinion, much has changed, since then." Clearly the founding parents of this journal were bucking the trend in the 1970s. Not only would the new journal promote teaching—unheard of at the time—but it would also explore teaching in OB, a discipline with no status. Furthermore, the founders of the journal were clearly more interested in relevance than in rigor, at least defined as empirical investigation. In fact, the first editorial published in 1975 indicates a possible bias against research amongst the journal's founders: "Somebody suggested, jokingly, that any article with extensive empirical data or a reference list longer than six items should be rejected" (Bradford, 1975, p. 3). We wondered, as we approached writing this chapter, could the same statement be made today? To investigate the relative importance of relevance and rigor in management education, this chapter explores how *JME* has evolved over time. In the first section, we trace the emergence of the concept of the scholarship of teaching and learning (SOTL) in management. The second section chronicles the *JME*'s journey from its original primary focus on relevance towards increasing rigor, while the third section provides anecdotal evidence of the Journal's relevance to the management education community from the perspective of the journal's readers. The fourth section juxtaposes these two constructs, rigor and relevance, as currently debated in management education, and the chapter concludes with our views on the future of the scholarship of teaching and learning in management.

EMERGENCE OF THE SCHOLARSHIP OF TEACHING AND LEARNING (SOTL)

The Scholarship of Teaching and Learning (SOTL), usually traced to educator Ernest Boyer's (1990) groundbreaking work, *Scholarship Reconsidered*, has attracted increased attention in higher education (Bernstein & Bass, 2005). Its emergence has helped establish the legitimacy of teaching in general as a scholarly pursuit and the work of the Journal of Management Education in particular (Schmidt-Wilk, 2007).

As noted above, the traditional job description of professors has been to conduct research, teach students, and provide service to the profession, to the community, and to the university. Boyer called for a new vision of scholarship that would be more directly related to contemporary institutions of higher education, and created what now is called the "Boyer Model" of scholarship. Boyer (1990) argued that contemporary professors actually engage in four separate, but overlapping, areas of scholarship: discovery, integration, application, and teaching. The scholarship of discovery is most related to what we have traditionally called "research," and involves knowledge creation and hypothesis testing. The scholarship of integration involves making connections across the discipline, thus weaving disciplinary knowledge into larger intellectual patterns (Boyer, 1990). The scholarship of application recognizes the work of scholars to apply disciplinary knowledge to solving real-world problems of consequence. Finally, the scholarship of teaching refers to disseminating knowledge in a way that transforms it and extends it, so that students effectively learn. This reformulation elevates the traditional view of teaching from a routine function to an essential component of a professor's scholarly life (Bruff, 2008).

If teaching is a scholarly pursuit, then it is important for teaching to become scholarly. Inherent in scholarship are at least three attributes (Shulman, 1999): it becomes public; it becomes an object of critical review and evaluation by members of one's community; and members of one's community begin to use, build upon, and develop it. Thus, peer-reviewed journals focusing on SOTL become an important part of the academy. To write an article that is accepted in a high-quality peer-reviewed journal implies that a scholar has taken the methods of scholarly inquiry from his or her discipline and has applied them to questions regarding teaching. Questions are framed and systematically investigated so that the practice of teaching is advanced (Hutchings & Shulman, 1999). The emergence of SOTL as a term and as a field of legitimate research has clearly influenced the amount of scholarly activity in teaching and has brought more attention to *JME* and management education.

With recognition of the field of teaching and learning as a field of legitimate research, pressures for rigor in SOTL have been increasing, as have outlets for publication-worthy manuscripts. Numerous stakeholders of higher education, including legislatures, educational institutions, parents, students, and accreditation agencies, are expecting assessment and assurance of learning, more quality in teaching, and evidence of that quality. Simultaneously, publications in SOTL have begun to count and are being rewarded in terms of hiring, promotion and tenure, and in decisions about faculty assignments, schedules, and pay. *JME* and its predecessor journals have been published since 1975. Although no other management education journals existed at that time in the United States, since then the number of management education journals has proliferated, suggesting that there is both a readership (demand) for quality publications in management education and an authorship (supply).

The Academy of Management, the largest worldwide professional organization of university-based management educators, has published *Academy of Management Learning and Education* since 2002. Other print journals exist: *Journal of Teaching in International Business, Journal of Education for Business, Journal of Accounting Education, The International Journal of Accounting Education and Research, Journal of Education for MIS, Journal of Information Systems Education, Journal of Public Administration Education,* and *Journal of Market-*

ing Education, to name a few. In addition, peer-reviewed online journals such as *Organization Management Journal* and *Journal of Behavioral and Applied Management* publish materials for and about management education. Pedagogical issues are also addressed in *Selections,* the journal of the Graduate Management Admission Council, and in *BizEd,* published by the AACSB. *Management Learning,* a European journal, was first published in 1970 and thus is the only management education journal to predate *JME.* However, the main focus of *Management Learning* is on the practice, contexts, processes, and outcomes of management organizational learning. Nonetheless, it frequently publishes research on student learning in management education settings. The rapid growth in available peer-reviewed journals has provided more opportunities for worthy articles.

Despite the abundance of management education journals, *JME* is considered to be one of the most prestigious outlets. A recent study of Anglo-American models of management education limited its investigation to three so called prominent journals: *The Academy of Management Learning and Education (AMLE), Management Learning (ML),* and *JME.* (Korpiaho, Päiviö, & Räsänen, 2007).

Beatty and Leigh (2006) have also reported results of an analysis of the differences and similarities in the content of these same three journals in two areas: subject area and methodology of articles. Their research suggests that these three journals each occupy a unique niche in management education. Using a qualitative mapping methodology, they concluded that there are common clusters across the three journals, but that each journal also has its own unique content themes. *AMLE* articles focused on higher education, covering business education, the academic life, programs, and curricular issues. Its articles focused on issues such as classroom dynamics and curriculum. *ML* articles tended to be about learning outside of higher education, predominantly at the organizational and broader management field level, and also at the individual level within organizations. Topic themes were organization, process, social, practice, reflection, and critique. *JME* articles were almost entirely in the domain of higher education, focusing on students, the classroom, exercises, methods, projects, and teams. Its articles focused on front-line teaching topics, dealing with course content and methods, classroom dynamics, and curricular issues. The relative strengths of *JME* are in articles dealing with students, including undergraduates; classroom and classes; methods, experiential activities and projects; teams; and behaviors and skills. They also found that each journal varied in the methodology used in its articles. *AMLE* articles relied primarily on quantitative methods. It also had higher proportions of conceptual, essay, and interview pieces. *ML* articles used qualitative methods, in addition to a large number of cases. *ML* was notable for offering critical, reflective, and action perspectives in addition to the default perspective of traditional positivism. In particular, *JME* articles used quantitative and mixed methods and published a great deal of narratives, which gave many of their articles a reflective first-person perspective (Beatty & Leigh, 2006).

JME'S JOURNEY TOWARDS INCREASING RIGOR

As noted above, the founders of the *Journal of Management Education* created the journal to serve practical, teaching-related needs of OB professors. Thus, the original emphasis of the journal was on relevance. Over time, there has been increasing emphasis on rigor as teaching-related ideas are developed into presentations of scholarly work. This section reviews *JME*'s mission and some of the distinctive genres published in the Journal that illustrate its commitment to relevance. It then explores the Journal's journey towards increasing rigor, as seen in the increasing expectation that articles will use sound methodology and provide evidence of effectiveness. Today the *Journal of Management Education* (*JME*) is dedicated to enhancing learning and teaching in all areas of management and organizational studies. It publishes six issues per year and has consistently reported a 10–15% acceptance rate. The *Journal*'s current mission states:

> The editors encourage contributions that respond to important issues in management education, including one or more of the following: How does learning occur? What should we be teaching? What should we be learning? What can be done to enhance learning effectiveness? How can management education delivery programs or systems be improved? What current educational assumptions or practices should be questioned or challenged? The overriding question that guides the review process is: Will this contribution have a significant impact on thinking and/or practice in management education? (*Journal of Management Education*, 2007, verso)

JME seeks to publish manuscripts that (1) explore theoretical and/or conceptual issues in management education, such as the questions noted in the mission statement above; (2) present empirical research findings that directly affect teaching strategies and learning; and (3) discuss commonly shared teaching challenges in the management classroom. The journal also publishes descriptions of innovative teaching strategies including original experiential exercises, activities and simulations.

This editorial vision is consistent with the original vision of the journal. An early *JME* editorial described the types of papers that the Journal would welcome: "conceptual pieces around the teaching of Organizational Behavior and descriptions of major course and training innovations" as well as "specific techniques that could be conducted in one or two [class] sessions" (Bradford, 1978, p. 3). Later editorials clarified that *JME* contributions would address the broader field of management education (Michaelsen, 1989–90) and could be "conceptual or empirical in nature" (Gallos, 1994, p. 136; see also Bilimoria, 1999).

Given the *Journal*'s emphasis on relevance, it is not surprising that the largest component of *JME* consists of articles describing innovative teaching strategies in management education. These innovative teaching strategies address a wide range of instructional elements: programs, curriculum, courses, projects, teaching approaches or methods, resources, exercises, activities and simulations. Although less prevalent, another distinctive type of article that appears in *JME* is the reflection paper. Since these two types of papers illustrate the Journal's commitment to relevance we discuss them in some detail below.

RELEVANCE THROUGH PUBLICATION OF INNOVATIVE TEACHING STRATEGIES

Articles describing innovative teaching strategies in *JME* have traditionally provided two key elements: (1) a rationale for the innovative teaching strategy that situates the work in a pedagogical perspective and literature, and (2) sufficient detail about implementation so that readers could (a) evaluate the suitability of the strategy for their own teaching and learning environments, (b) compare it to other approaches they might know or use, and (c) if desired, replicate it in their own teaching environments. Inclusion of these elements makes the journal contents relevant for its readers, management instructors and trainers.

As a longtime reader and former co-editor of *JME* captured this idea of relevance: "My primary decision to work with an author on a manuscript was based on whether I thought the teaching ideas were practical, relevant, useful and got to the heart of creating student comprehension." This editorial perspective was based on her experience as a reader of the journal:

> If I could take an idea or exercise and use it, if it wasn't too complex, too hideously labor-intensive to mount, if it was possible to see results.... I would continue reading. If not, I'd flip the page to the next article. I'm seriously into "Can I use this?" I don't have time to read anything that isn't directly related to what I'm doing, and I don't think I'm alone. If *JME* offers stuff that people need (can I take this design into the classroom tomorrow?) it'll be relevant. If not, I don't think so. (Susan Herman, personal communication, Feb. 26, 2007)

RELEVANCE THROUGH PUBLICATION
OF REFLECTION PAPERS

As SOTL scholars (Bilimoria & Fukami, 2002; Beatty & Leigh, 2006) have noted, *JME* has long had a rich tradition of publishing reflective work about teaching. The first person, narrative accounts in the journal have promoted this reflective perspective. However, the *JME* collection also includes articles that present the lessons learned from personally challenging experiences in teaching. These articles not only offer a counterpoint to the success stories of the descriptive innovative teaching strategies articles discussed above, they also serve readers who may be encountering similar challenges.

The reflection papers seem to be an outgrowth of the original request to share "disasters" called for in first editorial statement, which proposed a journal section to be titled "Major Disasters:"

A description of a course, project, or innovation that on the surface appeared very promising but turned out to be disastrous. The article should analyze what went wrong, and if relevant, suggest alternative approaches. (Bradford, 1975, p. 2)

More recent examples of reflection papers include forays into self-directed learning with students unprepared for it (Noel 2004), professors' reactions to students' language in a diversity course (Kirk & Durant, in press), and Rosile's (2007) discovery of widespread cheating in her business ethics class. In the last article, the author not only shared her lessons learned but also transformed her experience into an exercise that instructors can use to foster a classroom climate where cheating becomes discussable and students are supported to maintain their integrity.

It requires great honesty, courage, and humility to share these personal narratives with a community of peers, especially when that community is composed of scholars. Nonetheless, as Shulman (1993) has noted, it is crucial for teaching to become community property if it is to be considered as a scholarly act.

RIGOR THROUGH EVIDENCE OF TEACHING
EFFECTIVENESS

Today as editors of the *Journal*, we expect that an article describing a teaching innovation will also reflect a level of rigor identified by the three fundamental elements of instructional design: (1) articulating learning objectives, (2) specifying suitable pedagogical activities to facilitate the articulated learning objectives, and (3) identifying appropriate assessment methods to evaluate the learning outcomes (Fink, 2003).

Although learning objectives and pedagogical activities have long been regarded as standard elements of *JME* descriptive articles, the third element, evidence of effectiveness, appears to be a more recent trend in *JME* articles. Chronicling the development of the SOTL in ME, Bilimoria and Fukami wrote of *JME*, "the work is more cumulative and presented with more statistical rigor. More voices are included in the evidence provided. Yet, the work retains the balance of reflective and introspective scholarship that marked the beginning of this journey" (2002, p. 14).

As an example of an article where reviewers evaluated the evidence of effectiveness highly, we share the following comments from an anonymous reviewer of a manuscript about teaching statistics (Aguinis & Branstetter, 2007) that was accepted for and published in *JME*:

> The authors take an "unsexy" topic, and do a thorough job of describing an innovative approach and then (and this is the impressive part) conducting research that demonstrates the efficacy of the approach as a means of improving student learning. While most readers of *JME* do not teach statistics, there is a powerful lesson to be learned in this piece about how to move forward our efforts at improving teaching and learning. While we may not all be fans of AACSB's efforts around outcomes assessment, this article represents responsible scholarship that will help us meet the increasing scrutiny that is facing business education.

As editors, we have sometimes been surprised when authors of *JME* submissions overlook inclusion of their teaching objectives or evidence of effectiveness. As Roy Lewicki, long-term *JME* editorial board member and founding editor of *AMLE*, is wont to observe, authors would never omit hypotheses or results in a scholarly study in the scholarship of discovery, yet many aspiring authors in the scholarship of teaching continue to submit descriptive work that lacks learning objectives and/or evidence for the effectiveness of their proposed pedagogical contribution (Lewicki & Bailey, 2007): "It was astounding that all the PhDs we hired to teach, who had completed a rigorous research-oriented doctoral program and doctoral dissertation, seemed to forget (or ignore) all the research skills they learned when it comes to evaluating teaching effectiveness" (Roy Lewicki, personal communication, March 6, 2008).

RIGOR THROUGH METHODOLOGY

Although many scholars associate the term "rigor" with the use of empirical methods of assessment, as editors we also look for rigor in the logic of the manuscript, not only in its use of evidence. As one *JME* Associate Editor explained,

> I look for rigor in the conceptual development of a particular pedagogical idea/technique, rigor in its application and refinement, and rigor in the approach taken to sharing the technique via the *JME* submission. I want evidence that the author's idea is grounded in existing theory and practice, as evidenced by a thorough and comprehensive literature review.... I want evidence that the idea/technique has been fully fleshed out through repeated application and refinement.... I want evidence that the author is able to consider what the audience needs and wants by reflecting on his/her experience and going beyond to that experience to consider generalizability issues and variances in application. From my perspective, if the author can do these things (and of course if the idea/technique is relevant and applicable to our domain and potentially valuable to our readership), then the paper is publishable. (Courtney S. Hunt, personal communication, May 6, 2006)

Although there is no set structure for *JME* articles describing innovative teaching strategies, we have noticed that effective articles tend to follow the structure of a hypothesis-testing study in the scholarship of discovery: introduction and literature review culminating in hypotheses, method, results, discussion and conclusion. That is, the article begins with the identification of a problem, in this case pedagogical, and grounds the assessment of the problem in existing literature and known approaches to addressing the problem. The learning objectives serve as hypotheses as the paper introduces the authors' solution to the problem. A description of the actual teaching methods, which are sometimes relegated to appendices, serves as the methods section. The teaching methods are reported in sufficient detail so that readers can, if they wish, replicate the technique or exercise in their own classrooms. Assessment data provide evidence of the results of the proposed teaching method. Finally, in the discussion and concluding sections, the authors reflect on the effectiveness of their pedagogical solution, providing commentary about what lessons were learned, what conditions apply, and what variations are possible within other learning contexts, etc.

While the descriptive articles published in *JME* tend to follow the hypothesis-testing sequence described above, we were pleasantly surprised by a manuscript that presented these elements in an unusual sequence. The article opens with a discussion of the concept of organizational citizenship and a detailed description of an innovative approach to implementing this concept, and subsequently grounds the innovation in the relevant literature on organizational citizenship behaviors (Mazen, Herman, & Ornstein, in press). We note that this approach to presentation may more accurately reflect the process of conducting work in SOTL. That is, the process of generating reports in SOTL may often resemble more the qualitative tradition of generating grounded theory (Glaser & Strauss, 1967; Locke, 2001) rather than the hypothesis-testing tradition of positivist research. As Bass (1999) has noted that teaching innovations are often driven by needs or problems in one's teaching. Only later, after an innovation has been proven to be effective, does one think of "writing it up" for publication (Golden-Biddle & Locke, 2007). Thus, it is the process of scholarly writing that drives the search through the existing literature, not the practice of teaching.

RELEVANCE IN MANAGEMENT EDUCATION SCHOLARSHIP

In the absence of other institutions disseminating knowledge about teaching, *JME* has provided management educators with ideas and materials for practice throughout its 30+ year history. The innovativeness of the journal and its accessibility may account for its loyal readership. Although we cannot assess how many times readers adopt the ideas and exercises offered in *JME*, whether directly from *JME*'s pages or from the publication of *JME* materials in textbooks, we can offer some indications of how *JME*'s publications materials have shaped thought and action about management education. Below we offer some anecdotal evidence of the influence of *JME* on the actions of individual instructors and students of management, and on the dissemination of ideas within the intellectual community that may eventually lead to new structures within the institutions of management education.

Influencing the Actions of Individual Instructors and Students

In the first three accounts provided below, readers describe how *JME* has been used to enhance classroom teaching and learning, either to enliven existing courses or as starting points for course design. The first report describes an exercise designed to focus on themes associated with leading change for a course on leadership and organizational change. In the simulated context of a merger, students analyze, make decisions, and communicate information about a change as members of management or employee teams under conditions of environmental turbulence and uncertainty (McDonald & Mansour-Cole, 2000).

> I was looking for an experiential activity that would help my students experience organizational change instead of introducing the topic conceptually or abstractly. So naturally, I looked first at *JME*! This exercise (a merger of two hospitals) simulates an organizational change process and puts students in the roles of individuals that are being hit with multiple changes at a rapid pace. The exercise highlights issues of communication, organizational purpose, fairness and equity, anxieties produced by ambiguous circumstances, etc.

> I use it the first day of my Introduction to Organizational Change class as a way to provide students with a concrete example of what organizational change "feels" like. Although it is only a simulated exercise, students really get into the activity, and they continue to reference it relative to the organizational change concepts we learn throughout the course of the semester. I've used it four times now since last year, and each time it is a really rich way to introduce the topic at a visceral level. (Deborah A. O'Neil, Bowling Green State University)

In the next two examples, both of which engage students in building towers (albeit with different kinds of materials), the user describes exercises that reflect *JME*'s expansion into other management arenas: operations management and strategy. The first exercise illustrates foundational project management principles, allowing students to experience a complete project cycle from planning and design, through construction and evaluation of the best performing team (Cook & Olson, 2006). The second example allows students to apply a strategic management concept to explore how different combinations of resources and capabilities may explain differences in the performance of firms (Sheehan, 2006).

> The week after I read the spaghetti and marshmallow exercise in *JME*, I used it successfully in my class and have continued to use it each term since in a course that covers operations management topics. This particular class has Saturday sessions that run from 8:00–4:00, which is a long day for the students and the instructor. The exercise breaks up the day. I have found the exercise an excellent means to energize the students and a perfect platform to review the concepts of planning, job specialization, TQM, and time management. Students learn from it, and it's also fun. I plan to continue to use the exercise for this course and will incorporate it into a traditional operations management course I am slated to teach next fall.

> On a related note, I've used the paper clip tower exercise that was in that same issue in each delivery of my strategy class since its publication. This exercise was positioned as a means to present the resource-based view (RVB) of the firm. In my deployment, we almost always pick up the secondary learning that having the resource isn't enough; it has to be leveraged appropriately for competitive success. (Michael A. Dutch, Greensboro College)

Articles about innovative teaching strategies also have the potential for launching course design and development. This example, contributed by former *JME* co-editor Susan Herman, describes her experience with Thompson and Beak's (2007) "Leadership Book," a course-long activity in which students interview leaders and managers and then write and publish a book based on their findings.

As the "leadership" associate editor for *JME*, articles on this topic tend to fall into my folder of assignments. I read them with great interest because they relate to a topic of great relevancy for me. My administrative responsibilities are to direct the University of Alaska's new Northern Leadership Center, an organization whose mission is to enable current and emerging leaders to gain a fundamental understanding of leadership practice and theory, develop and articulate their own values on leadership and society, and contribute to the future of Alaska in meaningful and positive ways; and to create a culture of leadership and engagement, through partnership, cooperation, civic duty, and ethical practice. My teaching responsibilities are to offer academic courses relating to leadership development, so I am continuously scanning the environment for ideas to make the topic lively; engage the students; and provide activities, readings, and exercises that engage their minds and hearts.

One such idea came across my desk. Karen Thompson and Joel Beak offered an activity for their classes that involved writing a book on leadership. Long before the article came back from its first review and was revised and ready for publication, I put the idea to work in my Leadership for Alaska Scholars: Making A Difference course. Twenty-five students and their mentors, all recognized state leaders, worked together to look at what makes leading in Alaska unique, and the students used the information gained from reading, personal experience and the experience of their mentors to write a book which was then published by the University of Alaska Press. It was a tremendous undertaking, accompanied by joy, complaining, discouragement, and ultimately forward momentum to the final project. It wasn't easy. But the outcome was outstanding.

The book is a source of pride to its authors and to the mentors who supported them; and a tremendous PR piece for the School of Management at UAF, under whose auspices the book was written. While we don't claim to have a best seller, the book has had wide circulation in the state due to the support of our mentors and has led to the funding of our second project, the writing and publication of a set of leadership workshops, each of which will be developed and written up by a team of this year's Leadership Alaska scholars. The workshop idea came from a session at the 2007 Organizational Behavior Teaching Society conference at Pepperdine University. I have encouraged the workshop presenters to write up the exercise as a *JME* article, and look forward to seeing how they do. (Susan Herman, University of Alaska Fairbanks)

A final example at the individual level shows how a conceptual article has the power to engage readers in deeper, more personal levels—to illuminate personal challenges in the teaching profession and promote personal learning and growth. The example comes from an anonymous professor who signed on for an international teaching assignment. Upon arrival, he discovered a mismatch between personal and institutional expectations. A colleague from OBTS alerted him to a published *JME* article describing a similar situation, where he found the following passage:

> Having a host institution, particularly one that understands your mission and goals, is critical to maximizing the foreign experience. Although it is in the best interest of all parties to ensure the coordination and planning for visiting faculty, there have been far too many horror stories of talented and expensive faculty who have been misplaced or misused. (Elbert, 1996, p. 71)

Reading these reflections helped him articulate his frustration, understand the broader context, and justify his decision:

> [The article]...certainly describes my situation perfectly. It was never a fit. On Monday they started talking to me about teaching cost accounting and financial management—courses I am not qualified to teach. I have repeatedly told them: That is not what I want to do. They just never heard me. It was never a fit....Reading the article reminded me of the bureaucratic challenges. All international teaching assignments are not created equal, and it made better sense to not prolong a misfit. (Anonymous, personal communication, Sept. 27, 2007)

Influencing the Community of Scholars towards Educational Policy and Practice

While the above examples reveal *JME*'s contribution to individual faculty in their daily professional activities, on occasion *JME* articles also have the opportunity to create a broader influence as they disseminate ideas and proposals about the discipline and its processes. A contemporary example comes from a conceptual article originally published in *JME* in 1994. The article challenged the professional societies in management education to recognize the mobility of educators and increase their market value by creating a peer-review infrastructure for teaching, parallel to that which exists for research (Van Fleet, 1994). Based on the initial publication, the author was invited to present the idea at a symposium at the Western Academy of Management (Van Fleet, 1995). About 10 years later, another long-time OBTS member contacted the author and suggested expanding the ideas and exposing them to a wider audience. The resulting article was published in *AMLE* (Van Fleet & Peterson, 2005).

The following year, the Chair of the Management Education and Development Division of the Academy invited to authors to discuss the ideas with the MED Executive Committee: "We invited Dave and Tim to meet interested parties of the MED exec for a debate about the contents of their article. At that meeting it was decided that the issues under debate were so important that we should try to keep the debate alive" (S. Armstrong, personal communication, October 8, 2007).

At a caucus at the 2007 Academy meetings (Williams et al., 2007), the Value In Teaching Initiative through MED was created. As of the time of this writing, the following actions are planned:

1. Promotion of research that examines how to measure the value in teaching.
2. Development of a Symposium for the 2008 AOM regarding the research being conducted.
3. Development of professional development workshops that address becoming a master teacher.
4. Discussions regarding the development of an external review process for teaching. (J. Williams, Personal Communication, October 19, 2007).

In summary, although these ideas, originally published in *JME* in 1994, have not yet been implemented as educational policy or practice, they are gaining more attention and more momentum as more members of the larger community of scholars recognize their relevance.

THE CURRENT DIALECTIC: RIGOR AND RELEVANCE IN MANAGEMENT EDUCATION SCHOLARSHIP

The evolution of scholarship identified in *JME* has come about with some controversy among the journal's core readership. It is fair to say that the journal is beloved by many because of its rich tradition of sharing of observation and reflection about what constitutes effective teaching and learning. Some have feared that an evolution in the sophistication of methodology and rigor will result in a loss of the reflection and introspection that marked the beginning of the journal and continues to differentiate *JME* among its sister journals (Beatty & Leigh, 2006). After all, as we noted earlier, *JME* was founded by individuals who felt disrespected by their academic colleagues. One way to understand this controversy is simply from the perspective of change, and that it is human to resist change (Bridges, 1991). Alternatively, another perspective from which to understand this controversy is from the point of view of the development of a science. In our opinion, *JME* is facing a rather predictable dilemma. As we have traced above, *JME* has experienced an increased trend in scientific rigor in the articles it has published. Does this mean that there must be a concomitant decrease in relevance? In other words, as rigor is increased, will relevance be sacrificed? Is it possible to have both?

As noted earlier in this chapter, discovery scholarship was conceptualized by Boyer to be characterized by hypothesis generation and testing. In addition, we have traditional measures for the quality of discovery scholarship (Campbell & Stanley, 1963). Thus, it is tempting to argue that we should take lessons learned from evaluating discovery scholarship and apply these lessons to teaching scholarship. Is SOTL different than discovery scholarship, and if so, how?

Judgments of the worth of scholarship strongly influence the continuing vitality of any field of research (Mahoney, 1985). The quality, sophistication, and significance of research are often connected with the age and stage of development of a discipline or paradigm. At early stages, quality criteria tend to be less stringent (Mahoney, 1985) and the discipline grants more slack in evaluating quality. A study in a new area with few precedents would therefore be allowed more methodological flaws or ambiguities than manuscripts within well-worked territories (Staw, 1985). Therefore, given the relative newness of inquiry in SOTL, significant contributions have been made with less stringent quality criteria. Until more stringent standards are developed and attained, the scholarship of teaching and learning may remain a stepchild in one's scholarly dossier.

As noted earlier in this chapter, discovery scholarship was conceptualized by Boyer to be characterized by hypothesis generation and testing. In addition, we have traditional measures for the quality of discovery scholarship (Campbell & Stanley, 1963). Thus, it is tempting to argue that we should take lessons learned from evaluating discovery scholarship and apply these lessons to the scholarship of teaching and learning. To be sure, there is some advantage to be gained from doing so. For example, our training as scholars exposed us to methodologies that allow for strong inferences to be made from observations. We know how to design research so that internal validity is strengthened (Campbell and Stanley, 1963), to include multiple operationalizations of our variables, to rule out alternative explanations for our results, and to provide several independent tests of a given hypothesis (Staw, 1985). We also learned to strive for multiple checks of hypotheses from relatively independent or at least non-overlapping data sources. In short, we learned to strive for objectivity, independence, and cumulative effort. These are clearly appropriate aims for any and all scholarly efforts, and closely mirror those suggested by Shulman (1999) for SOTL.

On the other hand, we would do a disservice to SOTL by acting as if its pursuit is not different than discovery work. For example, research articles are the standard fare for discovery work. In SOTL, a written paper may not be possible or appropriate as the documentation of work.

In addition, as teachers, we are practitioners in our classrooms, not abstracting from theory and testing it independently. The teacher/researcher is not independent but in fact interdependent with the phenomena of interest. This interdependence introduces sources of bias that potentially reduce the strength of inference, hence the rigor (and perceived quality) of research on teaching.

The issue is not just one of qualitative versus quantitative research. Statistics and methods don't matter so much as expertise in a subject matter, sound measurement, appropriate procedures, and clear exposition (Campbell, 1975). Qualitative methodology may generate evidence and rich insight. Rigor may be demonstrated in case studies, for example, by incorporating multiple observations across a series of case studies (Campbell, 1975). The key is that qualitative research must be separated from "journalism" (Schneider, 1985).

In short, the process of evaluating the quality of research in discovery and in teaching is the same—that is, we must build a ladder or continuum of quality for SOTL. Some of our outputs will be of lesser quality, and some of our outputs will be of higher quality. In its infancy, less stringent criteria were acceptable but eventually, to be taken seriously, standards needed to be raised and we needed to become more rigorous in our approaches to SOTL.

However, we can't "throw the baby out with the bath water," and lose relevance. In other words, the steps on our SOTL quality ladder may be different than we would find on the quality ladders of the other three types of scholarship. Do gains in rigor inevitably result in losses of relevance? Can this paradox become a strength, as opposed to an impediment, to SOTL?

THE FUTURE OF SOTL IN MANAGEMENT EDUCATION

In this chapter we have seen that the history of the scholarship of teaching and learning in management, as pioneered in the *Journal of Management Education*, has reflected both relevance and rigor, with relevance taking the lead and rigor following over time. As the discipline continues to develop, will or should rigor overtake relevance? What should be the response of those scholars who seek to make a contribution to SOTL in general, and to management education in particular? To address this issue, we conclude this chapter by offering our views on the future of SOTL in management education in general, and for *JME* in particular.

1. Scholarly contributions in SOTL will increasingly involve the development of theory, constructs, and paradigms.

> Innovation is meaningless in a field with undeveloped paradigms. In the absence of paradigms, people have little agreement on criteria by which to judge innovation. When people work with an undeveloped paradigm, all work is innovative. The problem with an underdeveloped

> paradigm is not innovation, the problem is that there is little normal
> science. (Weick, 1985, p. 368)

Contributors to SOTL can no longer be practitioners or engineers. Practitioner journals follow an "engineering" model: There is little concern toward theory—they treat specific situations and get things done. The early days of SOTL were marked by atheoretical work and eventually, the atheoretical work was broadened. More explicit theory will naturally lead to theory-testing, which will result in innovation.

2. Contributors to SOTL should practice what we're preaching. Howard Gardner argued that deep understanding in our students comes from using multiple perspectives and requiring our students to apply learning in new settings (Gardner, 1999). Starting from this inspiration, it follows that we should use multiple perspectives when assessing classroom innovations. It will no longer be sufficient to assert, "This worked for me." We need to provide evidence from multiple perspectives and perhaps in multiple settings in order to move SOTL forward.

3. There is an opportunity for contributions that derive from interdisciplinary relationships, both in methodology and in theory. Action learning, participant-observation, or perhaps even work by therapists who do research on their own patients, may provide appropriate methodology for high rigor and high relevance. Similarly, SOTL scholars could find theoretical models from other disciplines to help produce quality contributions. To illustrate, one of us, with her colleagues, built a model to understand internship effectiveness based on the knowledge transfer literature (Narayanan, Olk, & Fukami, 2006). Many other such opportunities exist for grounding SOTL research.

4. SOTL outlets must find a balance between rigor and relevance. Rigor exists not only in empiricism, but also in logic. The early era of *JME* was marked by rich self-reflective essays. These were compilations of wise observations gleaned from teachers' own experiences in their own classrooms. While this was a good place to start and has a fair amount of quality, we can't leave it at that. We need to move beyond reflective essays and self-study to methods and evidence that permit stronger inference. Yet we strongly believe that *JME* should retain its distinctive competence in self-reflection. After all, self-reflection is a place for theory-building to start. In addition, too much of an emphasis on rigor might result in work that makes irrelevant contributions. To maintain a balance between relevance and rigor, *JME* will continue to seek conceptual and empirical work that addresses contemporary issues in management education, as well as commonly shared challenges of teaching management and the organizational sciences. *JME* will also continue to seek articles

on innovative teaching strategies that integrate creativity, reflective thought, and evidence of effectiveness.

Aristotle (n.d.) argued that virtue was the mean, or balance point, between opposing vices. If we consider rigor and relevance to be opposing vices, then *JME* defines the virtue in the middle. *JME* aims to be the journal that is "rigorously relevant."

REFERENCES

Aguinis, H. & Branstetter, S.A. (2007). Teaching the concept of the sampling distribution of the mean. *Journal of Management Education, 31*, 467–483.

Aristotle (n.d.). Nicomachean ethics. Retrieved March 28, 2008 from http://classics.mit.edu/Aristotle/nicomachaen.2.ii.html

Bass, R. (1999). The scholarship of teaching: What's the problem? *Inventio, 1*(1), http://www.doiiit.gmu.edu/Archives/feb98/rbass.htm.

Beatty, J. & Leigh, J. (2006). *Comparing management education journals: Academy of Management Learning and Education, Journal of Management Education, and Management Learning.* Paper presented at the annual meetings, Academy of Management, PDW, Atlanta, GA.

Bernstein, D. & Bass, R. (2005). The scholarship of teaching and learning. *Academe, 91*(4), 37–43.

Bilimoria, D. (1999). The editor's corner: The *Journal of Management Education*'s sections: Editorial mission and guidelines. *Journal of Management Education, 23*, 334–337.

Bilimoria, D. & Fukami, C. (2002). The scholarship of teaching and learning in the Management sciences: Disciplinary style and content. In M. T. Huber & S. P. Morreale (Eds.), *Disciplinary styles in the scholarship of teaching and learning: Exploring common ground* (pp. 125–142). Menlo Park, CA: The Carnegie Foundation for the Advancement of Teaching and the American Association for Higher Education.

Boyer, E.L. (1990). *Scholarship reconsidered: Priorities of the professoriate.* Princeton, NJ: The Carnegie Foundation for the Advancement of Teaching.

Bradford, D. L. (1975). Editorial Statement. *The teaching of organizational behavior: A journal of teaching theory and technique.* 1, 3.

Bradford, D. L. (1978). Editorial. *Exchange: The Organizational Behavior Teaching Journal, 3*, 3.

Bridges, W. (1991). *Managing transitions: Making the most of change.* Cambridge, MA: Perseus Books Group.

Bruff, D. (2008). Vanderbilt Center for Teaching: Scholarship of Teaching and Learning (SoTL). Retrieved March 6, 2008 from http://www.vanderbilt.edu/cft/resources/teaching_resources/reflecting/sotl.htm

Campbell, D.T. (1975). "Degrees of freedom" and the case study. *Comparative Political Science, 8*, 178–193.

Campbell, D.T. & Stanley, J. (1963). *Experimental and quasi-experimental designs for research.* Boston: Houghton Mifflin.

Cook, L. S. & Olson, J. R. (2006). The sky's the limit: An activity for teaching project management. *Journal of Management Education, 30,* 404–420.

Daft, R. L. (1995). Disaster in Commerce 353. *Journal of Management Education, 19,* 17–30.

Elbert, N. E. (1996). Management education in post-socialist Hungary: Observations on obstacles to reforms. *Journal of Management Education, 20,* 70–79.

Fink, L. D. (2003). *Creating significant learning experiences.* San Francisco: Jossey-Bass.

Fukami, C. (2007). The third road. *Journal of Management Education, 31,* 358–364.

Gallos, J. (1994). The editor's corner. *Journal of Management Education, 18,* 135–138.

Gardner, H. (1999). *The disciplined mind.* New York: Simon & Schuster.

Glaser, B. G., & Strauss, A. S. (1967). *The discovery of grounded theory: Strategies for qualitative research.* New York: Aldine De Gruyter.

Golden-Biddle, K. & Locke, K. (2007). *Composing qualitative research.* Thousand Oaks, CA: Sage.

Hutchings, P. & L. Shulman. (1999). The scholarship of teaching: New elaborations, new developments. *Change. 31*(5), 10–15.

Journal of Management Education. Aims and Scope. Retrieved March 25, 2008, from http://www.sagepub.com/journalsProdAims.nav?prodId=Journal200931

Korpiaho, K., Päiviö , H. & Räsänen, K. (2007). Anglo-American forms of management education: A practice-theoretical perspective. *Scandanavian Journal of Management, 23,* 36–65.

Lewicki, R. & Bailey, J. (2007). A Narrative of the founding of the Academy of Management Learning & Education. Presentation at the Academy of Management, August 7. Session 1140.

Locke, K. (2001). *Grounded theory in management research.* Thousand Oaks, CA: Sage.

Mahoney, T.A. (1985). Journal publishing in the Organization Sciences: An analysis of exchanges. In L.L. Cummings & P. J. Frost. (Eds.), *Publishing in the organizational sciences* (pp. 14–34). Homewood, IL: Irwin.

Mazen, A., Herman, S., & Ornstein, S. (2007). Professor delight: Cultivating organizational citizenship behavior. *Journal of Management Education,* Pre-published November 7, 2007. DOI:10.1177/1052562907307642

McDonald, K. S. & Mansour-Cole, D. (2000). Change requires intensive care: An experiential exercise for learners in university and corporate settings. *Journal of Management Education, 24,* 127–148.

Michaelsen, L. (1989–90). Editorial statement. *Organizational Behavior Teaching Review, 14*(4), iii.

Narayanan, V., Olk, P., & Fukami, C. (2006). Determinants of internship effectiveness: An exploratory model. *Best Paper Proceedings of the 2006 Annual Meetings of the Academy of Management,* August, 2006.

Noel, T. W. (2004). Lessons from the learning classroom. *Journal of Management Education, 28,* 188–206.

Rosile, G.A. (2007). Cheating: Making it a teachable moment. *Journal of Management Education, 31,* 582–613.

Schneider, B. (1985). Some propositions on getting research published. In L.L. Cummings & P.J. Frost (Eds.), *Publishing in the Organizational Sciences.* (pp. 238–247) Homewood, IL: Richard D. Irwin.

Schmidt-Wilk, J. (2007). Editor's Corner: Why should my JME count? *Journal of Management Education, 3,* 439–441.

Sheehan, N. T. (2006) Understanding how resources and capabilities affect performance: Actively applying the resource-based view in the classroom. *Journal of Management Education, 30,* 421–430.

Shulman, L. (1993). Teaching as community property: Putting an end to pedagogical solitude. *Change, 25*(6), 6–7.

Shulman, L. (1999). Taking learning seriously. *Change. 31*(4), 11–17.

Staw, Barry M. (1985). Repairs on the road to relevance and rigor. In L.L. Cummings & P.J. Frost (Eds.), *Publishing in the organizational sciences.* (pp. 96–107) Homewood, IL: Richard D. Irwin.

Thompson, K. J. & Beak, J. (2007). The leadership book: Enhancing the theory-practice connection through project-based learning. *Journal of Management Education, 31,* 278–291.

Van Fleet, D.D. (1994). Instruction, scholarship, and tenure. *Journal of Management Education, 18,* 77–85.

Van Fleet, D.D. (1995). *Increasing the market value of good teaching.* Symposium on Scholarly Criticism of Management Education at the Western Academy of Management meetings, San Diego.

Van Fleet, D.D., & Peterson, T.O. (2005). Increasing the value of teaching in the academic marketplace: The creation of a peer-review infrastructure for teaching. *Academy of Management Learning and Education, 4,* 506–514.

Weick, K. (1985). Editing innovation into Administrative Science Quarterly. In L.L. Cummings & P.J. Frost (Eds.), *Publishing in the Organizational Sciences* (pp. 366–376). Homewood, IL: Richard D. Irwin.

Williams, J.K., Brennan, L.L., Gaylor, K.P., Van Fleet, D.D., Goldman, E.F., & Sarkar, R. (2007). *Measuring value in teaching.* Caucus at the Academy of Management meetings, Philadelphia, 2007.

CHAPTER 9

THE CHALLENGE OF CHANGE IN BUSINESS AND ECONOMICS EDUCATION

Lessons Learned from the ED*i*NEB Network

W. H. Gijselaers and R. G. Milter

ABSTRACT

There is no shortage of good ideas and good practices in business education. But as soon as it comes to research about business education, spreading these ideas within a school, and communicating them to a larger audience, there is a major problem. The ED*i*NEB Network grew out of the need to rethink how a good researched teaching and learning practice could be implemented program or school wide. When we started our efforts to implement innovations in business and economics education at the program and school/college level, few resources were available to inform us, provide guidelines on change processes, or offer meeting points to connect with people encountering simi-

Being and Becoming a Management Education Scholar, pages 157–173
Copyright © 2010 by Information Age Publishing
All rights of reproduction in any form reserved.

lar issues. The present chapter addresses the issue of how to support change in business schools by encouraging research and by going beyond publication of research results. We describe the importance of engaging teachers and other participants in active experimentation in their teaching context. The EDiNEB Network provides a platform to further teachers' understanding of the innovation and development of ownership.

INTRODUCTION

EDiNEB Network: Initially an organization where educators could learn about Problem-Based Learning (PBL) and share experiences of both successful implementations and challenges with its use. Membership in EDiNEB has involved educators reporting on the practice of implementing PBL and other innovative approaches to management education. Researchers targeting new learning methods and innovative curriculum approaches have also been actively providing their findings at EDiNEB conferences and in EDiNEB sponsored publications since 1993.

How can higher education achieve success in developing, adopting and implementing new education initiatives? Faculty, teachers, and administrators are well aware that it is not too common to hear people talk enthusiastically about the change that is needed and look forward to the change that will come in the end. Thinking about change requires also thinking about how to deal with obstacles that will appear whenever teachers develop good ideas and implement them in the classroom. Not surprisingly, change is also about resistance to change: People avoid change, or simply wait till the wave of change is over, or demonstrate support by saying that the innovation was indeed a success elsewhere but cannot possibly work in your own institution or for your own course. But change may cause success as well. Many examples have been reported about individual success to implement changes in the classroom. Yet the risk remains that change stays at the single-course level, never reaching school-wide acceptance. In that particular case the innovator becomes the lone ranger who paves his or her own way. Few examples seem to exist demonstrating successful curriculum-wide implementation of innovative approaches to teaching and learning. Unfortunately, the difficult nature of implementing change is not restricted to education. It has been estimated that within business about 70% of all change programs either stall prematurely or fail to achieve their intended result (Boonstra, 2004).

While substantial progress has been made to understand change processes within higher education (e.g., Bland et al., 2000) a paucity of research exists about how to scale up innovations at the program level. One of the few exceptions that reports research on this issue is contained in the book *Scaling Up Success: Lessons From Technology-Based Educational Improvement*

(Dede, Honan, & Peters, 2005). It addresses the central question of how to scale up technology-based innovation. These researchers realized that in many cases there is no shortage of good ideas, good practices, and good research about education and technology, but there is a major problem as soon as it comes to spreading these ideas within a school.

The authors' contribution to this area grew out of the need to rethink how a well-researched teaching and learning practice could be implemented program- or school-wide. When we started our efforts to implement innovations in business and economics education at the program and school/college level, few resources were available to inform us, provide guidelines on change processes, or offer meeting points to connect with people encountering similar issues. The present chapter provides the outcome of our learning journey that brought us to the development of a network for innovators in business and economics education. We will address the question of how educational change can be supported by offering opportunities to share experience and research about good practices, as well as providing guidance by coaches and consultants. This chapter describes some of the challenges we faced when scaling up one of the most profound educational innovations in professional education developed in the past 30 years: problem-based learning. We will present the case of the ED*i*NEB network that was founded in 1993 to provide support to innovators in business and economics education facing the challenge of change.

WHEN CHANGE HAPPENS

In 1983, Maastricht University—Maastricht, the Netherlands—created a new Faculty of Economics and Business Administration. It developed a wide range of programs in international economics, econometrics, business economics, and international business. From its start, an innovative educational approach was to be used throughout its entire four-year programs, an approach now known globally as problem-based learning (Gijselaers et al., 1995; Wilkerson & Gijselaers, 1996). By doing so, it built further on the ideas underlying the problem-based program design of the medical faculty of Maastricht University. The medical faculty of this university was a newly created medical school that followed curriculum developments at McMaster University, Canada. Only two years later, Ohio University launched a similar initiative at the College of Business (Milter & Stinson, 1995; Stinson & Milter, 1996). They moved from a traditional course-based, discipline-divided MBA to a problem-based driven curriculum program. Also, the College of Business of Ohio University was heavily influenced by the ideas that had proven to be very successful at the Medical School of McMaster University. The irony was that both schools didn't know about each other's efforts to adopt and implement this education initiative. Only years later, after a coincidental meeting at a conference, we realized we were addressing similar challenges and facing similar problems with respect to the development of course materials, teacher training workshops, course evaluation systems, and building capacity to maintain the innovation.

In hindsight, it was probably not a coincidence that curriculum reform in medical education influenced reform in business education. Both can be considered as professional education programs that require a strong connection with professional practice; struggle with the balance between basic sciences and applied sciences; and require students to develop skills such as problem-solving skills, self-directed learning skills, and team skills. They also deal with short life cycles of knowledge due to ongoing innovations in practice, and both encounter strong counterparts in practice through their clients, legislation, and professional association. While business education seemed to accept case-based learning (Harvard Case Method) as a gold standard for curriculum reform in their profession, medical educators kept seeking other ways to prepare students for practice. The awareness to rethink the role of medical education was fueled by its excessive emphasis on memorization, its fragmentation, and its failure to equip graduates with the problem-solving skills required for a lifetime of learning. Barrows (1996) was one of the outspoken proponents in medical education arguing that professional practice required acquisition of skills in problem-solving application, as opposed to only conceptual understanding. This particular issue led to the development of instructional methods and curriculum design that could narrow the gap between professional practice and professional education and equip students with enhanced problem-solving skills. Later, many professions (e.g., architecture, engineering, management, law, and social work) adopted the ideas from these medical educators and implemented various versions of problem-based learning (Boud & Feletti, 1991; Wilkerson & Gijselaers, 1996; De Graaff & Kolmos, 2003; Knowlton & Sharpe, 2003). The use of problem-based learning within business schools has been documented in a U.S. university accounting course (Barsky, Catanach, & Stout, 2002), an economics course in Ireland (Forsythe, 2002), a cross-curricular experience at a university in the UK (Brassington & Smith, 2000), a corporate MBA program in Malaysia (Yost & Keifer, 1998), and an undergraduate business program in Sweden (Söderlund, 1998).

PROBLEM-BASED LEARNING AS STARTING POINT
FOR THE EDINEB NETWORK

Today we consider Problem-Based Learning (PBL) as an educational practice offering many strategies for educators to enhance student learning.

It is considered one of the forerunners of constructivist views on teaching and learning. PBL engages the learner actively in the learning process; it recognizes the idiosyncrasy of the learner's knowledge, the importance of changing students' misconceptions about science, and the need to prepare students for professional practice by paying explicit attention to the transfer of learning to practice. Even more important, it has a substantial educational research basis as published in many academic journals and has produced many new and profound insights on how people learn within and outside schools.

But this research knowledge doesn't necessarily break down the barriers for change because it requires from practitioners, administrators, teachers, and students more than the knowledge about this innovation. Stone-Wiske and Perkins (2005) remark that it is important to engage the teachers and other participants by emphasizing active experimentation in their teaching context, using various constructivist frameworks to ensure the teacher's understanding of the innovation and development of ownership. In their view the key to improving education lies not in simply transferring knowledge about an innovation but in helping educators to understand this knowledge relative to the teacher's context and needs—to see its power, but also to see where modifications are necessary. For purposes of demonstrating how difficult it is to move toward understanding the nature of a profound educational innovation as PBL we will give a brief overview. Those who are familiar with the Harvard Case Method, or other established educational methods based on case analysis, will probably wonder how PBL differs from the Harvard Case Method. In our institutions this caused confusion many times because academics felt they had always been using PBL in the past, the only difference being that case analysis took place in smaller groups (8–12 students) than usual.

Problem-based learning typically involves students working on problems in small groups of five to twelve with the assistance of a faculty tutor. Problems serve as the context for new learning. Their analysis and resolution result in the acquisition of knowledge and problem-solving skills. But it is important to realize that problems are encountered *before* all relevant knowledge has been acquired, not just after reading texts or hearing lectures about the subject matter underlying a problem. This feature reflects one of the essential distinctions between problem-based learning and other problem-oriented methods (Gijselaers, 1996). The role of the faculty tutor is to coach the group by providing support to make student interaction productive and to help students identify knowledge needed to resolve the problem. As a result of the problem-solving process, students generate questions (learning issues) about what kind of knowledge is required to explain the mechanisms underlying the causes of the problem. After leaving the meeting, students do research on the learning issues using a variety of resources. Significant time is available for independent study. The PBL process is completed when students report in the next meeting about what they have learned. The students' first goal is to relate newly acquired knowledge to the problem at hand. Their second focus is moving to a more general level of understanding, making transfer to new problems possible. After completing this problem-solving cycle, students will start to analyze a new problem, again following the procedure outlined above.

A typical problem for students entering undergraduate business education may look as follows:

> For more than fifty years the Lee Company of Merriam, Kansas, did a good steady business. In the 1960s and 1970s, Lee Riders were riding high as jeans became fashionable among women as well as men. Lee couldn't make jeans fast enough. Recently, however, ten plants were closed down. Furthermore, Lee's international sales decreased despite enormous demand in foreign countries. Nowadays, Chief Executive Officer Fred Rowan is struggling to re-orient Lee to suit the changes in the external environment. In order to make a sound reorientation, what is the first thing Fred should do?

Analysis of this problem takes place through several stages. The first step is to make sure everybody understands all the concepts and terms used in the problem. Students can raise questions about the concepts of organizational environment, dynamics of market behavior, and market share. During the next step, students define and analyze the problem. For example, in discussing the problem, students may question why in a stage of growing market demand, Lee Jeans Company is not able to sell jeans. At this point, students are confronted with conflicting information: (1) there is a substantial market demand; (2) in the past Lee was more or less "surfing" on market demand because production could not keep pace with demand; and (3) now market demand is still growing, but Lee is unprofitable. This problem increases their interest in knowing more about organizational behavior and market analysis because the information in the problem conflicts with their naïve beliefs about market demand and opportunities to sell products. Their naïve belief says that if market demand is large, a company operating in this market should not have the problems that Lee Jeans Company is encountering. The usual outcome of the discussion of the problem is that students study the relationships between the environment of an organization and organizational behavior. Possible learning issues are: "How does the environment of organizations influence organizational behavior?; "What kind of organizational strategies are most effective given certain market features?"; and "How do you conduct a marketing opportunity analysis to determine how a company can be restructured in response to market demands?" The PBL process is completed when students report in a subsequent group session about what they have learned.

New faculty may question the effectiveness of this approach, because in PBL the problem comes in first and then reading relevant literature. While the case method uses the case to apply the knowledge learned, in PBL it is the other way around. Another difference lies in the emphasis on collaborative learning. Small-group work is the key process to make learning happen, while in the case method it is the interaction between teacher and students that determines whether the case analysis results in fruitful learning. Finally, a PBL curriculum is defined by the series of problems presented to students, and not by the conceptual structure of disciplines.

It is one thing to start with problem-based learning as a leading curriculum design principle; it is quite another to implement it and sustain the innovation. It requires rethinking the role of higher education, redesign of traditional courses, developing new instructional methods and instruments for student assessment, and last but not least training of faculty in new teaching skills. Moreover, attention must be paid to support mechanisms for student learning (e.g., through adapted library resources and modified assessment practices) and organizational support by the administration. It may not be a surprise that maintenance of the innovation can become a new concern for an organization. When inappropriately used, it will not lead to desired student learning but rather may even distort faculty capabilities and attitudes toward the program design (Stinson & Milter, 1996).

PBL AND THE EDINEB NETWORK

Following years of excitement on what was accomplished, a growing need developed for sharing experiences with other business schools involved with innovations such as problem-based learning. Several curriculum and instructional issues remained unsolved with respect to (1) management of the educational organization, (2) effective faculty development, (3) guidelines for continuous curriculum improvement, and (4) development of new assessment procedures. As a consequence, growing awareness emerged of the need to get in touch with others to share knowledge, research ideas, and get tools for addressing these unsolved issues to keep the innovation alive and sustainable. For that purpose the Faculty of Economics and Business Administration of Maastricht University decided to organize an international conference around the theme "Educational Innovation in Economics and Business: the Case of Problem-Based Learning." The idea was to share experiences in similar innovations as problem-based education in business.

The authors of this chapter met at this conference in December of 1993. It was a serendipitous meeting in that we found we shared many common curriculum experiences in the process of implementing radical program changes based on the values of problem-based learning. Before our meeting we were more or less acting as the "lone rangers" in the field of business education. Journals in management or business education didn't pay attention to problem-based learning, while at the same time, plenty of research articles about this approach were published in medical education journals. Many other conference participants felt the same way and expressed the need to continue organizing this kind of event. At the end of the conference, it was decided that an international network organization should be founded that would provide a platform for exchanging ideas, knowledge, and experiences in the field of innovative business education: the EDiNEB Network.

EDiNEB is an acronym for **ED**ucational **IN**novation in **E**conomics and **B**usiness. The *i is* emphasized in the name because of the emphasis of the network on innovation. Since its launch in 1993, we have moved from an organization dedicated to the improvement of problem-based learning in schools of economics and business to a network organization that offers a place of learning and knowledge exchange in many areas related to educational innovation. In 1993, we started without a clear road map, but along the way we became more and more interested in and passionate about sharing thoughts on issues of innovation in the fields of business education, corporate training, and professional development of business professionals. We believe we have gained some insights that may be of use to others attempting to innovate in learning, whether it is within higher education or in the corporate training of business professionals. It is in this spirit that we share our story.

DRIVERS OF CURRICULUM CHANGE
IN BUSINESS EDUCATION

> *You need substance to make an impact. In our case: research and publications. In the spirit of continuous improvement we followed the mantra that if we ever thought we had it right, it would be time to retire.*

Many innovations in business education seem to be driven by the idea that "content is king." The underlying assumption is that through making changes in course content, improvements can be made in students' learning and the graduates' proficiency in a subject area. Relatively few changes seem to focus on improvement of instructional methods. Changes in assessment practices, incorporation of technology in instruction, or integrating work experience in graduate education get even less attention. As a consequence, attention to faculty development, or other curriculum support mechanisms such as course and curriculum evaluation, seems to go as far as requirements set by accreditation agencies.

A typical observation about the impact of the "content is king" idea in business education is provided by Ball (2006). Recently, he noted in his review on curriculum change in management education:

> Yet, an extensive review of the suggestions of business program faculty in the 1990s for improving their programs showed that business faculty overwhelmingly see their curricula as primarily *content* (what will we teach?), *pedagogy* (how will we teach?), and sometimes *sequencing* (in what order will the content be taught?). Other important curriculum elements are generally short-changed. As a result graduate management curricular reforms are often cosmetic at best. (Ball, 2006, p. 94)

We have also observed in educational practice that innovations that seem to work in one business school are difficult to implement in another. It is even more difficult to copy best practices from one profession to another. For example, it took years at our two business schools to find out that some successful elements of problem-based learning in medical schools simply didn't work in our business programs.

A typical case of such is provided by Maastricht University. When its faculty of economics and business administration was established, it was decided at the level of the president's office that this faculty should adopt the successful problem-based learning philosophy implemented by the medical faculty of the university. Programs in economics and business were developed that copied best practices from the medical faculty and were based on findings from educational research conducted in medicine. Typical for the innovation process was that next to its emphasis on changing curricular contents, much attention was paid to developing new instructional methods. Special attention was paid to nurturing student learning, fostering student progress throughout programs, and strengthening the link between programs' content and professional practice. But we soon realized that different disciplines foster different values about education. For example, while medical education journals gave considerable attention to student assessment and evaluation of course and curriculum outcomes, this was hardly an issue in business education. The latter was much more concerned with issues of how to make sure students acquire relevant course content.

Curriculum change at the College of Business at Ohio University was prompted by criticism of graduate business education. The popular business press published several reports critical of business education during the early 1980s (e.g., Business Higher Education Forum, 1985). Business schools were chastised for being too theoretical and out of touch with business realities, for producing narrow-minded technicians who lack interpersonal and communication skills, and for concentrating on esoteric research that has little if anything to do with the business world (Stinson & Milter, 1996). While some of the reports were sensationalized and demonstrated a lack of understanding of both business schools and the business world, there was some merit to the concerns expressed (Porter & McKibbin, 1988). Many business schools heard from members of their executive advisory boards that graduates were not well prepared for the business world. They noted that graduates did not have a realistic understanding of the business world, they criticized graduates for ineffective communication skills, they noted the lack of leadership skills, and they commented on the need to train new graduates and teach them concepts they had supposedly learned in school. In response to those concerns, a complete redesign of the Ohio University curricula was performed that included both content changes and development of new learning methodologies (Milter, 2002).

In our view, it is only more recently that a growing awareness has developed in management education—or more broadly the domain of business education—that innovation should be an inherent process of business schools. Despite few noted examples—for example, the curriculum change process at the Weatherhead School of Management in the early 1990s (Boyatzis, Cowen, & Kolb, 1995)—it is our impression that many innovations may occur at the course level, but few exist at the program level. Current criticisms on the nature of business education seem to be fueled by two leading arguments (Mintzberg, 2004; Bennis & O'Toole, 2005). First, the question is raised whether business school curricula overemphasize that management is a science and not a profession based on best-evidence practices. Authors such as Mintzberg (2004) and Bennis and O'Toole (2005) claim that business schools are overly scientific and out of touch with business realities, concentrating on research that has little to do with the needs of business world. Second, it has been argued that business graduates do not have a realistic understanding of the business world. These critics argue that graduates are not prepared to approach work situations in ways that respond to the key demands of the business (Bigelow, 2001). Although critics do not seem to offer profound empirical basis in educational, methodological, or psychological research, they do provide food for thought about how business curricula may contribute to student acquisition of managerial competencies. Researchers such as Isenberg (1984, 1986), Wagner (1991, 2002), and Walsh (1995) are among the few who have tried to address practical aspects of managerial work and investigated its implications for the development of managerial expertise by conducting research with a strong basis in cognitive psychology.

The leadership of the ED*i*NEB Network recognized from its very start the need for educational research that addresses critical issues in business and economics education. For that purpose we started the book series called Educational Innovation in Economics and Business, published by Kluwer Academic Publishers (today, Springer Publishers). This book series contains selected and peer-reviewed papers from the annual international conferences. Since our start in 1993, the ED*i*NEB Network has published ten volumes, each addressing different themes. For each volume we collected both research-driven papers and examples from best practices regarding innovation in business education. More information about this book series can be found at: http://www.springer.com. In 2006 we introduced our new publication initiative the book series "Advances in Business Education and Training" (again published by Springer Publishers) that allows us to function more as a peer-reviewed journal. Our book series is no longer solely based on selected conference papers, as editors may decide to invite authors or to include special sections in a book on key issues. This book series is considered to be the successor of our book series Educational Innovation in Economics and Business.

INNOVATION AS A LEAD

As soon as you structure the process it becomes a routine. Once you think you have it, you lost it. You can't be a purist as an innovator.

In the beginning of the ED*i*NEB Network our thinking was dominated by people who were involved with research and development of problem-based learning. Clearly, in those days there was a definite need for knowledge about how to implement one of the most successful innovations in medical education that seemed to be very suitable for business education. But it soon became clear that business educators were looking for a variety of innovations that may address different elements of business education. The introduction of new Web technologies also served as a catalyst in this development because it allowed educators to experiment with an unmatched availability of new approaches to course and program design. As a consequence, a strong move occurred toward understanding elements of the innovation process. Educators wanted to design their new educational approaches themselves instead of copying established practices. Contributions to our annual conference shifted toward questions around how to implement change, how to sustain change, how to keep track of changes in other environments, and how to build bridges with the corporate world.

The issue of building bridges with the corporate world has been a source of constant debate within our network. Pure academics (representing the domain of economics) doubted the value of including business practitioners in our mix. Others in our ranks believe that collaborating with leaders in the corporate and government sectors is vital to developing the types of educational environments that produce leaders with the requisite knowledge and skills to meet future challenges. This debate reinforces our earlier point that insights from educational research should provide the basis for future curriculum reform.

Since research in the domain of business education is relatively underdeveloped, we call for research on effects of innovations in business education. In addition, research on innovation in business education is also very justified. Understanding the process of implementing innovation is crucial, because it has been claimed that many innovations fail, stall prematurely, or achieve unintended results (Boonstra, 2004). Recent business research demonstrates how difficult it is to disseminate knowledge to others in the same firm, meeting little success in sharing expertise when aiming to innovate business processes (Hinds & Pfeffer, 2003).

Next to its emphasis on educational research and theory development in the field of business education, the ED*i*NEB Network has paid substantial attention to issues that are inherent to innovation and change processes. It is our experience that many individuals who are leading change processes within their organization are lone rangers without sufficient support from their deans or directors. Our network organization offers them an opportunity to meet others, become aware of best practices and relevant research findings, receive feedback regarding their own reports on practice and/or research findings, and publish their work in our book series.

THE EDINEB NETWORK: WWW.EDINEB.NET

It is a true community. It is kind of homecoming for the old members. For the new members, they realize they have an opportunity to reflect upon what they are doing. They commiserate on the struggles of the innovator.

The ED*i*NEB Network was founded at the end of the 1993 conference organized by a scientific committee that was passionate about educational innovation and problem-based learning. The Faculty of Economics and Business Administration of Maastricht University decided to support this committee by provision of a substantial grant, the help of a skilled conference secretariat (Mrs. Mieke van Zutphen), and support of a managing director (Mr. Rene Verspeek). After the conference the members of the scientific committee served as editors for our first book publication (Gijselaers et al., 1995). This conference was a success for its participants and provided crucial support for Maastricht University to continue its efforts in developing problem-based programs in business and economics. Soon after this conference, an international board was established representing various international partner institutions interested in innovation: Maastricht University (Netherlands), Napier University (UK), Ohio University (USA), and Uppsala University (Sweden). The home office for this network was provided by Maastricht University, which took care of its secretariat (Mrs. Ellen Nelissen), and the EDiNEB foundation supported the international board. In 1994 we launched our first international workshop on the design of problem-based learning in business education, soon followed by our second international conference at Uppsala University, Sweden. From that time forward, EDiNEB has successfully organized annual international conferences in Europe and North America. Although conference participants can include representation from as many as 25 countries from across every continent (except Antarctica; for some reason educational innovation isn't a draw there), we purposefully remain a fairly small international community, attracting a total of between 100 and 200 international visitors at our conferences. Our workshops are typically limited to 25 participants. Each conference spurred the composition of an edited volume of selected "best of class" conference papers for our book series.

The EDiNEB Network was initially supported by the EDiNEB Foundation at Maastricht University and led by the executive board. The executive board enjoyed membership from both academic and industry leaders of innovation in both Europe and the United States. The authors of this chapter have each had the privilege of serving as the only two chairs of the board since its founding. The executive board worked closely with the foundation and the secretariat in developing the mission, goals, venue selection, and schedule of each year's activities as well as leading in structuring the peer-review process for the selection of paper presentations and organizing the annual conference. The editors of the quarterly newsletter and book series also came from within the ranks of the executive board.

Most recently the EDiNEB Network has sought to gain additional corporate support as its members seek to more deeply integrate their research and teaching with the realities of business practice. There have been bold and exciting partnerships formed by its members as they seek to reinvent their processes to train future business professionals. The value of the annual conferences and workshop offerings is clear and remains appealing to a wide spectrum of business educators in both academic and industry settings. Moving toward the use of other sharing and collaborative options via technology has been a major agenda item for the past several years. We have moved to an online newsletter and have provided our conference content including abstracts and papers on our website: www.edineb.net. We have also provided a password-protected platform for discussion between members regarding research efforts and consulting options. The difficulty with our online collaboration is providing a compelling reason for members to make a regular visit to the site.

CONCLUSION: BEING AND BECOMING A SCHOLAR IN MANAGEMENT EDUCATION

You need substance to make an impact.

"Publish or Perish" also counts for educational innovation. Making a true impact on the processes of educational innovation in any domain or profession requires that work on best practices, theoretical reflections on practice, or research on theory or practice needs to get published. Starting broad discussions about curriculum philosophy, instructional methods, or teaching is a necessary but not sufficient condition to keep an innovation going or to sustain and improve the innovation. Publications serve an important role in this because it legitimizes the innovation and opens it up for external validation by peers, institutions for business education, and accreditation agencies. It is for that particular reason that the EDiNEB network has developed the book series Educational Innovation in Economics and Business and its successor Advances in Business Education and Training that selects and publishes the best work of our members.

The book series plays a key role in the network because it promotes advanced understanding of the most important activity of business schools: preparing people for business practice. However, our understanding of what contributes to the development of qualified business professionals is still fairly limited. Criticisms on what business schools do in preparing students for practice are substantial (e.g., Crainer & Dearlove, 1998). Unfortunately, these criticisms lack sufficient guidance for redesign of business curricula. We should not rely on our intuition when designing curricula, but apply the same academic scrutiny on our curriculum thoughts as we do in business research (Milter, 2000).

In hindsight, we notice that the book series started as a set of volumes addressing issues of innovative instructional methods. Later, a shift was made to target more strategic issues focusing on the impact of globalization on business curricula, assessment of links between the workplace and education, and development of alliances in university education. Research and educational development have been the drivers for many articles in our book series. Contributions draw upon a rich array of international business educators who are standing with their feet in the clay of educational practice and who are capable of building impressive learning designs upon it.

"Meet the lone ranger" has become another crucial element for innovators working alone on course changes. Organizing support from others in various ways is essential in order to keep the efforts going. Getting inspiration from leaders in the field or by reading daring publications on reform in business education is one part of the story. The other part is that innovators recognize similarities in experience of others, get support from the leaders who did it, and develop research ideas that help them gain external validation. It has always been the aim of the ED*i*NEB network to provide such a platform.

REFERENCES

Ball, S.R. (2006). Bridging The Gap: A model for graduate management education. In C.Wankel & R. DeFilippi (Eds.), *New Visions of Graduate Management Education* (pp. 87–106). Greenwich, CT: Information Age Publishing.
Barsky, N.P., Catanach, A.H., & Stout, D.E. (2002). A PBL framework for introductory management accounting. In A. Bentzen-Bilkvist, W.H. Gijselaers & R.G. Milter (Eds.), *Educating knowledge workers for corporate leadership: Learning into the future* (pp. 3–20). Boston, Dordrecht, London: Kluwer Academic Publishers.
Bennis, W.G, & O'Toole, J. (2005). How business schools lost their way. *Harvard Business Review, May,* 1–9.
Bigelow, J.D. (2001). Preparing undergraduates for organizational situations: A frames/problem-based approach. Unpublished paper, Boise State University.
Bland, C. Starnaman, S., Harris, D., Wersal, L., Moorhead-Rosenberg, L., Zonia, S., & Henry, R. (2000). Curricular change in medical schools: how to succeed. *Academic Medicine, 75,* 575–594.
Boonstra, J. (Ed.) (2004). *Dynamics of organizational change and learning.* Sussex: John Wiley.
Boud, D., & Feletti, G. (1991). *The challenge of problem-based learning.* London: Kogan Page.
Boyatzis, R.E., Cowen, S.S., Kolb, D.A., & Associates (1995). *Innovation in professional education: Steps on a journey from teaching to learning.* San Francisco: Jossey-Bass Publishers.
Brassington, F., & Smith, A. (2000). Competition and problem-based learning: The effect of an externally set competition on a cross-curricular project in marketing and design. In L. Borghans, W.H. Gijselaers, R.G. Milter & J.E. Stinson (Eds.), *Business education for the changing workplace* (pp. 187–208). Boston, Dordrecht, London: Kluwer.
Business Higher Education Forum (1985). America's Business Schools: Priorities for Change, Report to the President.
Crainer, S. & Dearlove, D. (1998). *Gravy training: Inside the shadowy world of business schools.* Oxford: Capstone Publishing.
De Graaff, E., & Kolmos, A. (2003). Characteristics of problem-based learning. *International Journal of Engineering Education, 19*(5), 657–662.
Dede, C., Honan, J.P., & Peters, L.C. (Eds.) (2005). *Scaling up success: Lessons learned from technology-based educational improvement.* San Francisco: Jossey-Bass.
Forsythe, F.P. (2002). The role of problem-based learning and technology support in a "spoon-fed" undergraduate environment. In T.A. Johannesen, A. Pedersen & K. Petersen (Eds.), *Teaching today the knowledge of tomorrow* (pp. 147–162). Boston, Dordrecht, London: Kluwer.

Gijselaers, W.H. (1996). Connecting problem-based practices with educational theory. In L. Wilkerson & W.H. Gijselaers (Eds.), *Bringing problem-based learning to higher education: Theory and practice* (pp. 13–22). San Francisco: Jossey-Bass.

Gijselaers, W.H., Tempelaar, D.T., Keizer, P.K., Blommaert, J.M., Bernard, E.M., & Kasper, H. (Eds.) (1995). *Educational innovation in economics and business administration: The case of problem-based learning.* Dordrecht, Boston, London: Kluwer.

Hinds, P.J., & Pfeffer, J. (2003). Why organizations don't "know what they know": Cognitive and motivational factors affecting the transfer of expertise. In M. Ackerman, V. Pipek, & V. Wulf (Eds.), *Sharing expertise: Beyond knowledge management* (pp. 3–26). Cambridge, MA: MIT Press.

Isenberg, D.J. (1984). How senior managers think. *Harvard Business Review, 62*(6), 80–90.

Isenberg, D.J. (1986). Thinking and managing: A verbal protocol analysis of managerial problem solving. *Academy of Management Journal, 4,* 775–788.

Knowlton, D.S., & Sharpe, D.C. (2003). Problem-based learning in the information age. *New Directions in Teaching and Learning, 95.*

Milter, R.G. (2000). Innovation in learning methodologies for adult learners: Implications for theory and practice. *Virtual University Journal, 3*(6), 228–236.

Milter, R.G. (2002). Developing an MBA online degree program: Expanding knowledge and skills via technology-mediated learning communities. In P. Comeaux (Ed.), *Communication and collaboration in the online classroom: Examples and applications* (pp. 3–22). Boston, MA: Jossey-Bass, Anker Publishing.

Milter, R.G. & Stinson, J.E. (1995). Educating leaders for the new competitive environment. In W.H. Gijselaers et al. (Eds.), *Educational innovation in economics and business administration: The case of problem-based learning* (pp. 30–38). Dordrecht: Kluwer Academic Publishers.

Mintzberg, H. (2004). *Managers not MBAS.* London: Prentice Hall.

Porter, L., & McKibbin, L. (1988). *Management education and development: Drift or thrust into the 21st century.* New York: McGraw-Hill.

Söderlund, M. (1998). Problem-based learning, interpersonal orientations and learning approaches: An empirical examination of a business education program. In D.T. Tempelaar, F. Wiedersheim-Paul, & E. Gunnarsson (Eds.), *In search of quality* (pp. 155–170). Dordrecht: Kluwer Academic Publishers.

Stinson, J.E. & Milter, R.G. (1996). Problem-based learning in business education: Curriculum design and implementation issues. In L. Wilkerson & W.H. Gijselaers (Eds.), *Bringing problem-based learning to higher education: Theory and practice* (pp. 13–22). San Francisco: Jossey-Bass.

Stone Wiske, M., & Perkins, D. (2005). Dewey goes digital: Scaling up constructivist pedagogies and the promise of new technologies. In C. Dede, J.P. Honan, & L.C. Peters (Eds.), *Scaling up success: Lessons learned from technology-based educational improvement* (pp. 27–47). San Francisco: Jossey-Bass.

Wagner, R.K. (1991). Managerial problem solving. In R.J. Sternberg & P.A. Frensch (Eds.), *Complex problem solving: Principles and mechanisms* (pp. 159–184). Hillsdale, NJ: Lawrence Erlbaum Associates.

Wagner, R.K. (2002). Smart people doing dumb things: The case of managerial incompetence. In R.J. Sternberg (Ed.), *Why smart people can be so stupid* (pp. 42–63). Yale: Yale University Press.

Walsh, J. P. (1995). Managerial and organizational cognition: Notes from a trip down memory lane. *Organizational Science, 6,* 280–321.

Wilkerson, L., & Gijselaers, W.H. (Eds.) (1996). *Bringing problem-based learning to higher education: Theory and practice.* San Francisco: Jossey-Bass.

Yost, E.B., & Keifer, J.L. (1998). Application of problem-based learning pedagogy to management education. In R.G. Milter, J.E. Stinson, W.H. Gijselaers (Eds.), *Innovative practices in business education* (pp. 283–300). Dordrecht: Kluwer.

CHAPTER 10

THE DIVERSITY OF TRAJECTORIES IN MANAGEMENT EDUCATION RESEARCH

Charles Wankel

ABSTRACT

The highways and byways by which one can enter into and traverse management education scholarship are quite diverse. This chapter displays how a career focus on management education scholarship can be grounded in professional service as an official of scholarly societies, such as the Academy of Management, Management Education and Development Division; serving as an editor of journals and book series on management education research; textbooks translating management research for educators and learners; and virtual communities that act as forums for management education researchers to partner and share information about meetings and other activities. Management education research is increasingly an endeavor of global teams who report on management education phenomena that are increasingly convergent.

Being and Becoming a Management Education Scholar, pages 175–182
Copyright © 2010 by Information Age Publishing
All rights of reproduction in any form reserved.

175

TEXTBOOKS AS CONDUITS OF MANAGEMENT RESEARCH INTO MANAGEMENT EDUCATION

My first writing endeavor in management education was as coauthor with James Stoner of Fordham University of an introductory management textbook for Prentice Hall (Stoner & Wankel, 1986) more than twenty years ago. The research grounding this book was planned from a number of directions. We wanted to understand all the topics covered by all of the other management textbooks and decide which topics were probably expected by adopters, and of the less common topics, which ones did we feel would be interesting to use. This benchmarking helped us create structures for our chapters that we were confident about. For each topic, we made a list of all of the original sources that had been used by the gamut of competitor textbooks as a way of understanding the primary literature that would be best to write from. Those included classic articles and books, as well as the literature critiquing and extending them. We also used the ISI Social Sciences Citation Index (SSCI, Social Scisearch) and other periodical indexes to identify cutting-edge material. To receive these articles quickly we typically leveraged the affiliation and addresses included in the SSCI by sending off a request to the corresponding author of each article for a copy, as well as copies of any related articles or working papers that they might provide. We had access to the libraries of many large universities including NYU, Columbia, Fordham, and Yale, as well as the large New York Public Library system. Our textbook succeeded in the market, and we would like to think it was due to our thoroughness in benchmarking and researching the topics that would be most appreciated by instructors and students.

A NEW TEXTBOOK FOR THE TWENTY-FIRST CENTURY

I am currently leading the development of *Management through Collaboration: Teaming in a Networked World* (Wankel et al., in press), a new introductory management textbook for Routledge Publishers. This leverages the opportunities and expectations of the second decade of the twenty-first century. I wished to work with a global team to create a textbook that would transcend the U.S. mindset and provide the richness of extensive international examples, cases, and perspectives. My initial thought was to look at the programs of important conferences to locate people who are experts in topics covered in an introductory management book. I found many prospects who I thought would be ideal. I then searched through my connections in LinkedIn and Facebook and found hundreds of others whom I recruited (I have almost 6000 such connections). However, when I finally tallied acceptances, I found I had recruited 930 coauthors in 90 nations. Though

I did not know the term at the time I initiated the project, I agree with the *Chronicle of Higher Education* when they characterize it as crowdsourcing (Young, 2008). The coauthors include management professors in far-flung places such as Iran, Botswana, Peru, Tonga, Iceland, and Grenada. I found scholars in more remote nations to be more likely to be enthusiastic about a global collaboration than those in leading western nations.

Wanting to provide a truly 21st century experience to our learners, I endeavored to develop teams of people to bring in new media in important ways. Andrei Villarroel of the Sloan School of Management at MIT agreed to head up the Facebook part of the project. A Facebook group was set up and people in the project were invited to join. Exercises involving the use of Facebook are being planned for the book and its ancillaries. A key idea in this respect is to have learners create announcements of events using the Facebook events utility. For example, students might be instructed to use Facebook to construct teams for class projects or to create co-curricular events involving their universities' larger population of students on Facebook for such endeavors as service learning related activities.

I enlisted William "Bill" Sodeman of Hawaii Pacific University in Honolulu to head up an effort to develop LinkedIn exercises for the book. He started a LinkedIn group for members of the project that enables us to understand their backgrounds better and also serves as a backup for tracking changes and their affiliation and contact information. The sorts of exercises that we are experimenting with include having learners join their university's alumni group and then connect with alumni, adding them as contacts, asking them for career advice, and so on. Using the LinkedIn query utility, learners will be required to ask topical questions in LinkedIn forums on issues that they are interested in and develop dialogues with those respondents who seem most informed. Using geographical, industry, current position, past positions, and so on as search dimensions, learners will be instructed about developing and using contacts in LinkedIn. Bill has also taken on the development and management of our book project's website.

I see streaming media as very important for a book at this time. A key purpose will be to film interviews with managers around the world to be edited into multimedia case studies. Also, video discussion of topics, available as podcasts, will be produced. Guest e-lecturers from around the world will be provided in this medium too. My initial thought was to have a management professor head up this effort, so I appointed Jon Billingsley of the Open University (now of the University of Coventry) to take this on. However, we realized that the scope of it was beyond a single faculty member's time and abilities. I then came up with the notion of using LinkedIn to locate a world-class expert in streaming media. I went through several hundred who came up in targeted searches. I decided upon a 2007 Webby Award honoree with experience in successful YouTube program development who headed up a leading media firm: J. Sibley Law of Saxon Mills in Stratford, CT. Sibley has provided many great ideas such as using the very inexpensive but high quality Flip cameras to readily equip book project members. Also, he has developed video tutorials on selecting and using equipment. Andy Ngo, A member of the project in Ho Chi Minh City, Vietnam, has worked with Sibley to develop a site to which videos made by project members around the world can be uploaded for Sibley to download in his office.

Jūratė Stanaitytė of Stockholm University has taken on the role of book project manager. She has used Survey Monkey software to collect contact information for all the members of the project as well as information on their topical expertise and key publications. She has worked with website and wiki directors to make those efforts work. Truly she is a secret of the success of the project.

Charles Livermore, a colleague of mine at St. John's University, has created a wiki for our project. Its main structure reflects that of the book's chapters. Most chapter editors have directed their teams to add to versions of the chapters using this collaborative software. Also, chapter structures derived by the chapter editors benchmarking of a dozen competing books is communicated there too. Jūratė Stanaitytė has worked with Charles Livermore in troubleshooting problems in the wiki and facilitating access for members.

Yvonne "YL" Catino has taken on the role of Case Studies Director. She has conducted more than a thousand interviews in her career in human resources management and has distributed directions on case studies development to project members. She is working on coordinating teams who are working on important cases. She and Sibley are working together to mentor and facilitate members in creating video interviews and developing them into multimedia case studies. The intention is to have interviews done in a multitude of languages and at times use subtitles to share them beyond the linguistic group. However, since our book will be used in many nations it would be possible to have material, say, in Japanese that could be left in Japanese if the interest in it is perceived as being limited to Japanese-speaking people.

THE MANAGEMENT EDUCATION AND DEVELOPMENT DIVISION OF THE ACADEMY OF MANAGEMENT

One route to involvement in management education scholarship is through active involvement in the Academy of Management Management Education and Development Division (MED) or the Organizational Behavior Teaching Society (OBTS). I have been involved with both. However, my main involvement has been with MED. MED is a venue that welcomes both quantitative and qualitative scholarly research of management education. It sponsors scholarly paper sessions, symposia (which are either discussions among panelists or a coordinated sequence of paper presentations), and professional development workshops. I coauthored a paper on teaching quality management with Jim Stoner for the 1991 Academy of Management meeting that won MED's Best Paper in Management Development Award. This honor included an invitation to revise and submit a version of the paper to the *Journal of Management Development* (Stoner & Wankel, 1993). Through this experience I started attending the business meetings of MED and was nominated to run for Secretary of MED. It is possible to volunteer to run for many offices or to volunteer for appointment to other offices in MED, which has scores of positions. I volunteered in 1996 to initiate a virtual community (listserv) for MED called MG-ED-DV, which is ongoing under my direction. I found that running a virtual community for an AOM division like MED is a way to have many hundreds of people get to know you. So, for example, I signed messages for a while with the closing "cybercollegially" and when I would go to the annual AOM meeting I would have more than a hundred strangers wave and say "Hi, cybercolleague!" as they walked by.

I was nominated and elected to the top offices in MED in 1997 and served as MED Program Chair for the 1998 San Diego meeting and I was the Division Chair for 1999–2000. As Program Chair I was able to solicit management education research in areas that I felt were underrepresented. I found being Division Chair was an opportunity to bring into leadership positions about sixty management education scholars from around the world as liaisons for their countries or regions, or as the chairs of management education topical areas, such as simulations or service learning. These new officers were charged with creating interesting opportunities for symposia at the annual meeting or helping to arrange meetings in far-flung places with MED co-sponsorship. M. Omar Hefni of the United Arab Emirates University in Al Ain, UAE, agreed to cosponsor with MED a meeting in Al Ain in the spring of 2000. This was the only international meeting cosponsored by the MED division, and it was successful. Yugi Yoshida of the Chiba University of Commerce in Japan, as our Liaison to Japan, initiated a long-running series of annual exchanges between MED and the Nippon Academy of Management Education (NAME). Many MED and NAME scholars presented at each other's meetings in very helpful ways. I was one of the Americans from MED who participated in this exchange.

Another opportunity that derived from my leadership role in the MED Division was my appointment as an ad hoc special issue editor of the *Academy of Management Journal* millennial issue.

I encourage all AOM members to become active in a division. Most have roles even for doctoral students. All seek to maximize the involvement of those located beyond the U.S. and Canada. Certainly the MED Division has prided itself on being open to self-nominations of interested members.

THE RESEARCH IN MANAGEMENT EDUCATION AND DEVELOPMENT SERIES

In August 2000, I was approached by George Johnson of Information Age Publishing (IAP) with an offer to be editor of a series entitled Research in Management Education and Development. I invited Robert DeFillippi of Suffolk University to join me as coeditor. IAP is a great publisher to work with as they view their editors as the content experts and defer to their decisions readily. The initial volume, *Rethinking Management Education for the 21st Century* (Wankel & DeFillippi, 2002) was trailblazing in having a chapter on "Arts-Based Learning in Management Education," by Nick Nissley. We also pointedly include a number of chapters on corporate universities and executive education. Our second volume, *Educating Managers with Tomorrow's Technologies* (Wankel & DeFillippi, 2003), strove to include research on emerging management education topics such as "Innovations in Web-Format Case Teaching: Leveraging Dynamic Information," by Delwyn Clark and "Electronic Student Portfolios in Management Education," by David Chappell and John Schermerhorn. After having our introductory overview of the scope of management education research and our volume on research of new management education technologies, we decided on a volume on *The Cutting Edge of International Management Education* (Wankel & DeFillippi, 2004), which included articles on French and Chinese management education. Our volume *Educating Managers through Real World Projects* (Wankel & DeFillippi, 2005) included "*Real* real world projects," by Mats Lundeberg and Pär Mårtensson, which discussed research on making management education a revenue center for a corporation, rather than a cost center, by a university's working with a company to develop course work around important projects. Also, a chapter on "Work Embedded E-learning" by Paul Shrivastava of Bucknell University (now of Concordia University) was excitingly provocative. *New Visions of Graduate Management Education* (Wankel & DeFillippi, 2006) included research on "A Practice-Centered Approach to Management Education" by Mark Fenton-O'Creevy, Peter Knight, and Judith Margolis. *University and Corporate Innovations in Lifelong Learning* (Wankel & DeFillippi, 2007) included "Developing Learning Communities in Executive Education: A Case Study of a Global Senior Executive Program" by Schon Beechler, Lyle Yorks, and Rachel Ciporen. More recently the series has focused on the AOM 2009 annual meeting sustainability theme with *Management Education for Global Sustainability* (Wankel & Stoner, 2009). The volume you are reading now, *Being and Becoming a Management Education Scholar* (Wankel & DeFillippi, 2009) starkly shows us the limited venues for researching management education but also their quality and importance.

CONCLUSION

There are manifold ways to embark on a career as a management education scholar. This chapter shows examples of how management education scholarship can be based in professional service as an official of scholarly societies such as the Academy of Management, Management Education and Development Division; as an editor of journals and book series on management education research; as a textbook author translating management research for educators and learners; and as a member of virtual communities that act as forums for management education researchers to partner and share information about meetings and other activities. Management education is currently a global endeavor with opportunities to collaborate on comparative qualitative and quantitative research with partners from places as diverse, in my case, as Iran, Tonga, Peru, Botswana, Iceland, and Grenada.

REFERENCES

Stoner, J. A.F., & Wankel, C. (1986). *Management* (3rd ed.). Upper Saddle River, NJ: Prentice Hall.

Stoner, J.A.F. & Wankel, C. (1993). Putting total quality management into contemporary Polish management development" *Journal of Management Development. 12*(3), 65–72.

Wankel, C., et al. (in press). *Management through collaboration: Teaming in a networked world.* New York: Routledge.

Wankel. C., & DeFillippi, R. (Eds). (2002). *Rethinking management education for the 21st century.* Greenwich, CT: Information Age Publishing.

Wankel. C., & DeFillippi, R. (Eds). (2003). *Educating managers with tomorrow's technologies.* Greenwich, CT: Information Age Publishing.

Wankel. C., & DeFillippi, R. (Eds). (2004). *The cutting edge of international management education.* Greenwich, CT: Information Age Publishing.

Wankel. C., & DeFillippi, R. (Eds). (2005). *Educating managers through real world projects.* Greenwich, CT: Information Age Publishing.

Wankel. C., & DeFillippi, R. (Eds). (2006). *New visions of graduate management education.* Greenwich, CT: Information Age Publishing.

Wankel. C., & DeFillippi, R. (Eds). (2007). *University and corporate innovations in lifelong learning.* Greenwich, CT: Information Age Publishing.

Wankel. C., & DeFillippi, R. (Eds). (2009). *Being and becoming a management education scholar.* Charlotte, NC: Information Age Publishing.

Wankel. C., & Stoner, J.A.F. (Eds.). (2009). *Management education for global sustainability.* Charlotte, NC: Information Age Publishing.

Young, J.R. (2008, August 15). Management professor uses "crowdsourcing" to write textbook. *Chronicle of Higher Education (The Wired Campus).* Accessed July 30, 2009 from http://chronicle.com/blogPost/Management-Professor-Uses/4173

ABOUT THE CONTRIBUTORS

J. B. (Ben) Arbaugh is a Professor of Strategy and Project Management at the University of Wisconsin–Oshkosh. He received his PhD in Business Strategy from the Ohio State University. Ben currently is editor of *Academy of Management Learning & Education* and is a past chair of the Management Education and Development Division of the Academy of Management. Ben's online teaching research has won best article awards from the *Journal of Management Education* and the *Decision Sciences Journal of Innovative Education*. His other research interests are in graduate management education and the intersection between spirituality and strategic management research.

Steven Armstrong is Director of Research and Professor of Organizational Behavior at Hull University Business School in the UK. Steve is past president of the Management Education and Development Division of the Academy of Management and a council member of the British Academy of Management, where he serves as editor-in-chief of the Academy's *International Journal of Management Reviews* (Wiley-Blackwell). He is also a member of the Chartered Institute of Management and remains a Chartered Engineer and a member of the Institution of Engineering and Technology.

James R. Bailey is the Tucker Professor of Leadership and Chair of the Department of Management at the George Washington University School of Business. He has received numerous teaching awards and has published over 50 academic papers and case studies in several books. He served as associate editor of the *Academy of Management Learning and Education* from 2000–2004 and editor from 2004–2008.

Being and Becoming a Management Education Scholar, pages 183–187
Copyright © 2010 by Information Age Publishing
All rights of reproduction in any form reserved.

Joy E. Beatty is an assistant professor of organizational behavior at the University of Michigan–Dearborn. She received her PhD from Boston College. Her research interests are gender and diversity and management education. She is a member of the editorial board of the *Academy of Management Learning and Education.* Her pedagogy research has appeared in *Journal of Management Education* and *Academy of Management Learning and Education.*

Robert Chia is Professor of Management, University of Strathclyde Business School and Emeritus Professor of Management, University of Aberdeen. He received his PhD in Organization Studies from Lancaster University in 1992. Prior to entering academia he held senior management positions in manufacturing and human resources for a large multinational corporation based in the Asia-Pacific region. He is a Fellow of the Royal Society of Arts and Manufacture (RSA) UK. His research focuses on the complex educational process of transmitting knowledge, attitude and predisposition necessary for enhancing life chances and for engaging in productive and sustainable wealth-creating initiatives.

Laurence de Carlo, Ph.D., is Professor at ESSEC Business School, Paris. She teaches and conducts research in consultation, negotiation and mediation in complex decision processes. She progressively developed ways of teaching that include a personal development dimension. Part of her research reflects on these teaching methods. MBTI and Golden certified, she coaches students and participants in continuing education. She has also handled institutional projects related to pedagogical innovations at ESSEC. Her research has been published in the *Negotiation Journal, Conflict Resolution Quarterly, International Studies of Management and Organizations, Négociations, Revue Française de Gestion,* etc.

Gordon E. Dehler is on the management faculty at the College of Charleston. He received his PhD from the University of Cincinnati. His interests center on critical approaches to reform in management education and learning, managing, and organizing—that is, adopting positions that challenge established management orthodoxies. His work has been published in *Management Learning, Journal of Management Education, Academy of Management Journal,* and *Journal of Managerial Psychology,* in addition to several book chapters. He is a former associate editor of the journal *Management Learning* (2002–2008) and *Journal of Management Education* (2000–2002).

Robert DeFillippi is Professor of Management, Director of the Center for Innovation and Change Leadership and Academic Director for the Innovation and Design Management Executive MBA concentration at Suffolk University's Sawyer Business School in Boston. He is the author of over thirty-five journal publications and seven books. His research, teaching, and consulting practice focuses on creative collaborations and knowledge-based perspectives on innovation. Professor DeFillippi's empirical research typically compares U.S. and European practices, and he lectures regularly in Europe, with presentations at the following European business schools: Bocconi University, Cambridge University, Erasmus University Rotterdam School of Management, Free University of Berlin, Linkoping University, London Business School, Manchester Business School, University of Hull and University of Sussex. Moreover, he is a four-time visiting professor at City University (now Cass) Business School (London), an Advanced Institute of Management International Visiting Fellow at Tanaka Business School of Imperial College of London, a Research Fellow at the Freeman Innovation Center, Universities of Sussex and Brighton, and four-time visiting lecturer at Institut d'Administration des Enterprises–Aix-en-Provence, Universite de Marseille. Dr. DeFillippi is also associate editor for the *International Journal of Management,* and he has served as guest editor for special issues of *Management Learning* (2001), *Organization Studies* (2004) and *Journal of Organizational Behavior* (2007).

William P. Ferris is Professor of Management at Western New England College. As an original task force member, charter editorial board member, author of *Academy of Management Learning & Education* essays and a review, past MED Academy of Management chair, and reviewer, he has been in a unique place to observe the journey of *AMLE* during its first several years. Bill writes articles on management education, leadership, and other topics, and is currently editor-in-chief of *Organization Management Journal,* the official journal of the Eastern Academy of Management, published by Palgrave MacMillan.

Cynthia V. Fukami, PhD, is Professor of Management at the Daniels College of Business, University of Denver. In addition to her disciplinary contributions, Cindi has published some 12 articles and made over 25 presentations at scholarly meetings on the scholarship of teaching and learning. Cindi has served as chair of the Academy of Management's Teaching Committee, and on the board of directors (two years as board chair) of the OB Teaching Society. She was associate editor of the *Journal of Management Education* from 1997–2000, and again from 2005–2007, and was an associate editor of *Academy of Management Learning and Education* from 2001–2005. She remains on both editorial boards. Cindi was appointed as a Fellow of the Carnegie Foundation for the Advancement of Teaching in 1999. With Stephen J. Armstrong, she edited the *Handbook of Managerial Learning, Education, and Development,* published by SAGE in 2009.

Wim H. Gijselaers, professor of education, received his PhD from Maastricht University. His research interests are cognition and learning, expertise development in management, and team learning. His most recent publications have appeared in *Learning and Instruction, Contemporary Educational Psychology,* and *Small Group Research.* He chairs the international ED*i*NEB network (http://www.edineb.net/), which promotes advances in business education and training.

Jennifer S. A. Leigh is an assistant professor of management at Nazareth College of Rochester. Her research addresses management education and inter-organizational relationships, particularly cross-sector partnerships and corporate social responsibility. Recent publications focus on teaching philosophies, information literacy for undergraduate management students, the scholarship of teaching and learning, and responsible supply chain management. She teaches courses in organizational behavior, managerial ethics, leadership, organizations and society, gender in management, and organizational change.

Roy J. Lewicki is the Irving Abramowitz Professor of Business Ethics and Professor of Management and Human Resources at the Max M. Fisher College of Business, the Ohio State University. Professor Lewicki received his BA in Psychology from Dartmouth College and his PhD in Social Psychology from Columbia University. Professor Lewicki maintains research and teaching interests in the fields of negotiation and dispute resolution, trust development, managerial leadership, organizational justice, and ethical decision making.

Rick Milter, PhD, is Professor of Management and director of the MBA Fellows program in the Carey Business School at Johns Hopkins University. Rick has worked with faculty teams in several institutions around the globe in developing inquiry-based and action learning programs. Rick co-designed and served as director for a project-based action learning MBA program that achieved award recognition for "best practice" by the International Association for Management Education (AACSB) and "creative excellence" by the University Continuing Education Association (UCEA). Rick is a former chairman of the ED*i*NEB Network and currently serves as associate editor of the Springer Publishing series Advances in Business Education and Training; he also serves on the editorial boards of the Information Age Publishing series Research in Management Education and Development and the Springer Verlag Publishing series Innovation and Change in Professional Education.

Jane Schmidt-Wilk, PhD, is Associate Professor of Management, co-director of the PhD Program in Management, and director of the Center for Management Research at Maharishi University of Management, Fairfield, IA. Her workshop presentations and publications explore the role of development of consciousness in business and management education. She served on the Board of Directors of the OBTS Teaching Society for Management Educators from 2003–2005. She has been editor of the *Journal of Management Education* since 2005 and serves on the editorial boards of the *Journal of Management Spirituality, and Religion* and the *Organization Management Journal.*

Charles Wankel is Associate Professor of Management at St. John's University, New York. He received his doctorate from New York University. Dr. Wankel has authored and edited many books including the best-selling *Management,* 3rd ed. (Prentice-Hall, 1986), *Rethinking Management Education for the 21st Century* (IAP, 2002), *Educating Managers with Tomorrow's Technologies* (IAP, 2003), *The Cutting-Edge of International Management Education* (IAP, 2004), *Educating Managers through Real World Projects* (IAP, 2005), *New Visions of Graduate Management Education* (IAP, 2006), the *Handbook of 21st Century Management* (SAGE, 2008), and *Being and Becoming a Management Education Scholar* (IAP, 2008). He is the leading founder and director of scholarly virtual communities for management professors, currently directing eight with thousands of participants in more than seventy nations. He has taught in Lithuania at the Kaunas University of Technology (Fulbright Fellowship) and the University of Vilnius (United Nations Development Program and Soros Foundation funding). Invited lectures include 2005 Distinguished Speaker at the E-ducation without Border Conference, Abu Dhabi, and 2004 Keynote speaker at the Nippon Academy of Management, Tokyo. Corporate management development program development clients include McDonald's Corporation's Hamburger University and IBM Learning Services. Pro bono consulting assignments include re-engineering and total quality management programs for the Lithuanian National Postal Service. Email: wankelc@stjohns.edu.

David A. Whetten is the Jack Wheatley Professor of Organizational Studies and director of the Faculty Development Center at Brigham Young University. He received his PhD from Cornell University. His recent scholarship has focused on organizational identity and identification, theory development, and management education. He served as editor of the *Foundations for Organizational Science,* an academic book series, and the *Academy of Management Review,* as well as president of the Academy of Management. He is a founding editorial board member of the *Academy of Management Learning & Education.*

LaVergne, TN USA
03 March 2010

174838LV00002B/18/P

9 781607 523468